Beyond Political Liberalism

Beyond Political Liberalism

Toward a Post-Secular Ethics of Public Life

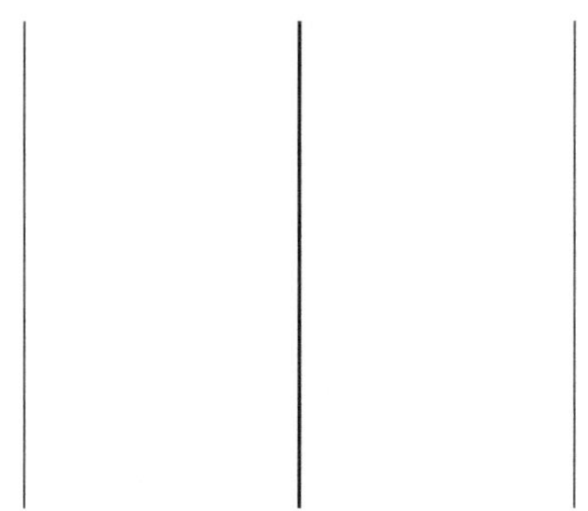

Troy Dostert

University of Notre Dame Press

Notre Dame, Indiana

Notre Dame, Indiana 46556
www.undpress.nd.edu

Published in the United States of America

Library of Congress Cataloging-in-Publication Data

Dostert, Troy Lewis, 1968–
Beyond political liberalism : toward a post-secular ethics of public life / Troy Dostert.
p. cm.
Based on the author's thesis (doctoral)—Duke University.
Includes bibliographical references (p.) and index.
ISBN-13: 978-0-268-02600-4 (pbk. : alk. paper)
ISBN-10: 0-268-02600-9 (pbk. : alk. paper)
1. Political ethics. 2. Religion and politics. 3. Liberalism—Religious aspects. 4. Religious pluralism—Political aspects. I. Title.
BJ55.D64 2006
172—dc22
2006023895

∞ *The paper in this book meets the guidelines for permanence and durability of the Committee on Production Guidelines for Book Longevity of the Council on Library Resources.*

For the members of the Church of the Abiding Savior,
Lutheran

Contents

Acknowledgments

This book originally took shape as my doctoral dissertation in political theory at Duke University. I must first, therefore, thank the members of my dissertation committee: Rom Coles, Ruth Grant, Stanley Hauerwas, Elizabeth Kiss, and Tom Spragens. I had hoped from the start to write something that would allow me to draw on my combined interests in political theory and theology, and each of them was graciously willing to help shepherd such a project. Individually and collectively they consistently offered judicious criticism and encouragement, and many of the core ideas of the book were influenced by their guidance. Special thanks are due to my advisor, Tom Spragens, whose sage advice was a constant resource through both the dissertation and the book-writing process.

I must also thank those who took the time to read portions of the book and whose reflections and criticisms were invaluable: Dan Bell, Bill Cavanaugh, Evan Charney, Eldon Eisenach, and Vivian Wang. I presented a number of early chapter drafts at the meetings of the American Political Science Association and Southern Political Science Association, and I benefited from discussions generated during and after those presentations. During 1998–99 I received a dissertation fellowship from the Kenan Institute for Ethics at Duke and had the pleasure of participating in its graduate colloquium in ethics. The members of that colloquium provided valuable feedback on an early version of the book's argument.

At the University of Notre Dame Press, Jeff Gainey and Chuck Van Hof both offered essential encouragement and support throughout the publication process. I also benefited enormously from the careful critiques of two anonymous reviewers, both of which made the book much stronger than it otherwise would have been.

I owe my first serious encounter with the rewards of scholarship to Alan Houston, who at the University of California, San Diego, supervised my undergraduate honors thesis on Isaiah Berlin. His friendship and counsel came at a crucial stage in my intellectual development and played a key role in my decision to pursue academic life as a calling.

Through the course of researching and writing this book I have become more cognizant than ever before of the ways in which we are indebted to the communities that sustain and shape us. In this light I must thank my parents, Bruce and Ardith Dostert, and my brother, Trent Dostert, for their unfailing love and support. I cannot begin to thank my wife, Manisha Dostert, for her boundless devotion and companionship. She has influenced this book in more ways than she knows, and she has shared in every triumph and frustration associated with it. Our son, Miles, was born right before I finished the first draft of the book. I am in his debt as well, for his sheer exuberance and delightful presence have become daily reminders that there are things more important than writing books.

I dedicate this book to a particular community that became our spiritual home during the last several years we spent in Durham, North Carolina. The Church of the Abiding Savior, Lutheran, is a remarkable example of a community dedicated to embodying the reality of the church as an alternative polis. The opportunity to witness its members' faithfulness and selflessness continues to give me hope that the vision of politics advanced in this book is an ongoing possibility. I am eternally grateful for the privilege of having shared in their journey.

Introduction

One of the most pressing dilemmas in contemporary political theory concerns how we should conceive of political life in light of the challenges posed by moral diversity. When citizens with widely divergent ethical or religious convictions clash in public debate, how can we approach such disagreements constructively? How can we work toward a stable and legitimate basis for political life, given that we do not share the same presuppositions about what constitutes the proper end of human activity? And to what extent should space be given to particular groups or communities to pursue their own distinctive practices and way of life, even when these might in some respects be at odds with public purposes as currently understood? Conceptualizing what is at stake in moral disagreements in public life and determining an appropriate response to them are political tasks of the first order, daunting though they may be.

These challenges are especially acute when they concern religious differences. The convictions that animate the lives of religious citizens touch upon the most crucial matters: the nature of good and evil, the path to salvation, the substance of a virtuous life. Citizens of diverse religious faiths, as well as those without religious commitments, disagree profoundly over such questions. And these disagreements cannot be neatly detached from the stuff of politics; indeed, they often reveal themselves most sharply in public debate. To be sure, religious diversity is not the only significant kind of moral diversity in political life. While contentious debates over multicultural education, school prayer, gay marriage, or capital punishment are frequently fueled by citizens' disparate moral convictions, these kinds of disagreements do not always have religious differences at their core. Nevertheless, in many respects, the differences that separate citizens as members of religious communities with divergent constitutive understandings and practices do exemplify the challenges of moral diversity, and they are apparent in many of today's most vexing public disagreements. How any conception of politics responds to the public presence of religious diversity is, therefore, one crucial test of its desirability.

The dominant approach to this question within contemporary liberal theory is that of political liberalism. Developed most fully and notably by John Rawls, political liberalism works within the tradition of theorizing the relationship between religion and politics initiated by John Locke in his work *A Letter Concerning Toleration* ([1689] 1983). Locke's approach to securing tolerance and church-state separation involved establishing a firm boundary between the civic and private realms. Within the latter realm churches would be free to carry out their distinctive purpose (defined by Locke as seeking "the Salvation of Souls"), while within the former the state would govern authoritatively, in the interests of the commonwealth as a whole (39). Rawls and other political liberals continue this project by theorizing a basis for political cooperation that can allow citizens with widely disparate convictions and ways of life to support a properly configured public sphere. Once liberal societies reach agreement upon an "overlapping consensus" of shared political norms and values, a conception of "public reason" becomes available through which citizens may deliberate together about political essentials. The boundary between the public and nonpublic realms can thus be legitimately established, and citizens are given a clear way to differentiate their obligations *qua* citizens from those, religious or otherwise, that they may recognize in their nonpublic lives. Via the shared political language of public reason, public discourse can be guided straightforwardly by distinctly political values, thereby circumventing the discord that can be occasioned when citizens bring their more comprehensive and contestable convictions forward in public life. The challenges raised by religious diversity are thus conclusively settled, as public reason allows citizens to approach their disagreements in a spirit of commonality, without allowing their conflicting worldviews to complicate the attainment of a just political order.[1]

My project in this book involves challenging this approach to public life. By examining political liberalism's conceptualization of religious diversity and its strategy for responding to it, I question the desirability of managing this diversity through the device of liberal public reason, and I suggest that a politics less devoted to a narrowly circumscribed public realm will be better suited for religiously diverse liberal societies. Indeed, I seek to contest the fundamental logic of political liberalism—that religion as such constitutes a distinctive threat to public order—and instead argue that religious communities themselves have a great deal to offer in approaching the challenges of religious diversity, and moral diversity more generally, in a responsible manner. Stated simply, my argument is that it is through engaging our diversity directly, rather than seeking to control it, that we stand the best chance of negotiating public space successfully. And I offer an alternative to political liberalism with this aim in view.

Political Liberalism's Appeal

It is not hard to appreciate why political liberalism has gained a substantial following. What it promises is a way to steer a course between two alternative theoretical frameworks, neither of which by itself appears to be fully compelling. The first is what has been called "perfectionist liberalism." Defended in different forms by thinkers such as Joseph Raz and Ronald Dworkin, this approach emphasizes the distinctive ethical attributes of a liberal way of life, for instance individualism or personal autonomy, and defends liberal political arrangements as a way to encourage those attributes in citizens generally. Dworkin contends that "the most plausible philosophical ethics grounds a liberal faith," and that "liberal equality does not preclude or threaten or ignore the goodness of the lives people live, but rather flows from and into an attractive conception of what a good life is" (2000, 242). Dworkin's own conception of liberalism is premised upon his ideal of "ethical individualism," which informs his particular defense of egalitarian justice, as well as his account of liberal citizens as self-determining beings (4–7). Similarly, Raz builds his defense of liberalism around the notion that personal autonomy is a "constituent element of the good life," and that liberal states should design public policy with an eye toward helping citizens achieve it (1986, 408).

Perfectionist liberalism traces its lineage not through Locke's *Letter*, with its primary emphasis on establishing a secure boundary between the political and the private spheres, but rather through thinkers such as John Stuart Mill and Immanuel Kant. It draws upon a rich tradition of liberal philosophical thought on the nature of the good life, thereby offering a robust depiction of the value of the liberal ideal. But as political liberals have pointed out, this way of life will not appeal to all citizens equally. Charles Larmore notes that a liberal politics that privileges the value of autonomy is deeply at odds with the Romantic values of "belonging and custom," and the life lived in obedience to a shared tradition (1990, 343–344). And Rawls stresses that a comprehensive commitment to autonomy or liberal individualism will inevitably prove to be "incompatible with other conceptions of the good, with forms of personal, moral, and religious life consistent with justice and which, therefore, have a proper place in a democratic society" (1985, 245). Would not the state's acting upon a perfectionist conception of liberalism lead to the kinds of paternalism and coercion that liberals have long resisted, carried out (ironically) in the interests of attaining a more perfect liberal political order? A perfectionist liberalism appears to pave the way toward making liberalism nonliberal.

Political liberalism thus reaffirms the public/private distinction invoked by Locke and limits its emphasis to obtaining *political* norms with which to regulate the public sphere, as opposed to wider ethical ideals that would inevitably generate disagreement among citizens with diverse worldviews. The virtue of "reasonableness" that undergirds political liberalism's conception of citizenship is considered a political virtue, connected to a political way of reasoning, and as such it may be very different from the way in which citizens reason personally about morality or ethics (Rawls 1996, 215). Similarly, while citizens must employ a version of *political* autonomy in their public lives, they are not obligated to view their nonpublic convictions and obligations through the lens of *personal* autonomy. They are free to regard those commitments as involving obedience to a shared faith or tradition (97–99, xliv–xlv). At the same time, however, political liberals insist that while this vision of liberalism is strictly political and not perfectionist in nature, it is nevertheless built upon a moral foundation. Rawls, for instance, stresses that citizens must affirm their allegiance to liberal justice on moral grounds (1996, xl), and Larmore also is at pains to emphasize that political liberalism rests upon a "core morality" (1990, 346). Why is this important?

Establishing a liberal regime on a moral foundation allows political liberals to differentiate their approach from the other competing liberal framework: modus vivendi liberalism. For modus vivendi liberals, political justification is pursued prudentially, in the hope of attaining provisional political agreements in societies deeply divided over the good life. What is most important is not that citizens share a commitment to particular political norms, let alone a commitment to a comprehensive way of life. Rather, it is simply to facilitate the negotiated compromises and strategic truces that allow citizens with widely disparate constitutive understandings to live amicably. Patrick Neal calls this "vulgar liberalism," and defends it as a "chastened and minimalist" liberalism best suited for polities in which citizens possess radically incommensurable worldviews (1997, 8). Similarly, John Gray argues that "the aim of *modus vivendi* cannot be to still the conflict of values. It is to reconcile individuals and ways of life honouring conflicting values to a life in common. We do not need common values in order to live together in peace. We need common institutions in which many forms of life can coexist" (2000, 5–6).[2]

Modus vivendi liberalism clearly evinces a significant attentiveness to the moral diversity likely to be present in contemporary liberal societies, especially when contrasted with perfectionist liberalism. But for political liberals it gives up far too much. It seems to rule out, for instance, the shared societal commitment to distributive justice that characterized Rawls's project in *A Theory of Justice*, a project that could only be successful if citizens were unified around the priority of social justice as a goal for liberal politics. Citizens whose allegiance to liberal justice involved "simply going along with it in view of the balance of political and social forces" would lack the deep-rooted attachment to social cooperation needed to realize liberal justice to the fullest extent (Rawls 1996, xl). What political liberalism seeks, in short, is "stability for the right reasons," and modus vivendi liberalism cannot promise this (xliii).

In its commitment both to rejecting the paternalist temptation of perfectionist liberalism and its insistence upon the ideal of a shared moral commitment to justice and political stability, political liberalism promises a way to incorporate citizens with wide-ranging moral and religious commitments within the liberal project. It aims not merely for civic peace but for a realization of the goods of mutual respect and, even, civic friendship (Rawls 1997, 771). As such it is an inspiring vision. But for my purposes in this study, it presents two central difficulties. Both have substantial implications for the status of religious citizens and their role in public life.

Where Is the Politics in Political Liberalism?

A number of recent analyses of political liberalism have focused on whether its emphasis on stability and a shared moral foundation for political life results in an attenuated democratic politics. Roberto Alejandro suggests that Rawlsian politics "is so concerned with the exclusion of divisive issues that might threaten the stability of a well-ordered society and so interested in removing any contingency that might impair the orderly application of the principles of justice that it might engender a passive citizenry, one willing to silence its criticisms rather than risk the instability of the political order" (1998, 134).[3] Stanley Fish contends that the principles embedded in political liberalism's ostensibly overlapping consensus are just a way of blanching political life. Like all approaches to liberalism that trace their inspiration to Locke, political liberalism claims to establish a common point of view to govern the public realm that can transcend the struggle between incommensurable worldviews. But such a strategy inevitably purges political life of the motivations that give politics its driving force: it requires us to abstract from our histories, our deepest convictions, and the commitments that propel us to conceptualize and strive to bring about our visions of justice and the good. This can only be done "by turning the highest things into the most ephemeral things (higher in the sense of 'airy') and by making the operations of the public sphere entirely procedural, with no more content than the content of traffic signals" (Fish 1999, 12).

Political liberalism's proceduralism is not limited to the workings of the public realm. It also shapes the manner in which political liberals consider the claims of those who may have reservations about its conception of politics. J. Judd Owen discusses the way in which political liberalism resists fully engaging the concerns of its critics, for if it did so "it would not then be on its own ground—the ground of reasonable democratic consensus—but rather on the ground of dogmatic assertion," which would involve offering the kind of "comprehensive" claims, à la perfectionist liberalism, that political liberalism has declared off-limits to the public sphere (2001, 120). Similarly, John Tomasi wonders why political liberals seem unwilling to address the concerns of religious citizens who may worry about their particular traditions being eroded by the "spillover effects" of a public realm governed by liberal rights and norms. Shouldn't political liberalism be more attentive to this concern, given its purpose of accommodating a wide range of citizens with diverse views of the good life, including those who (while otherwise remaining reasonable) may have religious commitments that are in tension with some aspects of liberalism? (2001, 21–22, 33–39).

Tomasi suggests that political liberals' neglect in this regard is largely a symptom of "the peculiarly narrow view most liberal theorists take concerning the boundaries of political theory." If we limit our concerns to establishing a legitimate conception of liberal justice, political liberals maintain, we can then sidestep questions concerning nonpublic life and the kinds of personal lives citizens lead, and we need not reflect upon the effects liberal political arrangements might have on the shape of those lives (37). Political liberalism thus adopts a kind of official agnosticism with respect to the substance of citizens' nonpublic convictions, and this radically restricts the scope of political liberals' theorizing, and the kinds of political possibilities that are conceivable as a result. There is much to be said for this explanation, although I believe Tomasi is wrong to argue that political liberalism can do otherwise if it is to remain within its core presuppositions.[4] Indeed, I will argue that political liberalism's general devaluation of politics and its insistence upon securing social stability are both principled stances that work powerfully to inhibit democratic engagement. And as I will seek to show, this stance toward politics has serious implications for our ability to negotiate public space amid the competing claims of radically diverse religious communities.

Singling Out the "Problem" of Religion

Although political liberalism is committed to a hands-off approach when it comes to negotiating the claims of religious communities politically, it is not the case that political liberals are silent on the question of religion. Indeed, religion has become an increasingly prominent preoccupation within political liberal thought. This is especially the case with Rawls and Stephen Macedo, both of whom have focused substantial attention on how political liberalism functions with respect to religion. The paradigmatic question Rawls poses in *Political Liberalism* is indicative: "How is it possible for those affirming a religious doctrine that is based on religious authority, for example, the Church or the Bible, also to hold a reasonable political conception that supports a just democratic regime?" (1996, xxxix). This emphasis is also reflected in the kinds of historical examples we find in political liberals' accounts of politics; these frequently concern religious groups and their involvement in public life.[5]

That political liberals have shown more willingness to confront these matters is a welcome development and, indeed, a crucial task if they are to take seriously their ambition to craft a commodious politics. Yet there is an aspect of much of this theorizing that is highly troubling. Ashley Woodiwiss identifies a constitutive tendency within liberalism to "police" communities of faith, in the interests of preventing them from disrupting social unity (2001, 68–71, 76–81). Such an impulse can be seen as the product of a distinctive narrative, in which liberalism is seen as the guarantor of civic peace in the midst of internecine religious conflict. Locke's project, on this view, is uniquely representative of liberalism as a political tradition. Political liberals exemplify this perspective, for when they write about religious diversity it is frequently with an eye toward controlling its politically "harmful" features.[6] When citizens offer religious arguments in public debate, we must worry that they may be trying to colonize the public sphere with their particular convictions. This is not to say that political liberals seek simply to confine religious expression to the private realm, for they acknowledge occasions in which citizens' religious arguments might work to support the overlapping consensus—for instance, if citizens can explain how their convictions are consistent with public reason. But such concessions serve only to make it clear that in order for religious citizens' political activity to be consistent with liberal norms, it is incumbent upon them to ensure that their convictions are properly expressed, governed by the primary logic of public reason—to which their religious or ethical appeals must always be offered in service.

Political liberalism thus relies upon the preeminence of secular political values as a way to suppress the dangers of religion's public presence. "Secular" here does not presuppose a self-consciously anti-religious worldview or explicit hostility to claims of religious faith. Indeed, in keeping with political liberalism's commitment to steer clear of contentious religious disputes about the good life, such a position would be clearly out of keeping with political liberalism's core principles.[7] For political liberalism, secular values are merely those that have been purged of religious particularity; they are thus able to serve as political values suitable for public discourse in a morally diverse polity. Unless we as a society can agree upon the public sufficiency of these values, political liberalism's project collapses, for there is no longer a way to guarantee the stability of the public sphere in the face of competing moral or ethical claims that citizens might use to justify their political positions. Political liberals thus advance a plausible claim to stay above the fray when determining the relative truth value of religious ways of life. But given the way in which religious claims are thus forbidden from contributing toward the definition of public ideals, faith communities are clearly faced with the imperative of tempering any assertions that might throw into question the self-sufficiency of secular political values or that might advance their faith tradition as offering a distinctive approach toward resolving public policy dilemmas. In this way, political liberalism assumes a hegemonic secular stance toward the political appeals of faith communities, even while refraining from endorsing a larger, more fully articulated account of "secularism" as a basis for its approach to politics.

When political liberalism's insistence upon the secular as a way to regulate public discourse is considered alongside its tendency to devalue democratic engagement, the difficulties this raises for an account of politics that would truly aspire to be a "home" for diverse communities of faith become evident. Are liberal justice and social stability fully desirable if, as a means to those ends, citizens are not welcomed in bringing their deepest convictions to bear in negotiating public space or defining public purposes? This is not simply a question of fairness to both religious and nonreligious citizens. Given the role that religious communities have historically played in the American context through shaping public space and public ideals, are we now to look upon this involvement as being inherently suspect, something to be carefully controlled or monitored?[8] Restricting religion's role in political life may not be as beneficial as political liberalism would have us believe.

The Objectives and Structure of This Book

While political liberalism's liabilities are significant, they are ultimately instructive. It is through a careful engagement with political liberalism that we can envision a route to a more compelling politics. My claim is that we can develop a politics better able to work through the challenges of moral diversity if we suspend political liberalism's assumption that *managing* moral diversity, and religion in particular, is the proper strategy. In other words, it is by inverting the logic of political liberalism—by *welcoming* democratic engagement over the good life, with all of its attendant messiness and uncertainty—that we stand the best chance of responding to our differences appropriately. Modus vivendi liberals are right to contend that in a context of radical moral diversity, the shape of public space must be negotiated rather than determined conclusively. We should proceed not by policing citizens' convictions but rather by bringing them forward and attempting to forge compromises and tentative agreements with those convictions in full view.

Yet I would not wish to suggest that political liberals' concerns about social stability are wholly unwarranted or that their desire for a politics characterized by civic friendship and moral commitment is misplaced. An agonistic politics without any guiding norms whatsoever could harmfully exacerbate social divisions, rendering the attainment of worthy political ideals a much more difficult undertaking. It is for this reason that I will offer an ethics of discourse that can allow us to envision a politics involving both significant contestation *and* a disciplined search for shared norms. As I will make clear, however, such an ethics must be a post-secular ethics: it must involve jettisoning the presuppositions that political liberalism relies upon for circumscribing religion's presence in the public realm. Once we do that, we are then freed to search out other moral resources for guiding political life—including those of theology.

I draw from theological sources for my constructive project for two main reasons. First, considering the substantial literature on public discourse written from a theological perspective better enables us to move beyond the view that religion is intrinsically problematic for political life, as well as the corollary premise that secular political values should be used to regulate public discourse in a liberal society. Because these understandings have come to play such a prominent role in liberal theorizing in general, they can hinder our ability to consider other ways of conceptualizing the public realm. As John Milbank has forcefully suggested, the way we theorize the political is always conditioned by the *narratives* we rely upon—it is never as simple as analyzing the social as a thing in itself. We cannot "'round upon' society as a finite object, and give an exhaustive inventory, valid for all time, of the essential categorical determinants for human social existence" (1990, 64).[9] If we are governed by the background assumption that religion constitutes a persistent threat to civic order, or that relying upon the primacy of a secular political language is a self-evident way to solve that problem, our conception of the political will be limited by those (often unquestioned) assumptions.

Second, if we are to take seriously the possibility of democratic moral engagement as a norm for political life, then it becomes crucial that we find ways in which citizens and their communities can sustain the practices needed for such a politics. Ecclesiological theology (theological reflection on the church as a community of faith) represents a sophisticated body of thought concerning how churches' social practices can themselves generate powerful and compelling political possibilities.[10] By considering the work of Mennonite theologian John Howard Yoder as well as the theological insights particular to the black church during the civil rights struggle, I suggest that these resources have much to offer by way of articulating and demonstrating the desirability of a post-secular ethics of moral engagement.

It is important to note that I am addressing these concerns within the context of American society and its longstanding struggles over the definition of public meanings and ideals. This is a significant qualification; the ways in which we understand the shape and limits of public life are crucially informed by the historical experiences of particular polities. As my analysis will show, the development of liberalism in America has been subject to a great deal of ongoing contestation, as communities with different moral convictions have sought to negotiate the challenges of sharing public space. This was as true of the eighteenth-century debates over religious freedom as it was of the twentieth-century struggle over civil rights. This has helped to give American liberalism its distinctive character, as it has always been subject to competing understandings and interpretations.[11] Indeed, I would suggest that it is by remaining attentive to the widest possible range of perspectives, even nonliberal ones, that liberalism possesses what potential it has to serve as a suitable framework for a noncoercive and capacious politics that can steer clear of totalizing and oppressive political possibilities.[12]

Seen in this light, much of the difficulty with political liberalism is its reluctance to concede the contestability and provisionality of liberal norms—to acknowledge that these depend for their vitality on the ongoing process whereby particular moral communities offer their distinctive moral and political visions in attempts to refine, reconceive, and give new meanings to political purposes. By offering a vision of liberalism that is safely immune from this democratic contestation, secure behind the static values of the overlapping consensus, political liberalism leaves us with a rigidified liberal politics unable to allow itself to be informed by broader ideals that are often indispensable to the viability and dynamism of political life. Rawlsian public reason thus works to foreclose possibilities of transformation within the liberal tradition, precisely by insulating core political values from the "corrupting" influence of religious or other moral languages that might be brought to bear in altering or developing our understanding of liberal political ideals. Certain of the adequacy of their particular conception of liberalism, political liberals deny that democratic engagement is necessary for navigating our way through the thicket of moral diversity. I contend, in contrast, that if we wish to remain both hopeful of approaching our moral disagreements constructively and open to the discovery of new political understandings and ideals, an ethics of engagement is our best option.

The chapters of the book can be divided into two main parts. In chapters 1 through 3, I consider political liberalism's approach to religious diversity, focusing principally on the thought of Rawls and Macedo. I discuss Rawls most extensively, both because of his prominence as the foremost and most respected proponent of political liberalism and because of the breadth and comprehensiveness of his analysis.

In chapter 1 I analyze political liberalism's strategy in managing moral diversity and the difficulties it raises for democratic politics. In chapter 2 I develop this criticism further, by looking specifically at Rawls's understanding of religious liberty. I consider the issues raised by the widely discussed *Mozert v. Hawkins* court case, a religious free-exercise dispute that involved several Christian fundamentalist families who were denied permission to have their children exempted from a reading curriculum they found to be in conflict with their religious convictions. Here I will turn to Macedo, whose analysis of the case from political liberalism's perspective reveals the ways in which political liberalism's resistance to democratic contestation renders it poorly equipped to recognize and respond to the challenges religious communities can sometimes face in negotiating their relationship with the wider liberal polity.

In chapter 3 I consider the implications of political liberalism's secular conception of public reason and its requirement that religion's role in public life should be constrained. I contend that, despite Rawls's and other political liberals' assertions to the contrary, this ideal of public reason entails very significant restrictions on the presence of religious communities in public debate. Moreover, it results in an impoverished public discourse, as communities with ennobling moral visions are precluded from offering those visions fully and compellingly.

Chapters 4 through 6 present the book's constructive project of formulating a post-secular ethics of moral engagement. For the first step in this process I devote chapter 4 to assessing the resources offered by three theological thinkers: David Tracy, Richard John Neuhaus, and Yoder. Each makes an argument for the positive role religious communities might play in public life. Of the three, however, only Yoder provides an account that is sufficiently able to move beyond the problematic presuppositions that animate political liberalism. Both Tracy and Neuhaus see the function of public discourse as maintaining shared conceptions of rationality, and in that light they make moves that parallel political liberalism's own restrictive view of public reason. Because Yoder is able to articulate a vision of inter-community discourse that does not rely upon a singular framework for public reasoning, Yoder offers the most valuable resources for my own conception of public life.

In chapter 5, I locate additional resources for developing this political vision, by way of the particular lessons to be drawn from the civil rights movement of the 1950s and 60s. The public witness of Martin Luther King Jr. and his fellow activists on the front lines of the struggle for racial justice reveals the promise and potential of a discourse in which our most fundamental convictions are linked to the pursuit of justice and shared public norms. Because the movement did not seek to offer support for political values that could be articulated in a "reasonable" secular language but instead brought its particular, religiously derived ideals forward to refashion and transform public meanings, it offers a valuable case study for considering how a post-secular ethics of public life might be conceptualized and sustained.

Finally, in chapter 6 I articulate and defend the distinctive practices at the heart of my ethical conception. What is critical to this approach is its emphasis on a genuine engagement among our moral traditions, a practice that allows us to present our political visions fully and sincerely, as opposed to subordinating them to a secular public language. With this approach in view, I reconsider the challenges of the *Mozert v. Hawkins* case. I argue that, rather than insisting on political liberalism's unyielding standard of reasonableness, a response of creativity and forbearance toward those like the *Mozert* families who find themselves at odds with public school curricula will better serve to ameliorate such conflicts. It will also help us avoid the divisive and tragic outcomes that can result when moral diversity is managed rather than negotiated.

I then explore two recent debates that suggest ways in which the ideals of religious communities, far from posing a threat to public debate, can provide indispensable resources for coming to terms with pressing public policy concerns. By considering the Jubilee 2000 movement for international debt relief and two recent analyses of the abortion debate, I argue that a politics of moral engagement, provided it is sustained by a disciplined and sincere attempt to discern what our moral communities can offer the search for public purposes, is preferable to one in which their insights are regarded with distrust or suspicion.

A conception of citizenship adequate to the challenges of moral diversity must entail the courage to present our core convictions truthfully, while being animated by a spirit of generosity and solicitude toward the contributions that very different communities might make to our political understandings. Developing such a conception will require great political imagination and should itself be informed by the insights of different traditions and worldviews, as well as the political experience of a wide range of moral communities. In what follows I offer my contribution to this project.

CHAPTER 1

Managing Moral Diversity in Rawls's *Political Liberalism*

In this chapter I delineate the essential features of political liberalism's project and begin to consider some of the exclusions and limitations that accompany its effort to secure political stability in the face of significant moral and religious diversity. Rawls's *Political Liberalism* is the canonical text for this study, as it involves the most systematic and comprehensive discussion of the concepts that have come to characterize political liberalism as a distinct body of thought. These include: (1) the notion of the "overlapping consensus," whereby citizens with diverse convictions converge in their support for core political values; (2) the standard of the "reasonable person," which is used to conceptualize citizens' responsibility in regulating their life plans in order to cohere with the requirements of justice; (3) the idea of the "well-ordered society," which concerns the way justice is realized in a political liberal regime; and (4) the ideal of "public reason," which governs public discourse in such a regime. I analyze public reason most extensively in chapter 3. My goal in this chapter and the next is to consider the first three features and the ways in which they work to circumscribe and, indeed, *manage* diversity in the political liberal state.

The charge that political liberalism seeks to manage moral diversity may seem a bit extreme, given that one of the more noteworthy features of Rawls's thought has involved its evolution away from the perfectionist liberalism that characterized his work in *A Theory of Justice*. In that book, where Rawls first presented "justice as fairness," his famous articulation of liberal egalitarianism, he expressed a less acute awareness of the significance of incommensurable moral difference or the possible tensions between faith communities and the political order. Rawls did acknowledge the diversity of individuals as reflected in their differing interests and talents, but ultimately he designed a theoretical edifice intended to submerge this diversity beneath an overriding, fundamental commitment to liberal justice. This was accomplished through the "original position," the thought experiment whereby citizens entrusted with designing principles of justice would be denied knowledge of their abilities, aspirations, and convictions in order to nullify the "effects of specific contingencies which put men at odds and tempt them to exploit social and natural circumstances to their own advantage," thus guaranteeing that the resultant principles would be regarded by all as legitimate (1971, 136). With individuals' particularities factored out of the equation, we could be certain of obtaining a conception of justice suitable for a liberal polity. Hence while Rawls took as a starting assumption the notion that "the plurality of distinct persons with separate systems of ends is an essential feature of human societies," he was nevertheless confident that a liberal society could, if guided by the proper theoretical framework, eventually unite around a substantive vision of justice that all individuals could honor and support (29).

The perfectionist aspects of Rawls's project in *Theory* became apparent through the manner in which citizens were to view their commitment to liberal justice: as the most deeply rooted aspect of their personality, a commitment that would shape their entire worldview. A society ordered by justice as fairness would be one in which citizens assign justice the highest priority, seeing it as an embodiment of their status as "free and equal rational beings with a liberty to choose," who reflect their autonomy by demonstrating "their independence from natural contingencies and social accident" (255–256). All citizens would view their individual life plans as being chosen in accordance with their shared commitment to rationality and personal autonomy. While differences in worldviews would undoubtedly exist, they would not extend into different ways of understanding justice or lead to conflicting appraisals of the value of personal autonomy in the pursuit of the good life. On these points there would be complete agreement. Thus moral diversity would be politically insignificant, incapable of disrupting the widely shared societal commitment to justice as fairness.

The changes in Rawls's thought after *Theory* were in large part a move away from these perfectionist characteristics toward a liberalism that would be less comprehensive and therefore more accommodating of a wider diversity of worldviews and moral commitments. In "Justice as Fairness: Political not Metaphysical," Rawls distanced himself from the Kantian conception of autonomy that pervaded *Theory.* He argued that in fashioning a workable conception of justice we must avoid "questions of philosophical psychology or a metaphysical doctrine of the nature of the self," since "no political view that depends on these deep and unresolved matters can serve as a public conception of justice in a constitutional democratic state" (1985, 231).[1] It was his appreciation of the contestability of autonomy as a personal ideal that led Rawls to insist that "justice as fairness deliberately stays on the surface, philosophically speaking," being applicable only to those matters that are essential to justice and political stability. It does not seek to transform citizens' nonpublic lives as well (230). Or as Rawls argues in *Political Liberalism,* citizens "usually have both political and nonpolitical aims and commitments," and a properly designed conception of justice does not insist upon a neat congruence between the norms regulating the public sphere and those that citizens value most highly in their personal lives. "It can happen that in their personal affairs, or in the internal life of associations, citizens may regard their final ends and attachments very differently from the way the political conception supposes," and that phenomenon is entirely consistent with political liberalism (1996, 30, 31).

These changes would certainly seem to offer more room for a diversity of worldviews to exist compatibly with a politically liberal regime. Traditionalist religious communities, for instance, would appear much more secure in such a regime than in a Kantian one. Insofar as these communities often resist or are at least ambivalent toward autonomy as a moral ideal, Rawls's turn from the Kantian self of *Theory* to the more complexly variegated self of *Political Liberalism* would seem more attractive to those citizens, and thus perhaps more likely to engender their commitment to a liberal regime.[2] Yet upon closer investigation of the core components of Rawls's framework, we will have reason to question how much has really been gained by these shifts in Rawls's thought. Indeed, there is considerably more uniformity in Rawls's ideal liberal society than one might expect.

The Overlapping Consensus

Given the presence of our different conceptions of the good life and the various ways in which these conceptions are reflected in our ultimate aims and purposes, the challenge facing political liberalism is to explain how this diversity does not threaten its quest for a mutually acceptable basis for societal cooperation and shared commitment to justice. If moral diversity is deep and extensive, would we not expect citizens to disagree strenuously about justice—concerning both its content and its relative importance?

The centerpiece of Rawls's response to this challenge is the "overlapping consensus." Rawls argues that contemporary democratic societies, despite the diversity they exhibit, have within their public culture a "shared fund of implicitly recognized basic ideas and principles" that can be used to formulate a common conception of justice (1996, 8). The difficulty is that these ideas and principles are not necessarily unified in a coherent theoretical framework. Assuming that "the public political culture may be of two minds at a very deep level," even over ideals as fundamental as liberty or equality, political liberalism seeks to reorganize these ideals, expressing them "in a somewhat different way than before," so that a particular approach to justice might be able to secure societal agreement. Rawls argues that justice as fairness accomplishes this task through one "organizing idea" in particular: the notion "of society as a fair system of social cooperation between free and equal persons viewed as fully cooperating members of society over a complete life" (9). This seemingly modest concept, which for Rawls is intrinsic to the idea of liberal democracy itself, provides the foundation on which principles of justice can be constructed and then embraced by all citizens.

This organizing idea of society as a fair system of social cooperation is for Rawls a *political* idea. It is not to include all that is important, but simply those matters that regulate our life in common. While as individuals we plan our lives around what Rawls calls "comprehensive doctrines"—cohesive systems of beliefs that effectively encompass every dimension of human life—Rawls contends that a conception of justice, insofar as it is expressly limited in scope and application, can remain *non*comprehensive. That is, while it is a moral conception insofar as it deals with aspects of life that are of fundamental importance, it is nevertheless limited to covering only "the basic structure of a constitutional democratic regime" (1996, 175).[3] It is intended for "the main institutions of political and social life, not for the whole of life" (175).[4] The overlapping consensus, therefore, does not involve a convergence around a particular conception of the good, or comprehensive doctrine. Since for Rawls it is our disagreements over comprehensive doctrines that can lead to moral conflict, thus threatening social unity and stability, justice cannot itself be based on such a doctrine. Rather, by remaining narrow in scope, a properly constituted conception of justice can secure a societal consensus by requiring only that extant comprehensive doctrines embrace its particular ideals concerning the overarching structure of political life and the limited demands of justice.

For Rawls, the plausibility of this convergence taking place is due to the fact that the vast majority of comprehensive doctrines that will thrive in a liberal society are "reasonable" ones. A reasonable comprehensive doctrine, for Rawls, has three key features. First, it is a product of theoretical reason—that is, "it covers the major religious, philosophical, and moral aspects of human life in a more or less consistent and coherent manner." Second, it is also a product of practical reason, whereby "it organizes and characterizes recognized values so that they are compatible with one another and express an intelligible view of the world." And third, it is derived from "a tradition of thought and doctrine," so that while it is more or less stable, "it tends to evolve slowly in the light of what, from its point of view, it sees as good and sufficient reasons" (1996, 59).

One can raise difficulties concerning the generalizability of these features of Rawls's understanding of reasonable doctrines.[5] However, Rawls goes on to elucidate two additional features that are significantly more controversial. First, Rawls contends that any reasonable comprehensive doctrine must recognize the importance of prioritizing a commitment to social cooperation. That is, it must appreciate that "it is by the reasonable that we enter as equals the public world of others and stand ready to propose, or to accept, as the case may be, fair terms of cooperation with them." We must be "ready to work out the framework for the public social world, a framework it is reasonable to expect everyone to endorse and act on, provided others can be relied on to do the same" (1996, 53–54).

The second additional aspect of Rawls's understanding of reasonable doctrines involves what he calls the "burdens of judgment." Reasonable comprehensive doctrines accept the idea that moral disagreement is an irreducible feature of moral and social life. This is so because the exercise of reason in the world as we know it is an ultimately fallible endeavor. We must wrestle with complex and sometimes contradictory evidence, and different values may be difficult to weigh consistently. Moreover, our assessment of moral and political values is always shaped by our life experiences, and these will inevitably differ. Given these conditions, "in a modern society with its numerous offices and positions, its various divisions of labor, its many social groups and their ethnic variety, citizens' total experiences are disparate enough for their judgments to diverge, at least to some degree, on many if not most cases of any significant complexity" (1996, 56–57). Reasonable comprehensive doctrines acknowledge these burdens of judgment, and therefore disavow any notion that they possess exclusive access to the true or the rational. "It is not in general unreasonable to affirm any one of a number of reasonable comprehensive doctrines. We recognize that our own doctrine has, and can have, for people generally, no special claims on them beyond their own view of its merits. Others who affirm doctrines different from ours are, we grant, reasonable also, and certainly not unreasonable" (60).

The implications following from these qualities of reasonable comprehensive doctrines are significant. Rawls argues that once we accept the idea that our divergent conceptions of the good life are to be viewed as an inevitable by-product of all moral reasoning, we will be much less inclined to suppress those views that are different from our own. In addition, we will be aware of the provisional, contingent status of all comprehensive belief systems, and we will be wary of advancing a particular comprehensive doctrine as providing principles suitable for the organization of society, given the inevitable disagreements we face concerning these matters and the practical impossibility of securing agreement on such a doctrine. We will likely, therefore, be favorably disposed toward a vision of politics in which we avoid relying on our comprehensive doctrines as a basis for arguments intended to challenge or redefine public norms. Instead, we will embrace a view of comprehensive doctrines that perceives their public value as playing an essentially supporting role in a consensus on a political conception of justice. This consensus is uncontroversial and legitimate precisely because it is, "as far as possible, *independent* of the opposing and conflicting philosophical and religious doctrines that citizens affirm" (1996, 9, my emphasis). What makes comprehensive doctrines "reasonable," then, is not simply their amenability to a liberal democratic political arrangement (that is, that they accept the importance of social cooperation among political equals). It is that, with the burdens of judgment in view, they are willing to allow political life to be governed by a conception of justice that excludes from political affairs any disputes over comprehensive views of the good life.

Rawls's ideal of the overlapping consensus thus envisions a convergence among reasonable comprehensive doctrines, in the interest of establishing a "freestanding" conception of justice that can stand apart from and independent of the doctrines that support it (1996, 140). And it establishes a conception of public reason, a "public point of view" from which disputes over justice can be approached on shared terms. Reasonable comprehensive doctrines can thereby flourish, provided that their features that lie outside the overlapping consensus of political values have normative relevance only in the realm of personal and associational life. They are not to contribute toward the definition of the boundaries of the political domain. Those matters vital to the political sphere are to be resolved solely by drawing upon the political values contained in the overlapping consensus (137–138).

The Reasonable Person

Rawls's idea of the overlapping consensus is further supported by the notion of the reasonable person. Since it is individual citizens who maintain and revise their comprehensive doctrines in the course of their pursuit of the good life, these citizens must ensure that these doctrines are able to contribute to and perpetuate an overlapping consensus. In other words, comprehensive doctrines are reasonable because the men and women who embrace them are reasonable. Thus, connected to Rawls's idea of a political conception of justice is a political conception of the person. This conception, like that of justice, is "political" because it applies to matters affecting the political sphere; it affects citizens in their capacity as political creatures (1996, 29).[6] It characterizes "how citizens are to think of themselves and of one another in their political and social relationships as specified by the basic structure" (300). This conception of the person entails two "moral powers," both of which are connected to citizens' duties and responsibilities and are integral to Rawls's conception of society as a fair system of social cooperation.

The first moral power is "a capacity for a sense of right and justice," which involves "the capacity to understand, to apply, and normally to be moved by an effective desire to act from (and not merely in accordance with) the principles of justice as the fair terms of social cooperation" (1996, 302).

This propensity, for Rawls, epitomizes reasonable persons, who "are not moved by the general good as such but desire for its own sake a social world in which they, as free and equal, can cooperate with others on terms all can accept" (50). This understanding of reciprocity, by which we collaborate with others in establishing just and fair political institutions, thus serves as a key moral basis on which liberal citizens are to guide their political activity.

The second moral power involves citizens' "capacity for a conception of the good," understood as "the capacity to form, to revise, and rationally to pursue a conception of one's rational advantage or good" (1996, 19). This moral power is given more specific content by the manner in which it works in conjunction with the first, for citizens who honor the importance of fair terms of social cooperation and who accept the burdens of judgment as Rawls defines them will tend to affirm only reasonable comprehensive doctrines. Citizens' "capacity for a conception of the good" thus entails more than simply the ability to acknowledge a particular religious or moral perspective as one's worldview or comprehensive doctrine. Reasonable persons must be able to determine which characteristics of their view of the good life require revision in order to meet the requirements of justice. That citizens are able to obtain the critical distance from their most fundamental convictions needed to carry out this task is a crucial presupposition behind the idea of the overlapping consensus, which requires citizens to differentiate between their moral, religious, or philosophical views that are unsuitable for political life and those that can legitimately serve as supports for an overlapping consensus.

With the moral powers of the citizen in view, we can see the way in which they support the vision of justice at the heart of political liberalism. Once it is assumed that all individuals possess these moral powers and have a fundamental interest in fulfilling them, it becomes possible to sustain a public conception of justice that aims to ensure that each citizen has the requisite resources and opportunities needed to do so. The substantive content of Rawls's justice as fairness can thus be presented as satisfying the crucial prerequisites for individuals' flourishing:

> The basic rights and liberties of a constitutional regime are to assure that everyone can adequately develop these powers and exercise them fully over the course of a complete life as they so decide. Such a society also provides its citizens with adequate all-purpose means (the primary goods, say, of income and wealth) to do this. Under normal cir-

> cumstances, then, we may suppose those moral powers to be developed and exercised within institutions of political freedom and liberty of conscience, and their exercise to be supported and sustained by the social bases of mutual and self-respect. (1996, 202)

Rawls argues that, from the perspective of the political conception of the citizen, the realization of one's moral powers is considered to be not only a fundamental goal but of the utmost importance. Citizens have "higher-order" interests in developing and exercising these powers, meaning that "as the fundamental idea of the person is specified, these interests are viewed as basic and hence as normally regulative and effective. Someone who has not developed and cannot exercise the moral powers to the minimum requisite degree cannot be a normal and fully cooperating member of society over a complete life" (1996, 74).

When people properly exercise their moral powers, then, they are capable of participating fully as citizens in maintaining a just political order. And in so doing, they achieve a certain measure of autonomy. They demonstrate to themselves and to one another their ability to promote social purposes in which principles of right and justice are firmly in place. Thus, while Rawls now eschews the more rigorous Kantian conception of autonomy he presented in *Theory*, it is nevertheless clear that in *Political Liberalism* the good of "political" autonomy remains a central aim (1996, xliv, 98). As this turns out to be a pivotal distinction in Rawls's framework, it will be helpful to explore in greater detail the practices required of citizens if they are to become "politically" autonomous.

In keeping with the idea of their moral powers as higher-order interests, citizens are required to recognize and effectuate the distinction between their public identity and their identity as persons committed to a more fundamental, comprehensive vision of life.[7] Rawls makes it clear that this is to be viewed not as a burden but rather as a practice that preserves individual freedom. As he states, citizens who are politically autonomous "claim the right to view their persons as independent from and not identified with any particular such conception [of the good] with its scheme of final ends. Given their moral power to form, revise, and rationally pursue a conception of the good, their public identity as free persons is not affected by changes over time in their determinate conception of it" (1996, 30). In this way, citizens are thus free from the concern that their private status as, for instance, religious believers might in any way impair their status as free public selves and the rights they possess in light of that status.[8] Yet to be sure, this also implies a great responsibility, for citizens must be able not only to maintain the distinction between the public and the nonpublic parts of their identity but also to reconcile them if they should happen to diverge. As Rawls observes, people "may have, and often do have at any given time, affections, devotions, and loyalties that they believe they would not, indeed could and should not, stand apart from and evaluate objectively. They may regard it as simply unthinkable to view themselves apart from certain religious, philosophical, and moral convictions, or from certain enduring attachments and loyalties" (31). This would present a potentially hazardous obstacle to political stability and justice, unless citizens are able to ensure that the convictions animating their "personal affairs," or "the internal life of [their] associations," are consistent with these political objectives (31).

Citizens, therefore, who recognize and appreciate the fact that their private identity is distinguishable and distinct from their public identity, and who honor the fair terms of cooperation as Rawls articulates them, will seek to ensure that their comprehensive convictions do not interfere with the pursuit of justice that exemplifies their political lives. In addition, they will recognize the freestanding nature of the principles of justice that govern a liberal political order, and they will refrain from subordinating these to their ends as determined by their wider conception of life. In fact, the opposite tendency is likely. Citizens who honor their higher-order interests in fulfilling their moral powers will abandon, or at least temper, any vision of the good life that could threaten the terms of political cooperation as established by the overlapping consensus.

The reasonable citizen's willingness to align his or her most fundamental aims with the public conception of justice is especially crucial for political liberalism, given that the overlapping consensus established on political principles of justice is, as noted earlier, a consensus built around a moral conception. It is not simply a modus vivendi that citizens perceive to be an expedient arrangement in their own interest, or a temporary balance of power. A properly constituted political conception of justice must be one that all citizens "may freely endorse, and so freely live by and come to understand its virtues" (1996, xl). It is essential, therefore, that each reasonable comprehensive doctrine have resources from which it may "endorse" the political conception of justice "from its own point of view" (134).

Given that the principles of justice are freestanding, however, it is essential that citizens be circumspect in identifying those points of connection between their more comprehensive views and the principles supporting the political order. "While we want a political conception to have a justification by reference to one or more comprehensive doctrines, it is neither presented as, nor derived from, such a doctrine applied to the basic structure of society, as if this structure were simply another subject to which that doctrine applied. . . . We must distinguish between how a political conception is presented and its being part of, or as derivable within, a comprehensive doctrine" (1996, 12). In their *personal* deliberations, however, citizens are permitted, and even encouraged, to draw precisely these kinds of connections: "All those who affirm the political conception start from within their own comprehensive view and draw on the religious, philosophical, and moral grounds it provides. The fact that people affirm the same political conception on those grounds does not make their affirming it any less religious, philosophical, or moral, as the case may be, since the grounds sincerely held determine the nature of their affirmation" (147–148).

The overlapping consensus is ultimately sustained because "citizens themselves, within the exercise of their liberty of thought and conscience, and looking to their comprehensive doctrines, view the political conception as derived from, or congruent with, or at least not in conflict with, their other values" (1996, 11). In this way, the political conception of the person is connected neatly to the idea of reasonable comprehensive doctrines. Reasonable citizens come to recognize that, just as their public and private identities must be kept distinct, so too must their comprehensive doctrines have components that are both public and private. That part of each comprehensive doctrine that supports a freestanding conception of justice is publicly relevant. The remainder is to be pursued by each individual and the associations he or she joins in the nonpublic realm.

The Well-Ordered Society

The ideas of both the overlapping consensus and the reasonable person are essential to political liberalism's conception of justice, but the project would not be complete without the notion of the well-ordered society. Rawls retains this idea from *Theory*, albeit with a significant revision. As Rawls explains, the idea of the well-ordered society in that book failed to distinguish "between comprehensive philosophical and moral doctrines and conceptions limited to the domain of the political" (1996, xvii). All citizens were assumed to embrace comprehensive ideals of autonomy and rationality. With the change of emphasis in *Political Liberalism* toward a more pronounced awareness of moral diversity, the principles regulating a well-ordered society are now said to be concerned merely with the presence of reasonable comprehensive doctrines and individuals' willingness to perform those particular (and limited) tasks entailed by liberal citizenship.

The principles of justice, as Rawls acknowledges, are far-reaching. They are "designed to form the social world in which our character and our conception of ourselves as persons, as well as our comprehensive views and their conceptions of the good, are first acquired, and in which our moral powers must be realized, if they are to be realized at all" (1996, 41). But rather than nurturing the values of autonomy or rationality in a fundamental, comprehensive sense, they require only that citizens acquire the *political* virtues needed for social cooperation. While a well-ordered society "is a society in which everyone accepts, and knows that everyone else accepts, the very same principles of justice," citizens agree to limit the sovereignty of these principles to the political sphere (35). In their nonpublic life, they are not required to view their commitments as either contingent or rationally chosen, as they would if they embraced a Kantian variant of rationality. It is expected that politically autonomous citizens have the ability to make this distinction, and they are encouraged to do so by participating in a society in which the public virtue of supporting the shared principles of justice is honored. Hence, in a well-ordered society, "citizens who affirm the political conception, and who have been raised in and are familiar with the fundamental ideas of the public political culture, find that, when they adopt its framework of deliberation, their judgments converge sufficiently so that political cooperation on the basis of mutual respect can be maintained" (156). Over time, they "acquire a normally sufficient sense of justice so that they comply with its just arrangements" (141).

Once the principles of justice are in place, then, and citizens engage in social cooperation with one another, comprehensive doctrines that are unable to support those principles or the conception of the public sphere they endorse will gradually lose their hold over citizens. When Rawls considers the presence of moral pluralism, he is explicit in noting that in a well-ordered society this is best described as *reasonable* pluralism. Unreasonable comprehensive doctrines that are unable or unwilling to support the principles of justice will continue to exist only with great difficulty in such a society. This is the case because, in shaping the contours of the basic structure of society, the principles of justice effectively determine the way political virtue is to be understood, and the kinds of associations individuals form will reflect this. "Even though political liberalism seeks common ground and is neutral in aim, it is important to emphasize that it may still affirm the superiority of certain forms of moral character and encourage certain moral virtues. Thus, justice as fairness includes an account of certain political virtues—the virtues of fair social cooperation such as the virtues of civility and tolerance, of reasonableness and the sense of fairness" (1996, 194). Citizens are effectively inculcated with these virtues in a well-ordered society, in which the political conception of the person, along with the capacities and responsibilities that accompany this conception, are infused throughout the culture. With the idea of the "political conception as educator," not only the institutions of political life, but also citizens' character and associative aims will be shaped, at least at the margins, by the values embodied in the overlapping consensus (71).

The idea of the well-ordered society enables Rawls to contend that he has provided a conception of a just liberal regime, all the while remaining sensitive to the constraints presented by the conditions of moral diversity. Citizens in such a society come to regard one another as fellow participants in a shared endeavor to achieve justice, despite the differences that characterize their nonpublic lives. This mutual quest for just political arrangements is considered beneficial for two important reasons. First, it is a good for individuals, in that it assures them a society in which they can fulfill their two moral powers. And second, it is a social good, since it enables citizens collectively to realize the satisfaction entailed in "establishing and successfully conducting reasonably just (though of course always imperfect) democratic institutions over a long period of time" (1996, 204). Yet at the same time, these goods are realized while respecting the differences that are an ineradicable feature of life in a liberal democracy. As reasonable persons, citizens recognize each other's shared commitment to justice and on that basis confer respect on one another; they need not inquire into the deeper aims and attachments that animate the nonpublic, nonpolitical lives of their fellow citizens. Citizens in Rawls's well-ordered society share the common values found in the political domain. In the interests of upholding the fair terms of social cooperation, they regard those as sufficient.

Managing Moral Diversity in the Well-Ordered Society

In responding to the challenge of seeking justice in a society characterized by moral diversity, political liberalism might initially seem to offer an ideal solution. By securing a political domain free of potentially divisive disputes over the good life, thereby ensuring a stable foundation not only for political institutions but for civil liberties as well, it holds out the promise of reconciling individuals and communities around a principled commitment to seek just political arrangements that can be defended and justified on their own terms. To the extent we value a shared and defensible basis for political life, this is a vision that cannot be easily dismissed or trivialized. Yet there are good reasons to question political liberalism's attractiveness as a response to moral diversity. A closer consideration of the idea of the reasonable within Rawls's thought reveals these most clearly.

As we have seen, Rawls presents the reasonable as a way to delineate *only* the political obligations of citizens. It is not assumed to represent an all-encompassing approach to life in general. But has Rawls really succeeded in presenting a view of citizenship that remains "on the surface"? In the first place, it is clear that citizens in a well-ordered society who are "educated" by the principles of justice have already been profoundly shaped in terms of their worldview and fundamental commitments. Since they recognize Rawls's burdens of judgment, they accept the thesis that moral differences are not simply pervasive, they are unavoidable; human reason is simply incapable of obtaining certainty in matters of morality. And moreover, given that these differences are a natural and inescapable by-product of human reason, citizens come to accept as a factual description the idea that "a diversity of conflicting and irreconcilable" comprehensive doctrines is a "permanent feature" of the culture of liberal democracy (1996, 36, 136). These are not uncontroversial presuppositions. Not only do many philosophical traditions reject the irreconcilability thesis, so also do many religious worldviews. Traditions diverge in considering the implications of moral disagreement as well. Rawls argues that citizens in a well-ordered society are to view moral diversity not only as unavoidable but also as a good. This perspective stands at odds with the perspective of religious traditions that consider the Tower of Babel to be a better metaphor for moral disagreement: a lamentable state of communicative distance and disruption resulting from God's punishment for the hubris and disobedience of human beings.[9] In assuming that individuals in a well-ordered society will share the same understanding of moral diversity, Rawls has from the outset significantly narrowed the scope of that diversity. Differences over how to interpret and evaluate moral disagreements are surely as fundamental as the subject matter on which the disagreements themselves are based.

Similarly, the political conception of the person at the core of Rawls's framework reflects presuppositions that significantly constrain the way individuals conceive of their moral identity. Once we recognize our higher-order interest in realizing our capacity to form and rationally revise our conception of the good (Rawls's second "moral power"), we will be enabled to "think of ourselves as affirming our way of life in accordance with the full, deliberate, and reasoned exercise of our intellectual and moral powers. And this rationally affirmed relation between our deliberative reason and our way of life itself becomes part of our determinate conception of the good" (1996, 313). Citizens will thus have an interest in regarding their life plan, or comprehensive doctrine, as something they have chosen and affirmed, rather than accepted on the basis of faith, authority, or tradition.

This understanding of a person's relationship to his or her worldview turns out to be largely reminiscent of the assumptions undergirding *Theory*, in which the ideal of the autonomous individual was central. Rawls is willing to concede that this mode of reasoning does not cohere well with religious traditions that reject the autonomy of the will: "Of course, many persons may not examine their acquired beliefs and ends but take them on faith, or be satisfied that they are matters of custom and tradition." In keeping with the ostensible aims of political liberalism to "stay on the surface," Rawls cannot explicitly condemn this, since within his framework "there is no political or social evaluation of conceptions of the good within the limits permitted by justice." Political liberalism must seek to remain agnostic with regard to the metaphysical underpinnings of people's comprehensive doctrines—at least insofar as they affect individuals' public duties (1996, 314). Nevertheless, it is clear that citizens whose moral formation has taken place in a society in which Rawls's political conception of the person is widely embraced would, at the very least, tend to regard it as strange that some citizens might persist in viewing their comprehensive doctrine as a life plan not chosen but consisting in an obligation to God, or to their religious community, that has little to do with personal choice. Here too then, just as with the burdens of judgment, citizens in a well-ordered society are understood to share particular moral assumptions that are more controversial than they might at first appear and that go well beyond the merely political.

Finally, it is important to stress that, despite Rawls's assertion that the commitment to justice remains simply one part of our individual comprehensive doctrines, this commitment is ultimately intended to be primary. Values or convictions within our comprehensive doctrines that might conflict with Rawlsian justice should be recognized to be "normally outweighed because they come into conflict with the very conditions that make fair social cooperation possible on a footing of mutual respect" (1996, 157). Citizens who are first and foremost concerned with realizing their two moral powers, and ensuring the perpetuation of a society in which that objective is the chief individual and public good, will simply be disinclined to challenge political liberalism's particular conception of justice. For this conception ensures the flourishing of not only their political identity but ultimately their moral identity as well.

These difficulties indicate that Rawls's attempt to avoid controversial presuppositions concerning the nature of morality or the self by staying within the realm of political values ultimately falls short. Rawls's burdens of judgment do not stay on the surface of political reality. At the heart of this concept is a contentious understanding of the nature of moral disagreement and rationality, one certainly not universally or perhaps even widely shared by citizens today.[10] Nor does Rawls's attempt to carve out a space for political autonomy fare any better. Here also, values that are said to be limited to individuals' public identity in actuality come to exercise significant influence over their moral choices and their ultimate commitments. As Patrick Neal argues, the idea that individuals "possess" a conception of the good is not a neutral or self-evident conceptualization; it differs markedly from understandings of the good life that are premised upon their being shared *essentially,* rather than contingently (1997, 39).[11] In these ways, therefore, it is evident that Rawls's understanding of reasonable diversity does make room for a certain range of views of the good, but only insofar as they are consistent with the priority of justice as Rawls has defined it, and with the core presuppositions that sustain it.

Political liberalism's idea of the reasonable thus turns out to be significantly more than just a means for specifying the bounds of liberal citizenship. It is a mechanism by which particular moral views (and the citizens who embrace them) can be pushed to the margins of public life. There is no question that were Rawls's burdens of moral judgment or understanding of political autonomy to be widely shared among citizens, conflict over the good life would be radically diminished. But such civic concord would come at the price of a significant decrease in diversity. Indeed, a Rawlsian society would be characterized by substantial uniformity concerning people's understanding of the nature of morality, the conditions of political cooperation, and the primacy of justice.

Such a society might also be characterized by a lack of politics—at least with respect to fundamental moral questions in public life. This would be due not simply to the narrowed scope of moral diversity. Even more fundamentally, it is unclear whether citizens who have learned to compartmentalize their comprehensive doctrines into public and nonpublic components in the way that Rawls recommends will even be able to *act* politically. From what resources will citizens derive their motivation to effectuate political change, if many of their most personal convictions are viewed as irrelevant to the regulation of the public sphere? It is this concern that leads Stanley Fish to claim that this logic of liberal personhood "displaces morality by asking you to inhabit your moral convictions loosely and be ready to withdraw from them whenever pursuing them would impinge on the activities and choices of others." This in turn generates a kind of moral and political lassitude, since it requires "that you suspend those very urgencies that move you to act in the world" (1999, 41). Can citizens thus constituted engage in the long and difficult work of bringing about meaningful political reform or taking the risks involved with presenting new issues for public deliberation? Would they have any interest in doing so? It is not clear that Rawls's politically autonomous citizens would make *good* citizens, all things considered.

What does seem clear is that it would be premature to declare this vision of liberal citizenship triumphant. There remain many citizens, religious or otherwise, who are not comfortable viewing the public sphere as a site governed by a freestanding logic and who would thus resist separating their public identities and obligations from their nonpublic convictions. How would these "unreasonable" citizens fare within a society regulated by political liberalism? We will take up this issue next.

CHAPTER 2

Religious Freedom within Political Liberalism?

The Implications of Avoiding Moral Negotiation

Questions surrounding religious freedom exemplify the challenges of moral diversity in a liberal polity. How far should the state go in accommodating particular individuals or groups whose religious convictions or practices are burdened by nondiscriminatory secular laws? Should freedom of religion extend beyond "freedom of belief," and if so, how far? And what is the venue through which appeals for religious freedom are most appropriately considered: democratic legislatures or the courts? The constitutional justification for religious liberty is derived from the religion clauses of the First Amendment, which hold that "Congress shall make no law respecting an establishment of religion, or prohibiting the free exercise thereof." But there is no agreement concerning how these provisions should be understood or instantiated. Jurisprudence surrounding religious freedom exhibits little coherence, and legal scholars have consistently disagreed sharply about what religious liberty means in theory or in practice.[1] The stakes could not be more significant. For societies such as our own in which religious diversity represents one of the dominant forms of moral difference, how we decide (if at all) to accommodate citizens' religious differences through public action has tremendous implications for religious communities whose way of life might hang in the balance.

Some have argued that the difficulties surrounding these questions render the very notion of religious freedom suspect in a liberal society. No one stands out more in this regard than Stanley Fish, who has aggressively sought to deflate liberalism's pretensions of offering a principled resolution to this dilemma. Today's liberals, Fish argues, are no more able than Locke to locate an uncontested "common ground" from which to establish the legitimate bounds of church and state.[2] Our differences over religion are real and deep, and they are not limited to matters of doctrine or belief, which can ostensibly be located uncontroversially in the private sphere. They extend into matters of conduct and, even more significantly, into the way we *conceptualize* the private and the public. What this suggests is that different religious communities will have radically different understandings of where the boundaries of religious freedom should be drawn. Any principled resolution to this dilemma, therefore, is ultimately going to rest not on uncoerced agreement but on an imposition and will leave some communities justifiably dissatisfied with the outcome.[3]

As Fish sees it, the problem in locating an uncontroversial principle of religious freedom stems directly from our inability to locate a clear distinction between faith and reason. Since faith and reason are not opposed binaries but are rather "mutually interdependent," liberals' desire to place politics on a foundation that is not itself conditioned by faith cannot succeed (1999, 263). This means, then, that when claims for religious freedom arise, the state has no impartial perspective from which to adjudicate those claims. The "project" of securing religious freedom is thus reduced to a kind of sleight of hand, in which the legislator or judge conceals the arbitrariness of the outcome in any given instance by insisting that his or her decision is really based upon an established precedent or principle that is both fair and objective (169–170). The conclusion Fish draws from this argument is bracing. He admonishes those religious citizens who would see the idea of religious freedom as a way to safeguard their genuine religious interests. Instead of seeking such an arrangement, Fish argues, a "strong" religious believer would be better off renouncing the separation of church and state and its invidious pretenses and seeking instead "a world ordered in accordance with the faith he lives by and would die for" (298).[4]

As will become clear in my argument in this chapter, I believe Fish is correct with respect to the unavailability of a neutral or uncontroversial way to adjudicate religious liberty claims. If we are to take seriously the differences separating diverse religious traditions' conceptualizations of the public sphere, it seems that *any* attempt to draw the boundaries between church and state conclusively will be fraught with uncertainty and disagreement. Steven Smith argues persuasively that formulations of religious freedom in the American context have always been multiple and conflicting, and never reducible to a singular theoretical standard (1995, 6–8).[5] Seen in this light, any prospects for a fully coherent justification for religious liberty are likely to remain dim.

Yet the conclusion Fish draws with respect to the value of the *concept* of religious freedom seems to go too far in discounting its importance. Indeed, as I will argue, attempts to define and protect religious freedom have furnished abundant opportunities for negotiating the moral differences that have characterized American life from the colonial period onward. While religious freedom has always remained a precarious achievement, particularly for minority religious communities on the fringes of mainstream American life, those successes that have been obtained should be taken seriously as opening up a way to come to terms with moral diversity that does not depend purely on vying for "the right to be supreme over this or that part of the public landscape," as Fish argues is inevitable (1999, 12).

It is not my purpose here to offer a definitive "theory" of religious freedom. Rather, I will consider the dynamics surrounding religious liberty claims and what implications we might draw from those dynamics in considering how moral diversity should be negotiated. My goal will be to contrast a more nuanced, *political* approach to negotiating religious liberty claims with political liberalism's more inflexible, *administered* approach. What political liberalism promises is a theory of freedom of conscience—one that can ostensibly be applied equally and fairly to all reasonable citizens, irrespective of their most fundamental convictions. This provides for a straightforward and unambiguous approach to religious liberty claims. Unfortunately, it also obscures the nature of those claims themselves and restricts the political space needed to approach such claims in a less imperial manner. Within the carefully demarcated realm of political liberalism's public sphere, claims based on contentious fundamental convictions, such as those of religious faith, are viewed as unreasonable. The difficulties inherent in disputes over religious freedom are thus neatly avoided—with the consequence that the public sphere is no longer a place where the claims of religious communities can be given a fair hearing. If we are committed to retaining the concept of religious freedom as having some value in ordering public space, political liberalism's conception of the reasonable will not help us.

Rawls's Defense of Liberty of Conscience

Rawls presents his account of freedom of conscience most extensively in *A Theory of Justice,* in which it is considered an aspect of justice as fairness. Although Rawls did modify some aspects of justice as fairness in the transition to *Political Liberalism*—most specifically, the way in which it is now defined clearly as a "political conception" of justice—for the most part justice as fairness remains intact (1996, 11). It also seems clear, moreover, that Rawls continues to regard justice as fairness as the paradigmatic "organizing idea" through which we can consider how society as a "fair system of cooperation" would be structured under political liberalism (14). In light of these presuppositions, how would a principle of religious freedom be conceptualized in a manner consistent with the idea of society as a fair system of cooperation?

Of the two principles of justice comprising Rawls's justice as fairness, the first, which secures basic liberties, is ranked prior to that which regulates the distribution of social and economic resources. Rawls asserts that the desirability of these principles is based to no small degree on the fact that "they provide the strongest arguments for freedom" (1971, 243). Furthermore, of the various freedoms Rawls specifies, "equal liberty of conscience" is considered of paramount importance, as it is "one of the fixed points of our considered judgments of justice." Rawls views religious freedom as being incorporated within that rubric (206). That Rawls seeks to provide a secure defense of religious freedom is therefore clear. But his specific understanding of the nature of this freedom, and how it is to be justified given the characteristics of political liberalism's conception of justice, significantly condition the role it plays in his political framework.

Since the basic liberties are part of the "basic structure" of society, they are to be decided upon by the parties in the original position. As we saw earlier, these individuals are deprived of knowledge concerning "the social position, or the conception of the good (its particular aims and attachments), or the realized abilities and psychological propensities, and much else, of the persons they represent" (1996, 305). They know only that they are to create conditions of justice whereby all citizens may have an equal opportunity to develop their moral powers. Hence, while they are aware that some citizens may embrace a religiously based worldview or comprehensive doctrine, they can have no way of knowing the content of those citizens' beliefs or what the overall distribution of religious communities in the greater society might look like. Knowing these features of social life might render the parties' deliberations subject to pragmatic considerations or lead to partial determinations on behalf of particular religious beliefs or groups. By staying within the constraints imposed by the veil of ignorance, the parties in the original position are able to ensure that the right of conscience, like all of the essential liberties, is placed on a secure footing immune from political wrangling or an unstable balance of social forces.

From these presuppositions, Rawls argues, "it seems evident that the parties must choose principles that secure the integrity of their religious and moral freedom" (1971, 206). This is because, while they lack specific information about their actual convictions, "they regard themselves as having moral or religious obligations which they must keep themselves free to honor," and "they cannot take chances with their liberty by permitting the dominant religious or moral doctrine to persecute or to suppress others if it wishes" (206, 207). Rawls's point makes clear why, within political liberalism's conception of justice, it is "freedom of conscience" that is protected, and religious freedom is seen only as a subset of that larger category. For the parties in the original position are aware that just as they might have religious interests they wish to pursue, it might just as likely turn out otherwise. They may espouse a conception of the good that does not meet conventional criteria for religious belief. Is their liberty to pursue their conception of the good to be jeopardized or placed at a relative disadvantage to that of other citizens, simply because the content of their beliefs is nonreligious? Rawls is unambiguous here. Within political liberalism, all religious, moral, and philosophical views of the good are to be given equal liberty, subject only to the requirement that these views be reasonable.

For political liberalism, therefore, religious freedom can only legitimately be considered a good because it is a good some citizens may have an interest in pursuing—not because there is anything peculiar about religious commitments that might render them particularly worthy of protection. It is the political conception of the person, with its two moral powers, that ultimately justifies any deference that is given to the claims of conscience. Liberty of conscience, along with freedom of association, is essential in order to "secure the full and informed and effective application of citizens' powers of deliberative reason to their forming, revising, and rationally pursuing a conception of the good over a complete life" (1996, 335).

Because this understanding of freedom of conscience is based solely on political values, for Rawls it is consistent with the notion that principles of justice should be based on public norms all can accept, consistent with the fair terms of social cooperation. We must acknowledge that "on matters of constitutional essentials and basic justice, the basic structure and its public policies are to be justifiable to all citizens, as the principle of political legitimacy requires" (1996, 224). Securing agreement on core civil liberties is a matter of the "greatest urgency," and having an unambiguous and clearly demarcated understanding of these liberties and their scope is vital (227). What political liberalism promises, then, is a broad conception of freedom of conscience that aims to accommodate both religious and nonreligious conceptions of the good on an equal basis, and thus in a manner that is politically uncontroversial and justifiable to all reasonable citizens.

Mozert v. Hawkins

To determine how Rawls's more general understanding of freedom of conscience might be applied specifically to matters concerning religious freedom, we can ask how it would approach appeals for free-exercise conduct exemptions (often referred to as "accommodations"), which involve special legislative or judicial measures undertaken on behalf of religious individuals whose convictions or practices are burdened by particular nondiscriminatory secular laws. Determining an answer to this question leads us directly to inquire how Rawls's political liberalism might be applied to "unreasonable" communities that stand outside the cultural and political mainstream. For surely citizens who are reasonable in the way Rawls defines it will rarely seek to avail themselves of free-exercise exemptions. In the first place, such citizens' convictions will infrequently conflict with the central norms of the community. And on those occasions when a conflict should arise, these individuals are able to adjust those features of their life plans that need to be realigned in order to comport with the principles undergirding the social order. Other less reasonable citizens, however, may not be as adept at or willing to perform this task. It is therefore by turning to consider the issues raised by the Christian fundamentalist families in *Mozert v. Hawkins* that we can gain a better glimpse of the practical implications of political liberalism's approach to religious liberty.

The seeds of the *Mozert* case were sown in 1983, when seven families in Hawkins County, Tennessee, filed a complaint against the local school board, asserting that the required use of a basal reading series in the county's elementary and middle schools violated their right to religious freedom. The Holt, Rinehart & Winston series, which in addition to teaching reading skills was intended to inculcate the values of tolerance and respect for diversity, was found objectionable by the parents on the grounds that its particular approach in presenting other cultures and worldviews directly jeopardized their own attempts to teach their children to rely exclusively on the Bible for guidance in their lives. The suit was filed after the school board rejected an "opt-out" arrangement that some of the parents had worked out with the schools, whereby their children were excused from class during reading periods in order to study from a different textbook. After a district court judge ruled in favor of the plaintiffs and the opt-out accommodation, the school board appealed, and a three-judge panel on the Court of Appeals for the Sixth Circuit reversed the decision, arguing that "mere exposure" to objectionable ideas did not constitute a constitutional burden on the free exercise of religion (*Mozert v. Hawkins*, 827 F.2d 1058). After providing a brief discussion of the plaintiffs' complaint and the appeals court's opinions, I will turn to consider the difficulties posed by political liberalism's own stance toward the *Mozert* families' claims.

The plaintiffs' objections to the reading series were based both on the content of the readers and their pedagogical approach. The *Mozert* families produced a lengthy list detailing the various offensive topics that they discovered in the readers and contended were damaging to the faith of their children. These included the depiction of witchcraft and occult activities, the endorsement of the theory of evolution, and the approval of feminism, as well as the presentation of a host of diverse cultural and religious practices that, as far as the plaintiffs were concerned, denigrated their Christian faith. The plaintiffs also vigorously objected to the fact that, while the religious beliefs of Buddhists and American Indians were found in abundance and treated respectfully in the readers, Christianity was rarely mentioned and, when it was, it was often disparaged (Bates 1993, 203–215).[6]

Despite the extensive attention the plaintiffs devoted to the objectionable subject matter of the readers, their larger concern had to do with the readers' underlying philosophy. For instance, the plaintiffs charged that the readers imparted a skeptical view of religion and taught children to "view Scriptural truth as myth," pressured children "to accept the view that all religions lead to God and are equally valid," and sought to influence the children's values, coercing them to adopt humanist beliefs (Stolzenberg 1993, 597). With these assertions, the plaintiffs went beyond the claim that there was merely some offensive material in the textbooks. On their view, the readers presented a direct threat to their children's faith by subjecting them to different cultural and religious belief systems with the implicit suggestion that none was intrinsically superior to any other. This aim ran directly contrary to the plaintiffs' efforts to instill in their children an unshakable faith in biblical Christianity. What the school board claimed was a benign attempt to teach the skills of critical reading and tolerance, the plaintiffs regarded as a hostile affront to their way of life.

The justices for the Sixth Circuit treated the case as involving a straightforward free-exercise claim. They therefore needed to determine whether the compulsory reading series constituted a burden on the plaintiffs' free exercise of their religion, and if it did, whether the government could demonstrate a compelling interest in requiring the children to continue using the readers. Chief Judge Lively, who wrote for the court, argued that while the plaintiffs might indeed have found material in the readers that offended them, their children were not required to do anything more than read the stories. They were not compelled to accept as true what they read or perform any actions that would signal their agreement with anything contained in the readers. Lively found persuasive the affidavit of the school district's superintendent, which maintained that "exposure to something does not constitute teaching, indoctrination, opposition or promotion of the things exposed. While it is true that these textbooks expose the students to varying values and religious backgrounds, neither the textbooks nor the teachers teach, indoctrinate, oppose or promote any particular value or religion" (*Mozert v. Hawkins*, 827 F.2d 1063).[7] The readers were taking what essentially amounted to a "neutral" approach to the whole question of religion and truth, choosing simply to present the students with a range of viewpoints that they could evaluate for themselves. Lively concluded that this could hardly be viewed as constituting a coercive environment for students, who were, after all, never encouraged to abandon or even question their own convictions. As he stated, "the requirement that students read the assigned materials and attend reading classes, in the absence of a showing that this participation entailed affirmation or denial of a religious belief, or performance or non-performance of a religious exercise or practice, does not place an unconstitutional burden on the students' free exercise of religion" (1065).

Having dismissed the plaintiffs' free-exercise claim, Lively found no reason to inquire into whether the state had a compelling interest in requiring the children to study from the readers. He did, however, go on to defend the reading program's basic aim of teaching "civil" tolerance, which as Lively saw it "does not require a person to accept any other religion as the equal of the one to which that person adheres. It merely requires a recognition that in a pluralistic society we must 'live and let live.' If the Hawkins County schools had required the plaintiff students either to believe or say they believe that 'all religions are merely different roads to God,' this would be a different case" (*Mozert v. Hawkins*, 827 F.2d 1069). The plaintiffs were wrong, therefore, in attributing a sinister animus to the school board's selection of the readers. The board members were not intending to sway the children's convictions away from their parents', but merely pursuing a legitimate civic goal. The readers' objective was simply to ensure that students became aware of and could learn to respect the fact that other people have different beliefs and look at the world in different ways. One of the other justices, Judge Kennedy, concurred with Lively in this regard and argued that even if the plaintiffs could demonstrate that their religion had been burdened by the readers, the civic aim of teaching tolerance would constitute a compelling state interest, since it is crucial to democratic citizenship. "Teaching students about complex and controversial social and moral issues is just as essential for preparing public school students for citizenship and self-government as inculcating in the students the habits and manners of civility" (1071).

Stephen Macedo has helpfully analyzed the *Mozert* case from political liberalism's perspective, concentrating principally on how the norm of the reasonable can be used to adjudicate the *Mozert* families' claims. Macedo follows Rawls closely in contending that political liberalism "focuses our attention on shared political values without requiring or expecting agreement on ultimate ends or a comprehensive set of moral values governing all of our lives" (Macedo 1995, 474). Moreover, Macedo argues, a political liberal society is responsible for securing citizens' allegiance to a political conception of justice and should thus foster the political values of tolerance and political autonomy, ensuring that reasonable citizens will recognize the importance of maintaining society as a fair system of social cooperation. Macedo differs from Rawls mainly in emphasis. Whereas Rawls generally casts political liberalism in as commodious a language as possible and tends not to address the implications surrounding how to respond to "unreasonable" citizens, Macedo favors a "liberalism with spine" (2000, 5). He takes a rather assertive posture in seeking to "put diversity in its place" by identifying comprehensive views of life that will not square with political liberalism's core features and urging that "the success of our civic project relies upon a transformative project that includes the remaking of moral and religious communities" (3, x). What Macedo provides, essentially, is a much-needed account of political liberalism's formative agenda—how to bring about a political liberal society and create political liberal citizens—by way of the "background statecraft" that encourages the development of the proper political capacities needed for life in such a society (6).

As I stressed in chapter 1, political liberalism's imperative to manage moral diversity in the interest of securing justice and social stability most certainly entails the formation of citizens who can successfully and willingly uphold political liberalism's core norms of citizenship, and it also exhibits a correlative tendency to resist or be wary of citizens whose fundamental commitments do not permit them to embrace these norms. So in this sense, Macedo's willingness to consider this matter at length sheds light on a crucial dimension of the political liberal project that Rawls himself does not explore.

It is important to recall, however, that Rawls does acknowledge that in light of its distinctive norms, a society ordered by political liberalism will inevitably come to have a deleterious impact on those comprehensive doctrines that are unable to adapt themselves to political liberalism's ideals. And indeed, in this regard political liberalism is no different from any other theoretical framework used to structure political society. As Rawls states in a passage worth quoting at length:

> If some conceptions will die out and others survive only barely in a just constitutional regime, does this by itself imply that its political conception of justice is not fair to them? Is the political conception arbitrarily biased against these views, or better, is it just or unjust to the persons whose conceptions they are, or might be? Without further explanation, it would not appear to be unfair to them, for social influences favoring some doctrines over others cannot be avoided by any

> view of political justice. No society can include within itself all forms of life. . . . As Berlin has long maintained (it is one of his fundamental themes), there is no social world without loss; that is, no social world that does not exclude some ways of life that realize in special ways certain fundamental values. (1996, 197)

Insofar as *Mozert* represents precisely the kind of situation in which a particular comprehensive doctrine collides with the justice of political liberalism, it will be helpful to consider Macedo's discussion of how to proceed in light of this conflict.

As Macedo observes, the justices' reasoning in *Mozert* is remarkable in its resemblance to political liberalism's approach in distancing itself from "comprehensive ideals of life" when determining legitimate civic aims (1995, 473). The justices concluded that the Holt reading series did not take a stand one way or the other concerning the nature of religious truth. By presenting the material in an objective, detached fashion, the curriculum "would in this way avoid directly confronting or denying the *Mozert* families' contention that the Bible's authority should be accepted uncritically" (1995, 475). Macedo stresses that "leaving religious questions to one side is the best that our educational establishment can do with respect to religion. Indeed, maintaining an educational establishment that teaches children that important public issues can be deliberated upon without considering religious questions is itself part of the education for liberal democratic citizenship properly understood" (2000, 121–122). Political liberalism does not enter into disputes concerning ultimate goods but remains committed only to political values and virtues. This stance is consistent with the justices' depiction of "civil tolerance," which Macedo characterizes as stipulating that "public schools may, in effect, teach that all religions are the same in the eyes of the state, not that they are all the same in the eyes of God" (1995, 473–474).

As Macedo sees it, then, the justices sought to defend a legitimate range of public values that can serve as a basis for the inculcation of civic virtue. "By simply leaving aside the religious question as such, Lively rightly leaves the school door open to reasonable fundamentalists—that is, to those willing to acknowledge *for civic purposes* the authority of public reasonableness" (2000, 175, emphasis in original). The virtues of tolerance and respect for diversity, and the "critical reading" methodology the readers used to try to instill those virtues, are consistent with public aims that can be defended on political terms alone. The plaintiffs, by denying the legitimacy of these aims, have thus jeopardized their participation in the project of liberal citizenship. As political liberalism views this state of affairs, the *Mozert* families were essentially unreasonable, since they rejected the norm of seeking just political arrangements on terms everyone can accept and were unwilling to set aside their nonpublic convictions in the pursuit of public purposes.

The *Mozert* case sheds light on political liberalism's treatment of religious diversity in two key respects. First, it allows us again to consider the extent to which the civic values at the core of political liberalism's conception of political life are able to steer clear of contentious norms and presuppositions concerning the self and the nature of the good life. If we follow Macedo in viewing the Holt series as one viable way in which political liberalism could be applied to a public educational curriculum, we can evaluate the extent to which it succeeds in establishing political values that can remain detached from more substantive disputes about morality or autonomy. The justices agreed with the school board's contention that the reading series was unobjectionable since it sought only to "acquaint students with a multitude of ideas and concepts" and did not aim to disturb the students' already rooted convictions (Macedo 1995, 473). This idea is consistent with political liberalism's ambition to "stay on the surface," so to speak, when it comes to fostering civic virtue. As long as the norms inculcated or encouraged are public ones, we need not fear that we are doing violence to the self, since the values that are most personal to us remain essentially undisturbed. But as Nomi Stolzenberg forcefully argues, the plaintiffs did not view the "mere exposure" of other worldviews and lifestyles as a benign activity. Indeed, they saw this as an attempt to change the way their children thought about morality itself, and that constituted the problem. "In their eyes, the standpoint of neutrality estranged the children from their parents' tradition by turning religious absolutes into matters of personal opinion," suggesting that individual choice was what mattered in determining religious truth (Stolzenberg 1993, 612–613).[8] The idea that people are better off having been given numerous options from which to choose in forming a plan of life was utterly foreign to the plaintiffs, who saw truth as consisting in a duty to God that was *not* chosen. For their children to embrace the view that what gave their beliefs validity was that *they* had tested them and then reaffirmed their commitment to them would be to change the very nature of their convictions.

> The point is not simply that the objective mode of exposure exhibits options, or even that it encourages rational selection among them. It is that even if the children adhere to their parents' beliefs, they do so knowing that those beliefs are matters of opinion. This knowledge enhances the likelihood that children will form their own opinions and deviate from at least some of their parents' beliefs. It also transforms the meaning of remaining (or in the case of children, becoming) attached to them. It is one thing for beliefs to be transmitted from one generation to another. It is another to hold beliefs, knowing that those beliefs are transmitted, that they vary, and that their truth is contested. (633)

We would do well to recall the role of the second moral power in political liberalism's political conception of the person, whereby individuals are said to have a "higher-order" interest in developing their capacity for having a conception of the good *as an end in itself*—that is, the idea that individuals should be able to "affirm" their way of life "in accordance with the full, deliberate, and reasoned exercise of [their] intellectual and moral powers" (Rawls 1996, 313). As we have seen, it is the importance of developing this ability that provides in part the grounds for Rawls's justification for freedom of conscience. But the challenge that the *Mozert* plaintiffs raise is that this "political" conception of the self, if made regulative of a school curriculum, actually has the power to undermine some religious worldviews by altering the basis on which students' deepest convictions are embraced. For the *Mozert* families, what gives their way of life its significance is not the fact that they have chosen it; it is that God *has shown them* the way to live.

The *Mozert* case thus illustrates in a particularly vivid way political liberalism's inability to refrain from taking sides on contested questions surrounding the nature of morality and rationality. The idea that to be fully cooperating citizens we must be able to hold our ultimate allegiances at a distance and subject them to critical evaluation is not an uncontroversial position that all individuals can easily embrace. Rather, it appears to involve a claim concerning the nature of the self that is perilously close to the "comprehensive" ideal of autonomy political liberals have renounced as a legitimate aim for political life.[9] In dismissing the *Mozert* parents' claim that their way of life had been threatened by the Holt curriculum, Justice Lively seems to suggest that the state can foster liberal virtues in an unobtrusive and innocuous fashion. But as Stolzenberg stresses, this notion is only plausible if we overlook the fact that the educational process is inherently about character formation and thus to some degree unavoidably "coercive"—particularly if it involves "the disruption of one culture's processes of socialization by another's" (1993, 634).

Macedo is willing to concede this point, acknowledging that political liberalism cannot be "nonpartisan, uncontroversial, or equally accommodating of all religious beliefs." Indeed, some groups are bound to fare better than others under this conception of political life and political virtue, and this reveals the extent to which political values influence nonpolitical norms and practices. "Promoting core liberal political virtues—such as the importance of a critical attitude toward contending political claims—seems certain to have the effect of promoting critical thinking in general. Liberal political virtues and attitudes will spill over into other spheres of life. Even a suitably circumscribed political liberalism is not really all that circumscribed: it will in various ways promote a way of life as a whole" (1995, 477). Or, as he puts it elsewhere, a task central to political liberalism is to "maintain political institutions and practices that work to transform the whole of the moral world in the image of our most basic political values" (2000, 151).

This leads us to the second, more pressing concern raised by the *Mozert* case. If political liberalism cannot in the end remain impartial toward different worldviews, what is to be done about it? To acknowledge that political liberalism cannot entirely transcend disputes about the good, or the nature of the self, and must ultimately encroach upon such terrain, might be simply to own up to the fact that no regulative social or political principles can refrain from doing so. Deciding how to proceed, however, when worldviews collide and moral communities run up against political norms that threaten their most cherished convictions and way of life is another issue altogether. It is here that the question of the merits of religious free-exercise exemptions arises most forcefully, and it is where we find some of political liberalism's most serious difficulties in responding to religious diversity.

After acknowledging that the reading program did indeed interfere with the *Mozert* parents' efforts to teach their religious convictions to their children, Macedo moves to consider whether this could be said to involve a violation of moral or constitutional rights that might justify the families' desire for an exemption from the curriculum on the grounds of religious freedom.

He concludes that such concerns in this instance are unwarranted, due to the fact that

> the source of the apparent "unfairness," the cause of the "disparate impact" here, is a reasonable attempt to inculcate core liberal values. . . . The program stands as a reasonable effort to familiarize students with diversity and teach toleration. The basic question of principle is: Do people have a moral or constitutional right to opt out of reasonable measures designed to educate children toward very basic liberal virtues, because those measures make it harder for parents to pass along their religious beliefs? Surely not. To acknowledge the legitimacy of the fundamentalist complaint as a matter of basic principle would overthrow reasonable efforts to inculcate core liberal values. (2000, 201–202)

To the charge that this position "appears to be at odds with religious freedom," Macedo responds with the following:

> It must be remembered that rightful liberty is civil liberty, or liberty that can be guaranteed equally to all. All of us must accept limits on our liberty designed to sustain a system of equal freedom for all. Each of us can reasonably be asked to surrender some control over our own children for the sake of reasonable common efforts to ensure that all future citizens learn the minimal prerequisites of citizenship. There is no right to be exempted from measures necessary to secure the freedom of all. (2000, 202)

It is by the standard of the reasonable that political liberalism approaches the claims of the *Mozert* families. As long as the state is implementing measures reasonably designed to further reasonable common purposes, the harmful effects these measures may have on some moral communities need not trouble us. In fact, from the perspective of the reasonable, the *Mozert* plaintiffs are not to be pitied in the least, since the burden they face is due to their vigorous opposition to political liberalism's core ideals. In seeking to deny their children's participation in a reading program designed to promote critical thinking and reflection about other worldviews, they are preventing them from developing their moral powers as citizens. As uncritical, nonautonomous beings, they will be unable to contribute to the perpetuation of a just society. The parents are also rejecting the importance of moderating their claims in accordance with the constraints of public reason. Instead of trying to sustain a system of "equal liberty for all," on terms all can accept, they are intent on introducing their nonpublic convictions as grounds for an exemption from legitimate public purposes. While we should "insist on political respect for fundamentalists who acknowledge the political authority of liberal public principles," we are under no compulsion to honor the wishes of communities or individuals who reject such principles (2000, 203).

What the forgoing strongly suggests is that political liberalism, in restricting public purposes to a rather narrowly defined commitment to furthering specific principles of justice and political virtue, has no standpoint from which it can move beyond those principles when it may be necessary to consider the claims of particular moral communities that may find such principles a threat to their worldview or core convictions. If the only publicly legitimate language we have at our disposal is that of the reasonable, then to offer the *Mozert* families an exemption from the Holt series may be seen as countenancing a rejection of the very principles that support a just liberal polity. Hence, while Macedo declines to insist that free-exercise exemptions should *never* be granted, he is clear that when "political basics" are at stake, these should "routinely trump religious complaints and warrant intransigent support" (2000, 203).

What allows Macedo to take this presumptive stance against a generous response toward free-exercise claims is his assumption, evident throughout his treatment of the *Mozert* case, that the core "political basics" we recognize as a society do not include a respect for religious communities' interest in maintaining their distinctive identity and practices. Only in this way can it be assumed that the *Mozert* parents are completely in opposition to public purposes, representing nothing more than a divisive attempt to disrupt the civic order. The principles of liberal justice, as political liberalism understands them, protect individuals' interests in being public citizens and determining their own life plans. They do not, however, justify reworking or redefining public purposes in the interests of crafting more accommodating arrangements on behalf of particular religious communities that might seek them. When Macedo insists that in encountering free-exercise claims we must "consider from a civic standpoint the nature and grounds of the complaints that are being advanced," this entails the expectation that civic purposes, defined exclusively in accordance with political liberalism's core values, will ultimately govern the way in which religious communities' appeals are perceived (2000, 196).

Macedo's defense of the idea that we can make determinations about something as complex and multifaceted as religious freedom *solely* by relying upon the civic language of political liberalism sheds light on his assertion elsewhere that "we should approach religiously and conscientiously based claims for exceptions without a strong presumption that they will be granted, *but with a determination that they will be listened to and seriously considered*" (2000, 200, my emphasis). The "listening" and "serious consideration" appealed to here might at first be viewed as opening up a possibility for a more expansive, flexible conception of civic purposes, one that could hold out the prospect of adapting public ends in light of the appeals of religious communities for justice. Macedo himself seems briefly to consider this possibility, saying that "we must listen to dissenters and be willing to learn from them," and that "we must also engage religious and other conscientious minorities in political conversation" (210). Yet this opportunity is quickly foreclosed as Macedo insists that

> the question of whether to make exceptions to public laws and if so, when, is vexing and complex but not really basic. The more basic point is that *we* must decide when we can afford to make exceptions in light of the full range of publicly accessible reasons as best we understand them. The grounds for exemptions and accommodation must be the principles and aims that *we* believe justified, and they should be consistent with—even supportive of—the preservation of a liberal civic order. We cannot allow that dissenters have a general right, on private, conscientious grounds, to opt out of generally applicable and publicly justifiable policies or rules. (211, emphasis in original)

Rather than displaying a genuine willingness to engage other perspectives that may not share political liberalism's vision of justice, Macedo consistently retreats to the fallback position of insisting that the purely "political" values of political liberalism must carry the day.[10] Claims that are based on religious viewpoints and at odds with public purposes, as political liberals have defined them, are deemed private and unworthy of "our" consideration.

Macedo rejects the suggestion that a "more substantial ideal of neutrality or fairness" might be needed to help assess the disproportionate impact of public policies on various groups, because doing so would require mitigating our reliance on political values alone. "Understanding the special burden that public rules sometimes impose on religious or cultural minorities requires adopting the minority perspective; that is, it requires dropping the resolute focus on public aims and shared secular interests" (2000, 190, 189). Pursuing such an approach would, of course, run directly against the grain of political liberalism's conception of political life. Taking seriously religious or other "comprehensive perspectives" and allowing them to have public significance in the shaping of policy issues concerned with fundamental liberties or other constitutional essentials jeopardize the distinctive logic and autonomy of the political sphere and are thus precisely what political liberalism cannot allow. As Rawls explains, the idea that crucial policy matters may in some instances be determined, even in part, by aspects of citizens' comprehensive doctrines that are independent of political values would invalidate the "completeness" of a political conception of justice (1997, 777).

It is thus clear that political liberalism's conception of the reasonable has a significant impact in reducing the scope of democratic negotiation of moral difference, at least as it concerns religious diversity. Appeals for religious liberty exemptions are practically denied in advance, insofar as those appeals by necessity move beyond the insular language of the reasonable. Political liberal elites—the "we" in Macedo's discussion above—are given the authority to adjudicate claims for exemptions solely with reference to a narrow and predetermined conception of public purposes, one that excludes the most essential concerns of the groups and individuals advancing those claims. Unreasonable religious communities such as the *Mozert* families are thus viewed as meddlesome interlopers, intent on disrupting the smoothly functioning societal system of cooperation that political liberalism offers as a way to manage religious diversity. Their concerns cannot be regarded as politically legitimate, or even worthy of democratic engagement, for to open up that prospect would be to introduce moral languages and values that exceed and challenge political liberalism's strictly political language.

It is crucial to recognize, however, that within the American context, legitimate public values have not been limited to those that unequivocally support a view of liberal citizenship in which free-exercise claims should be presumptively regarded with suspicion. The ability of religious communities to preserve the practices and convictions most central to their way of life has, after all, through military exemptions been recognized as a principle rivaling in importance even individuals' obligations to defend the polity.[11] Political liberalism's approach toward free-exercise claims thus privileges a statist understanding of political life out of keeping with that strand of American thought that views religious commitments as having greater importance than our temporal and civic obligations.[12] Since political liberalism is unable to grant any public weight to this perspective, it leaves the situation of the *Mozert* families and claimants like them on very unsure footing, to say the least.

Ultimately, then, the difficulties political liberalism faces with regard to the *Mozert* case are a direct result of its commitment to a static, unyielding vision of liberal justice that, in its effort to resolve questions of rights and justice as authoritatively as possible, ends up denying room for the political negotiation of conflicts in which those rights are subject to competing interpretations and meanings. The intricate articulations of freedom of conscience that one finds in Rawls's *A Theory of Justice* and *Political Liberalism* offer little guidance when we are confronted with hard cases that prompt imaginative responses beyond an unwavering reliance upon political liberalism's political values. Particularly illuminating is a brief section of *Theory* in which Rawls considers how, from the perspective of justice as fairness, acts of "conscientious refusal" might be regarded within a just society.

> It is a difficult matter to find the right course when some men appeal to religious principles in refusing to do actions which, it seems, are required by principles of political justice. Does the pacifist possess an immunity from military service in a just war, assuming that there are such wars? Or is the state permitted to impose certain hardships for noncompliance? There is a temptation to say that the law must always respect the dictates of conscience, but this cannot be right. As we have seen in the case of the intolerant, the legal order must regulate men's pursuit of their religious interests so as to realize the principle of equal liberty; and it may certainly forbid religious practices such as human sacrifice, to take an extreme case. Neither religiosity nor conscientiousness suffices to protect this practice. *A theory of justice must work out from its own point of view how to treat those who dissent from it. The aim of a well-ordered society, or one in a state of near justice, is to preserve and strengthen the institutions of justice.* If a religion is denied its full

> expression, it is presumably because it is in violation of the equal liberties of others. In general, the degree of tolerance accorded opposing moral conceptions depends upon the extent to which they can be allowed an equal place within a just system of liberty. (1971, 370, my emphasis)

From a perspective grounded solely in political liberalism's conception of liberal justice, the impartiality and inflexibility needed to secure justice in as unambiguous and mutually acceptable a way as possible ironically leave us instead with a restricted vision, precluding the kind of response that in the case of the *Mozert* families might have allowed their claims to gain a more equitable hearing. Only if we are willing to admit the possibility that civic purposes might at times require reformulation and may therefore be productively informed by the experiences and insights of diverse moral communities, can we hope for a less intransigent and exclusivist stance toward questions of rights and justice, particularly where matters of moral diversity are involved.

Religious Freedom in Context: American Struggles

Because political liberalism offers an understanding of freedom of conscience that is largely immune from contestation and political disagreement, it is unable to acknowledge the way in which religious freedom, like all matters concerning rights and justice, depends precisely on a political process of engagement and negotiation in order to define and instantiate it. This dynamic is revealed when we consider the historical development of the ideal of religious liberty in the American context. Rather than being derived principally on the basis of abstract principle, religious liberty in America became a reality only because religious communities in the seventeenth and eighteenth centuries were willing to wage visible struggles on behalf of their particular religious obligations. William Lee Miller reminds us that "the American achievements of religious liberty and the separation of church and state did not take place in a vacuum, but in a particular time and place, with specific historical and cultural antecedents and with specific historical and cultural results" (1986, 234).[13] By considering these contextual factors, we are afforded a glimpse into a process of defining public ideals that is less resistant toward the distinctive contributions that can be made by dissenting moral communities—even those whose claims cannot be translated neatly into a narrowly "political" public language.[14]

By the time of the revolution, America was characterized by a cultural Protestantism that thoroughly permeated both social and political life. To be sure, the states varied with regard to the composition of religious groups in their midst. The New England states, and Massachusetts in particular, had a preponderance of Congregationalist, or Puritan, churches, while other states such as New York, Rhode Island, and Maryland were characterized by greater diversity—in Maryland, for example, the presence of a large Catholic population led to a unique set of challenges. Despite the multiplicity of groups, however, most Americans' ideas about religious freedom had converged to the point that certain general norms were widely in place. Toleration of dissenting groups had become embraced as a matter of principle (although not always in practice, of course). The state was presumed to have no direct role to play in ecclesial matters, although provisions supporting Sabbath observance and other elements of civil religion considered essential for a healthy society were widely accepted as valid. The freedom *not* to believe was not explicitly recognized. The prevailing view was that religion mattered for the soundness of society generally, and thus, while commentators frequently championed the idea of "absolute" freedom of conscience, it was presumed that this freedom was grounded in the norms of a Christian and Protestant state (Curry 1986, 219, 78–79).

With this cultural context taken into account, it is all the more remarkable that religious toleration had become so widespread by the late eighteenth century. Absent the role played by dissenting religious communities in challenging the dominant religious norms of the greater society, it would have been unthinkable that more accommodating policies concerning religious liberty could gradually emerge in the various colonies, and then arise even more prominently during the postrevolutionary debates in the fledgling states. A noteworthy example of the latter was the 1784 struggle in the Virginia General Assembly over a proposed "assessment" to provide for the public support of clergy. Driven by a desire to reverse what was widely perceived to be a general flagging of religious observance in the state, Patrick Henry sponsored and labored on behalf of the bill, which would have implemented a general tax in support of religion, with taxpayers designating individually the denomination they wished to receive their share. The justification for the assessment was based on the notion that since "Christian knowledge hath a natural tendency to correct the morals of men, restrain their vices, and preserve the peace of society," the support of "learned teachers" for the dissemination of this knowledge was a genuine public good. The bill was widely popular, as it confirmed the prevalent idea that churches played an indispensable role in the maintenance of public virtue (Curry 1986, 140–141).

Henry's argument reflected one of two dominant perspectives on religion's relationship to the polity in eighteenth-century America. Many citizens found it inconceivable that a healthy society could be maintained without the public provision of moral instruction, and this was widely regarded as the province of the churches. In his "Memorial and Remonstrance," however, James Madison presented a very different view, questioning the wisdom of involving the state in matters of faith. His argument began with a quote from the religious liberty provision of the Virginia Declaration of Rights: "that Religion or the duty which we owe to our Creator and the manner of discharging it, can be directed only by reason and conviction, not by force or violence." It went on to contend that

> this duty is precedent, both in order of time and in degree of obligation, to the claims of Civil Society. Before any man can be considered as a member of Civil Society, he must be considered as a subject of the Governour of the Universe: And if a member of Civil Society, who enters into any subordinate Association, must always do it with a reservation of his duty to the General Authority; much more must every man who becomes a member of any particular Civil Society, do it with a saving of his allegiance to the Universal Sovereign. We maintain therefore that in matters of Religion, no man's right is abridged by the institution of Civil Society and that Religion is wholly exempt from its cognizance. ([1784] 1985, 56–58)

In addition to grounding the right to religious freedom on a duty all human beings have to God, Madison went on to stress that true religion is corrupted when it is used as an "engine of Civil policy" and that "the policy of the Bill is adverse to the diffusion of the light of Christianity" (57, 59).

Madison's argument exemplifies the other significant strand of thought on public life and religion during the late eighteenth-century debates over religious liberty. It draws heavily from the language of dissenting faith communities, those that had struggled against oppressive establishments throughout the colonies, and it must be seen against the backdrop of the struggles they waged. For it was within the individual colonies that concrete arrangements to instantiate religious liberty first came into being, well before the formal deliberations over the Bill of Rights took place. These "experiments" were sometimes characterized by significant social tension, as the presence of religious diversity challenged communities to come up with new ways of thinking about issues of church and state. Some colonies, such as Rhode Island and Pennsylvania, had from the start sought to initiate bold efforts to tolerate a wide range of dissenting groups. Roger Williams, who came out of the separatist strand of New England Congregationalism, founded Rhode Island to carry out his vision of a polity that would provide a welcoming haven for groups who were unable to find a home within the more constraining confines of Massachusetts (Curry 1986, 14–21; Miller 1986, 153–202; Murphy 2001, 27–73). Pennsylvania was founded by William Penn, who sought first of all an environment safe for Quakers but welcomed anyone into the community who affirmed a belief in God (Curry 1986, 72–76; Murphy 2001, 165–207). Both of these colonies were instrumental in providing examples of regimes in which religious freedom was intentionally, and for the most part successfully, pursued. During the debates in Virginia over the assessment bill, petitioners pointed to those colonies as proof that a policy of nonestablishment was beneficial for both civil society and religion (Curry 1986, 144).[15]

In those colonies with establishments in place, the attempt to secure religious liberty was a more perilous one and required the ongoing resistance of dissenting communities to gain recognition and respect, a goal that often went unachieved. In Massachusetts, for instance, Quaker and Baptist groups met particularly vehement opposition, particularly in the seventeenth century, when they were typically banished or, on occasion, put to death for their attempts to challenge Congregationalist establishments (McConnell 1990, 1422–1423; Murphy 2001, 56–64). Elsewhere dissenters enjoyed more success, but only after engaging in protracted efforts at resistance and enduring similar hardships.

Virginia provides the most pronounced example. Prior to the advent of the religious liberty provision in the Declaration of Rights of 1776 and the aforementioned Act Establishing Religious Freedom (which officially eliminated the establishment of the Anglican church), Virginia was one of the more hostile environments for unorthodox groups.[16] As dissenters increased in number and influence, they put mounting pressure on elites to secure their ability to worship and practice their faith without hindrance. It was from these dissenting groups, rather than the more firmly entrenched Anglican church, that the real push for religious freedom originated. As Michael McConnell puts it:

> The newer, more enthusiastic sects had the most to gain from breaking the monopoly of the old established church. This would allow new, often uneducated and itinerant preachers to conduct worship services and revival meetings and would make the financial support of a preacher dependent on the enthusiasm he generated among his adherents. The greatest support for disestablishment and free exercise therefore came from evangelical Protestant denominations, especially Baptists and Quakers, but also Presbyterians, Lutherans, and others. (1990, 1439)

Madison's remonstrance thus utilized an approach for coming to terms with religious liberty that had become thoroughly familiar to dissenting communities by the time of the assessment debate. In delimiting the state's legitimate authority before the greater sovereignty of the "Governour of the Universe," Madison essentially located all religious matters beyond the state's purview. It was this perspective that struggled against the view of Henry and others in favor of religious establishments, and it ultimately helped determine the eventual shape of the First Amendment. To be sure, the dissenting communities' justification for nonestablishment was not the only one that influenced the outcome; Jefferson's well-known concern to insulate politics from the divisive potential of religion was also an important view.[17] But it is doubtful that the nonestablishment forces would have triumphed so decisively without the distinct perspective offered by dissenting faith communities throughout the seventeenth and eighteenth centuries.

The impact of the dissenters' perspective can be measured in part by considering that with the lone exception of Connecticut, all of the early state constitutions contained provisions for religious liberty, which was "universally said to be an unalienable right," whereas "the status of other rights commonly found in state bills of rights, such as property or trial by jury, was more disputed and often considered derivative of civil society" (McConnell 1990, 1455–1456).[18] Moreover, a number of the colonial governments and state legislatures made exemptions for dissenting groups as a matter of policy. Exemptions for Quakers who refused to take oaths were common during the colonial period, and almost universally in place by 1789; accommodations for those who refused to bear arms, chiefly Quakers and Mennonites, were granted in several states; and those states that had established churches often spared dissenting groups from having to comply with compulsory tithes (McConnell 1990, 1466–1471).[19]

It must be acknowledged that free-exercise exemptions were never granted as basic rights in the same way that rights to belief and worship, narrowly construed, were understood. Nor were they extended equally to all groups; Catholics were often denied them as a matter of principle, for instance. It would not be until 1940 that the Supreme Court would begin to consider conduct exemptions as falling under the free-exercise clause; in its most prominent free-exercise case prior to that date, it emphatically denied the right to a conduct exemption.[20] The history of the development of religious freedom in America has thus been characterized by fitful steps and often-contradictory outcomes. It is best understood, therefore, not as a straightforward realization of a clear and unambiguous concept, but as an ongoing project—an attempt to continually redefine and reshape what religious liberty means and how it should be protected. It necessarily involves the effort of dissenting communities, in particular, who are able to challenge settled convictions and probe the limits of existing interpretations, in the hope that our collective understandings may be better defined and improved upon. Such a process is an intrinsically political one, whereby communities bring their insights and convictions to bear on public life in a direct way, exposing themselves to potential conflict but also holding out the possibility that they may gain respect through that struggle.

In pursuing the goal of a society characterized by a commitment to shared principles of justice, political liberalism seeks to manage, and thereby transcend, the obstacles and tensions posed by moral diversity. By securing public agreement on the norms regulating political life, political liberals argue, we can safely confine moral diversity to the nonpublic realm of voluntary associations, where, bounded by the constraints put in place by these shared norms, our differences will be unable to disrupt the process by which justice and rights are guaranteed to all. Yet this strategy ignores the way in which our differences are in large part responsible for new understandings of rights and new interpretations of justice coming about.[21] As this chapter has shown, our shifting understandings of freedom of religion have been deeply influenced by diverse religious communities that have insistently acted upon their most fundamental convictions in negotiating and shaping what has come to be regarded as one of our most privileged rights.

From political liberalism's perspective, the historical struggle over matters of religious liberty is relevant only as a cautionary tale, a way for us to recognize the dangers that accompany politicized religion. In no way is this historical context considered necessary for elucidating the nature or extent of the right to religious liberty, which like all rights is best justified by abstracting from history and contingency. This understanding of rights is a distorted one, however. Rights such as religious liberty have evolved to protect goods that are viewed as essential to human flourishing. They have therefore drawn upon our various ideas about human flourishing, and the particular traditions out of which these notions have arisen, for much of their justification and power. To leave that dimension out of our consideration of rights and justice may therefore not only result in faulty descriptions but deprive us of the broader normative understandings needed to give these matters their full weight and significance.

It is certainly true that acknowledging this context-bound aspect of rights presents difficult challenges, particularly when these rights are on contested terrain. There is indeed something paradoxical about the idea that a right such as religious liberty, which is in one sense intended to be a solution to the "problem" of moral diversity, is itself subject to the very tensions that arise out of it. But if we reject the temptation to assume that something as complex and multifaceted as religious liberty can be defined unproblematically and justified uncontroversially, we may be able to perceive this right (and its various incarnations) as, in part, an ongoing, unfolding reflection of the changing reality of moral diversity. We can appreciate the ways in which the altering of the religious landscape has helped contribute to the changing presuppositions underlying the right to religious freedom. Hence just as the "unorthodox" religious communities of the eighteenth century—the Quakers, Baptists, Mennonites, and others—were instrumental in helping to shape the understanding of religious liberty of that period, so too have groups outside the contemporary religious mainstream offered significant challenges to the way religious liberty is currently understood and protected. Jehovah's Witnesses, Seventh-day Adventists, the Old Order Amish, Christian Scientists, and various Native American communities have brought some of the most significant free-exercise cases to the courts during the post–World War II period. Others have sought to broaden the understanding of freedom of conscience by appealing for military draft exemptions on nonreligious grounds.[22] These efforts have not always been successful in effectuating change in the scope of religious liberty, but by challenging prevailing understandings, they illustrate one of the essential ways in which moral diversity is made publicly and politically relevant.[23]

The *Mozert* case is also exemplary in this regard. It brings to the fore many of the issues surrounding moral diversity in contemporary America, raising not only questions about how religious diversity should be addressed, but questions that go to the heart of liberal democracy itself, including the nature of civic virtue and current controversies surrounding civic education. It thus reveals that much remains to be determined about the best way to protect religious liberty and about liberalism's own self-understandings. Seen in this light, the "disruptions" occasioned by public contestation over moral diversity provide opportunities for considering larger questions that have either gone unexplored or been regarded as settled. They afford us the chance to respond to the changing composition of our moral landscape as it affects political life. The implications of moral diversity are thus to be continually wrestled with and worked out, as various notions of the good contend with one another in the quest to define and pursue political ideals. Acknowledging this requires us to recognize that the securing of rights and justice is a more inexact and turbulent process than that envisioned by political liberalism. But it also allows us to appreciate the possibility and merit of searching for more expansive understandings of public purposes, ones that involve engaging, not avoiding, the sources of our moral diversity.[24]

If we are to pursue this alternative approach to moral diversity, it is imperative that we move beyond the conceptualizations at the heart of political liberalism's vision of liberal justice. The particular understandings codified in its ideals of the reasonable, and the fair terms of social cooperation, result in the kinds of invidious distinctions that render it more difficult to engage a wide range of moral perspectives in the search for better understandings of public purposes. In the chapters to follow, I will consider how we might fashion an ethics of public life less prone to these liabilities.

CHAPTER 3

The Secularity of Liberal Public Reason

The issues surrounding the *Mozert* case and the contested nature of religious liberty serve to highlight the difficulties accompanying any attempt to establish the boundaries of political life that does not take into account the perspectives of those moral communities affected most directly by that process. Regardless of how they are approached, however, church-state questions seem to pose unavoidable challenges for coming to terms with our moral and religious differences. Yet these represent just one subset of the greater realm of questions concerning rights and justice, many of which touch upon our most fundamental and far-reaching convictions concerning the nature of human beings and the ultimate ends they should pursue. When conflicts over such issues emerge, it should not surprise us that they are often accompanied by heated rhetoric and passionate declamations. Public discussion of abortion, euthanasia, economic justice, human cloning, capital punishment, and other vital controversies reveals in a striking way the contrasting worldviews and moral traditions that characterize American society and help comprise its moral diversity.

For political liberals, this moral diversity necessitates the search for a shared political language, a way to carry out public discussions on terms all reasonable citizens can accept. Once an overlapping consensus on principles of justice is obtained and set in place, a "public point of view" is made available to assist us in approaching contentious policy issues in a spirit of commonality and civility. By virtue of their shared commitment to reasonableness, citizens can be confident that their political disputes will not evolve into a bare-knuckled struggle between incommensurable worldviews. Instead, by remaining within the horizon of liberal public reason, our disagreements can be made less divisive and intractable.

I have thus far raised a number of concerns about this project and its prospects for helping us negotiate the challenges of moral diversity. This chapter will pursue the matter further, by exploring in greater depth political liberalism's conception of public reason and the arguments that support it. It is here that we see most clearly the implications of political liberalism's commitment to managing moral diversity and restricting democratic engagement. For while political liberalism has gradually moved in a more accommodating direction in its view of public discourse, it remains the case that there are deeply rooted impulses within it that mandate a vigilant policing of the public realm, to ensure that citizens' comprehensive views cannot interfere with the orderly pursuit of liberal justice. As I argued in the previous chapters, political liberals rely upon highly contestable principles for their vision of liberal rights and justice. But this is hardly their greatest failing. It is in their effort to insulate those principles from contestation by religious and other kinds of comprehensive doctrines that political liberals reveal their approach to public life to be both invidious *and* at odds with democratic politics.

Political Liberalism's Search for a Public Language: Is Religion Welcome?

As we observed in chapter 1, Rawls's *Political Liberalism* takes for its starting point the fact that contemporary liberal societies are radically divided by a multiplicity of comprehensive doctrines. We cannot, moreover, expect "that in the foreseeable future one of them, or some other reasonable doctrine, will ever be affirmed by all, or nearly all, citizens" (Rawls 1996, xviii).[1] Given the need for a stable and purposeful basis for social cooperation, this diversity requires us to obtain a shared political language that can facilitate the creation of a public space that is equally available to all of us, one free of invidious or unjustifiably coercive exercises of political power. For political liberalism, this is made possible by the "publicly recognized point of view" brought about by the overlapping consensus on a political conception of justice. From this perspective, "all citizens can examine before one another whether their political and social institutions are just. It enables them to do this by citing what are publicly recognized among them as valid and sufficient reasons singled out by that conception itself." The fact that this perspective is truly public, truly shared, ensures that it is equally accessible to all citizens: "society's main institutions and how they fit together into one system of social cooperation can be assessed in the same way by each citizen, whatever that citizen's social position or more particular interests" (9). Political liberalism thus seeks to make possible a transparent and demystified public realm.

> The political order does not, it seems, depend on historically accidental or established delusions, or other mistaken beliefs resting on the deceptive appearances of institutions that mislead us as to how they work. Of course, there can be no certainty about this. But publicity ensures, so far as practical measures allow, that citizens are in a position to know and to accept the pervasive influences of the basic structure that shape their conception of themselves, their character and ends. . . . That citizens should be in this position is a condition of their realizing their freedom as fully autonomous, politically speaking. It means that in their public political life nothing need be hidden. (68)

In helping to bring about a public realm that rests on a publicly transparent foundation, political liberalism's "public point of view," or public reason, serves both to limit and to justify the state's coercive authority. As Rawls puts it, "our exercise of political power is fully proper only when it is exercised in accordance with a constitution the essentials of which all citizens as free and equal may reasonably be expected to endorse in the light of principles and ideals acceptable to their common human reason" (1996, 137). And since public reason produces this constraint on the legitimate exercise of coercion, the willingness to rely upon it in our political activity constitutes a fundamental norm of citizenship. Citizens have a responsibility to "live politically with others in the light of reasons all might reasonably be expected to endorse," and in taking this responsibility seriously citizens exhibit the liberal virtue of civility (243).

For this project to succeed, we would need to be able to determine fairly precisely the boundaries of the political sphere—the realm within which public reason is to be regulative—as well as stipulate the kinds of reasoning that should be admitted there. Doing this would allow us to be confident that religious and other kinds of controversial reasoning will be unable to disrupt the stability of the political domain. As political liberals conceive it, this task is integral to the liberal project itself, as they identify its origins in the response to the novel set of conditions created by the Reformation and subsequent wars of religion of the sixteenth and seventeenth centuries. As Rawls argues, these events posed the problem that liberalism was designed to solve. Societies came to be inhabited by clashing rival faiths characterized by "authoritative, salvationist, and expansionist" impulses, and the political imperative soon became finding a way to end internecine conflict by establishing a basis for social unity other than that provided by religious tradition (1996, xxiv–xxxi). This problem was exacerbated by the "transcendent" element of religious faith, an element "not admitting of compromise," which "forces either mortal conflict moderated only by circumstance and exhaustion, or equal liberty of conscience and freedom of thought" (xxviii). Rawls contends that it was within this dilemma that the possibility of a solution became manifest to the early moderns. Religion would have to relinquish its civic authority, giving way to a distinctly public reason allowed to regulate those concerns properly falling within the newly constituted, autonomous, public realm.

Of course, if the situation giving birth to liberalism is portrayed in these terms and continues to shape our understanding of the liberal project, the ensuing conception of public reason would seem to require an exclusively secular foundation, with religious reasoning playing no legitimate role in public discourse. And indeed, some articulations of public reason by contemporary liberals do seem to take this position. Macedo, for instance, has argued that the reasons liberal citizens offer to one another as being politically authoritative "must be *public* in the sense of being widely and openly accessible; appeals to inner conviction or faith," in addition to other forms of "inaccessible" reasoning, are ruled out (1992, 46, emphasis in original). Similarly, Thomas Nagel contends that public reasoning must meet the criterion of "impartiality," so that only "evidence that can be shared" is properly introduced into public deliberation. Beliefs that are based on "personal faith or revelation" can never meet this requirement and should therefore be excluded from the process of public justification (1987, 232). Robert Audi makes the point clearly: public reason is *secular* reason, particularly when public deliberation involves coercive legislation. Liberal democracy should be "committed to the *conceptual and epistemic autonomy of ethics*," a commitment that would be jeopardized if citizens were unwilling to exclude their religious convictions from the process of public debate (1993, 697, emphasis in original).[2]

This kind of thoroughgoing secularist understanding of public reason has recently been put on the defensive, however. Many critics have noted the unfairness inherent in secularist conceptions of public reason: citizens with religiously formed worldviews, if they are to be good citizens, must examine and modify their convictions and censor their public speech in a way not required of their secularist fellow citizens.[3] It is noteworthy, therefore, that more recent defenses of political liberalism evince a recognition that requiring citizens consistently to divorce their most comprehensive convictions from their political activity may not be wholly defensible. Rawls, in particular, seems eager to convince would-be detractors that political liberalism does not pose a threat to most religious citizens. He indicates, for instance, that he has gradually altered his understanding of public reason from an "exclusive" view, which would preclude citizens from ever offering religious arguments in public debate over fundamental political issues, to an "inclusive" view, which would selectively allow such appeals, and finally to an even more expansive view: what he now calls the "wide view of public reason." Rawls's "wide view" framework allows citizens' religious arguments to be presented alongside their more purely "public" claims, rather than simply requiring religious kinds of reasoning to be categorically excluded from the public realm (1996, 247–248, li–lii).[4] Similarly, Macedo has sought to counter the notion that religious citizens' viewpoints are entirely off-limits in political life. He asserts that critics who argue that political liberals "seek to exclude religious people from the public realm or to curtail their political speech" are mistaken. Religious citizens must only agree to accept the idea that "the most basic political rights and institutions should be justified in terms of reasons and arguments that can be shared with reasonable people whose religious and other ultimate commitments differ" (1995, 480, 475). This, Macedo argues, is a reasonable expectation to place on religious citizens who enjoy the particular benefits of living in a liberal society, and he seems confident that for the most part religious citizens should have no real difficulty in making this accommodation.[5]

When contrasted with the more unapologetically secularist versions of liberal public reason, these more recent articulations can be seen as embodying attempts to modify public reason in a more inclusive direction, or at least to placate those who are less enthusiastic about removing religion's presence from political life. This "softer" stance toward religion is reflected both in political liberalism's conception of the circumscribed limits of the language of public reason and in the correlative boundedness of the political domain itself. After discussing these features, I will proceed to evaluate whether political liberalism's more inclusive framework offers a satisfactory way to establish a widely shared and workable public language.

Political liberals stress that public reason is intended only to govern our deliberations concerning the most fundamental political matters. It is not to regulate all of public life. It covers what Rawls calls "constitutional essentials" and "questions of basic justice," those areas most central to the foundation of the political order itself (1996, 214). On these kinds of issues it is of the utmost importance that citizens share the same political vocabulary. Constitutional essentials include anything pertaining to "the general structure of government and the political process," as well as the "equal basic rights and liberties of citizenship that legislative majorities are to respect" (227). The "basic justice" rubric covers "the principles regulating basic matters of distributive justice, such as freedom of movement and equality of opportunity, social and economic inequalities, and the social bases of self-respect" (228). Those issues not included in these categories, and therefore of less political urgency, are not subject to the constraints of public reason. Rawls maintains that "many if not most political questions do not concern those fundamental matters," and he notes by way of example that some forms of tax legislation, as well as environmental protection statutes and legislation establishing parks or designating funding for the arts would fall outside the purview of public reason (214). Religious comprehensive doctrines, like other comprehensive views, could be introduced in public deliberation over these kinds of issues without difficulty.

In addition to being applicable to only a certain range of political questions, public reason is intended to be confined to the space Rawls calls the "domain of the political." That is, it is intended to govern our actions when we as citizens "engage in political advocacy in the public forum," but it does not "apply to our personal deliberations and reflections about political questions, or to the reasoning about them by members of associations such as churches and universities, all of which is a vital part of the background culture" (1996, 215). Within the context of the "background culture," or civil society, other kinds of reasons are properly used, consistent with the distinctive aims of each association. Following the work of David Hollenbach, Rawls suggests that a great deal of significant discourse takes place in this realm in an unencumbered fashion, precisely because the institutions involved stand outside the political sphere narrowly understood (1997, 768).[6] And although the arguments presented in these contexts are, politically understood, "nonpublic," they are not therefore considered private or nonsocial. They are "public with respect to their members, but nonpublic with respect to political society and to citizens generally" (1996, 220). As Rawls puts it elsewhere, the background culture is "the culture of the social, not of the political" (13–14).[7]

Rawls also suggests that, in keeping with the distinction between the public political forum and the background culture, the strictures of public reason apply most heavily to those in positions of public authority. The public political forum includes "the discourse of judges in their decisions, and especially of the judges of a supreme court; the discourse of government officials, especially chief executives and legislators; and finally, the discourse of candidates for public office and their campaign managers, especially in their public oratory, party platforms, and political statements" (1997, 767). Citizens not in these positions of public responsibility are less encumbered in their discourse. Since their political activity does not typically take place in the political forum, their primary support of public reason entails "doing what they can to hold government officials to it" (769).[8]

Finally, Rawls has stipulated that it can be acceptable for citizens to advance religious arguments *even in* situations in which constitutional essentials are being discussed and in which the discourse taking place is conducted in the public political forum. Rawls insists only that this discourse be subject to what he calls "the proviso": "reasonable comprehensive doctrines, religious or nonreligious, may be introduced in public political discussion at any time, provided that in due course proper political reasons—and not reasons given solely by comprehensive doctrines—are presented that are sufficient to support whatever the comprehensive doctrines introduced are said to support" (1997, 783–784).[9] Rawls even allows that on some occasions religious argument might not simply be acceptable in public debate but in fact be helpful. Particularly in societies that are moving toward a consensus on principles of justice but in which such a consensus remains yet to be firmly established, citizens who rely upon widely shared religious views to frame their public defense of justice can help influence their fellow citizens to place a higher value on justice (1996, li–lii).[10] Along these lines, Macedo grants that "if religious people wish to bear witness to the justifiability of political liberalism from the point of view of their religious perspectives, this may be not only appropriate but also helpful on certain occasions" (1995, 492). By declaring to other citizens the features of our comprehensive doctrines, it becomes possible to solidify support for an overlapping consensus, by showing "how, from our own doctrines, we can and do endorse a reasonable public political conception of justice with its principles and ideals. The aim of doing this is to declare to others who affirm different comprehensive doctrines that we also each endorse a reasonable political conception belonging to the family of reasonable such conceptions. . . . In this way citizens who hold different doctrines are reassured, and this strengthens the ties of civic friendship" (Rawls 1997, 786). Rawls stresses that "there is, or need be, no war between religion and democracy" (803–804). Where reasonable religious comprehensive doctrines can work to sustain a societal commitment to liberal justice, they should be encouraged to do so.

With these qualifications in view, political liberals are able to make a plausible claim that in proposing this conception of public reason, they are not seeking to banish religion from public life or confine it to the realm of personal belief, strategies that have been favored by less circumspect liberals. Indeed, for political liberalism to be internally consistent, it must refrain from taking sides at all on questions concerning the nature of religion or religious truth. To argue, for instance, that religion is inherently a private phenomenon would be an unacceptable violation of political liberalism's own self-imposed constraints on public discourse. By removing these questions altogether from the sphere of public reason, Rawls argues, we are able to apply "the principle of toleration to philosophy itself" and ensure that the principles regulating the political order rest on as uncontroversial a foundation as possible (1996, 10).[11]

In agreeing to rely upon public reason in our political activity *as citizens,* then, we are not embracing the view that religion is of no value in shaping our communities. Nor are we claiming that religious traditions have nothing to say about the crucial issues of our day. We are simply ensuring that they do not interfere with the distinctly political logic that must govern our most essential political practices. Our commitment to establishing the primacy of public reason, and allowing it to govern our use of our comprehensive views in public discourse, does not stem from doubts about the truth of our deepest beliefs. Rather, it reflects an understanding that "politics in a democratic society can never be guided by what we see as the whole truth," and that we are therefore much better served by trying to "live politically with others in the light of reasons all might reasonably be expected to endorse" (1996, 242–243).

We are to agree, therefore, that on that certain range of issues falling under the categories of constitutional essentials and basic justice, we are to justify our activity in the political domain by relying upon "political values." These include both "values of political justice," such as equal liberty and opportunity, and "guidelines for public inquiry," such as the political virtues of reasonableness and civility (1996, 224).[12] To refuse to structure our public arguments around political values would risk jeopardizing the basis for social unity that is maintained by our shared devotion to a political conception of justice. On this view, it is our commitment to the reciprocity at the heart of "civic friendship," not suspicion toward the claims of religion, that leads us to regulate our reliance on our comprehensive convictions in accordance with public reason (1996, li). By offering public arguments that others can accept as consistent with their own exercise of reason, we demonstrate respect for our fellow citizens' status as political equals and recognize their shared role in maintaining just social and political institutions.

These observations would suggest that, rather than seeking to banish religion from the public realm, political liberals are merely attempting to work out an amicable arrangement whereby reasonable religious viewpoints can converge, as part of the overlapping consensus, on a political conception of justice that all citizens, regardless of their religious or philosophical convictions, can embrace on the same grounds. The restraint in reason-giving political liberalism requires of citizens is on this reading to be seen merely as the price we must pay for securing a mutually acceptable basis for social unity consistent with each citizen's rationality. The autonomy we grant to the "domain of the political," reflected in freestanding principles of justice that are established and justified by reference to political values alone, would then be necessary simply because it is the only way in which a society divided by incommensurable comprehensive doctrines can proceed to transcend these divisions.

Difficulties with Circumscribing Public Reason's Scope and Proper Domain

Might political liberalism, even considering these important qualifications, still go too far in seeking to constrain the role of religion in public life? As I take up this question, the first set of issues I will address involve the descriptive conceptualizations at the heart of political liberalism's model of public reason. These concern the scope of public reason as well as the distinction between the public political forum and the background culture. Both of these conceptualizations have crucial implications for how we understand the purpose of public discourse and the responsibilities of citizenship.

First, political liberals claim that because the purview of public reason is limited to constitutional essentials and questions of basic justice, it is suitably circumscribed so as to allow for a wide range of arguments to be presented in public discussion concerning all but the most essential foundational matters of the polity itself. However, closer examination of what is to be included under these rubrics leaves some doubt about public reason's narrowness. Not only discussions concerning economic justice or the structure of governmental institutions are to be regulated by public reason; any attempt to specify or delineate the scope of particular human rights would seem to be similarly constrained. All of those issues that confront our understanding of life and death—abortion, euthanasia, human cloning, and capital punishment, among others—would also have to be considered bound by this requirement. Indeed, this group of issues in particular involves concerns that have widely been regarded as those in which theological ethical reflection has the most to offer—those matters that are centrally connected with our understanding of life's origins, purposes, and limits. If theological arguments on these questions are to be governed by Rawls's proviso, such that they must be offered alongside political values in order to have legitimacy, this would go substantially beyond a minimal restriction on public discourse.

Political liberalism's distinction between the public political forum and civil society, or the "background culture," is also problematic. There are indeed advantages to recognizing the importance of civil society as a space where public discussions can be more open-ended and wide-ranging and where considerations of political expediency and tactical bargaining are secondary. Much of contemporary politics is inherently adversarial, and it is helpful to remember that there are other contexts for public discourse beyond the floor of Congress, ones that offer various options for moral communities to present their convictions without having to worry about winning political battles. At the same time, it is essential to recognize that there can be no hard and fast separation between the spheres of civil society and the political, such that we could be assured of knowing when we have crossed the boundary between them. Difficulties arise if we try to envision such a separation, and Rawls leaves these difficulties for the most part unexplored.

To address this point, we might consider the public statements issued by the National Conference of Catholic Bishops. Can we regard such forms of communication as existing comfortably within the background culture, as Rawls would contend?[13] On one level it is clear that the bishops, whose advocacy has covered issues ranging from economic justice to abortion and foreign policy, are addressing first of all the Catholic community in America. Their statements could thus be seen as falling squarely within the domain of "churches and universities" and the reasoning specific to them that Rawls identifies with the background culture. But the bishops are also addressing office holders and Americans generally, and they typically frame their arguments both in language specific to the Christian tradition and with forms of reasoning they clearly intend to be accessible to a broader audience. It would seem, then, as though the bishops' engagement can fairly be portrayed as public discourse in the broad civil society sense and also as a more narrowly political form of discourse, intended to influence policymakers' decisions about matters directly concerning constitutional essentials and justice.[14] In this case, we have an example of public advocacy that is confined neither to the background culture nor to the public political culture but is instead an attempt to shape the convictions both of those in the Church and those outside it, and citizens in general as well as those directly responsible for crafting public policy.[15] The complexity of the bishops' statements is poorly conceptualized by political liberalism's suggestion that the realms of politics and civil society can remain neatly distinct. If in fact they cannot, we should question the desirability of trying to erect an unyielding boundary between the kinds of reasoning appropriate to nonpublic associations and those suitable for addressing the polity as a whole.

Rawls's depiction of the public discourse taking place in the background culture is in general rather underdeveloped. Only rarely, for instance, do we get a sense that part of what goes on within civil society involves moral *communities* attempting collectively to remain faithful to a particular comprehensive doctrine. More often it is implied that *individuals* are occupied there with the task of deciding for themselves the manner in which their most fundamental convictions are relevant or irrelevant for dealing with public questions. Once the norms regulating the political domain have been established, it is "left to citizens individually—as part of liberty of conscience—to settle how they think the values of the political domain are related to other values in their comprehensive doctrine" (1996, 140). We observed in chapter 1 the way in which comprehensive doctrines are generally characterized by political liberals as the possessions of individual citizens, who develop, revise, and rely on them as they choose to orient their individual life plans. If this understanding is applied to the way comprehensive doctrines function in the background culture, we are left with only an incomplete characterization at best.

Most citizens are not isolated individuals, in charge of fashioning their own comprehensive doctrines by their own powers alone. Within civil society, citizens typically find themselves part of a web of various communities and associations, some of which are, like churches, communities of moral formation, in which they are shaped and engaged in a collective attempt with others to pursue a way of life consistent with the community's ongoing tradition. Since many moral traditions have at their core a broader social vision as well, this collective effort can include attempts to reorient societal priorities in accordance with the tradition itself. Bearing in mind this shared, communal, and *political* aspect of "comprehensive doctrines" is important, and it makes it harder to sustain political liberalism's distinction between the spheres of the political and the background culture. Citizens, depending on the context, may be faced with shifting social settings in which they encounter relatively unstable boundaries between what might be considered purely "cultural" public environments and those that take on more pronounced "political" aspects.

For example, whenever church groups organize pro-life rallies or assemble outside a federal prison to protest the execution of a death row inmate, are they safely within a cultural realm or a more explicitly political one? In what realm would we locate a public school board meeting in which curricular materials concerning civic education are being debated? How would we categorize a gay pride march? These contexts seem to have features of both the background culture and the political sphere. While they do not necessarily involve political debate among public officials or Supreme Court justices issuing opinions, they do involve moral communities contesting constitutional essentials and matters of basic justice, issues Rawls locates squarely in the political domain. Such instances thus seem to reflect an intrinsic porousness between the spheres of civil society and the political, and they suggest that firm boundaries for determining where civil society ends and the political sphere begins are unattainable.

Seen in this light, Rawls's political division of labor between public officials and ordinary citizens, wherein only the former are formally charged with adhering to public reason in their political speech, works to obscure the political significance of the background culture. On an intuitive level, it seems appropriate to say that if there are to be principles guiding public discourse, politicians and judges should bear the heaviest burden in honoring those principles in their political conduct. But Rawls's particular separation between the background culture and the public political forum goes beyond that, as it suggests that the discourse of ordinary citizens is politically insignificant—at least with respect to the definition and maintenance of public norms and values. Because the two realms are "distinct and separate," it is unclear how the unhindered discourse in the background culture can have a meaningful impact on the public forum, which is always to be carefully monitored and regulated through public reason (1997, 768).[16] It is also difficult to perceive how citizens would be encouraged to take seriously the significance of their own political activity if they shared this understanding of the public realm. Would this not be likely to contribute to citizens' disengagement from public life, rather than to lead them to invest themselves more substantially in it? There is a distinctly anti-democratic impulse running through this conceptualization of the political realm, given the way in which citizens' political responsibility is so heavily attenuated.

This difficulty becomes especially poignant for Rawls, whose thought has an otherwise pervasive emphasis on the crucial importance of all citizens being morally committed to upholding fair terms of social cooperation. He stresses that

> without citizens' allegiance to public reason and their honoring the duty of civility, divisions and hostilities between doctrines are bound in time to assert themselves, should they not already exist. Harmony

> and concord among doctrines and a people's affirming public reason are unhappily not a permanent condition of social life. Rather, harmony and concord depend on the vitality of the public political culture and on citizens' being devoted to and realizing the ideal of public reason. (1997, 803)

If Rawls is correct about citizens' attitudes and capacities being essential to political stability and social concord, then a more nuanced conception of the political sphere would seem much more appropriate than one in which the background culture and the political domain are seen as neatly distinct.

As it stands, Rawls's evident effort to make liberal public reason less burdensome to religious and other kinds of moral communities appears to be a bit of a mixed blessing. Their freedom to engage in unrestricted discourse in the background culture is protected, but only by being predicated on that realm's safe separation from that of the public political forum, which is governed by an altogether different logic.

Public Reason's Secular Telos

The conceptual difficulties with political liberalism's ideal of public reason are significant, and they begin to illuminate some of the problems with the constraints such an ideal places on the role of religion in public life. But we must now take up the central normative question. How desirable is it to treat religious ways of reasoning as being presumptively suspect in the public realm, in need of regulation by the device of public reason? Or, put somewhat differently: Is it defensible to regard religious arguments as only *conditionally* public, subject to their meeting the criteria of the reasonable? For Rawls stresses that, while he is not altogether averse to allowing comprehensive theological or philosophical views to be presented in public discourse, "it is normally desirable that the comprehensive philosophical and moral views we are wont to use in debating fundamental political issues should give way in public life" (1996, 10).[17] Is such a stance warranted, given the manifold ways in which religious traditions have influenced and spurred the reform of American social and political norms?[18] Why should political liberals continue to insist on placing restrictions on public discourse, to the extent that political values must be viewed as the dominant language through which political fundamentals are discussed?

Rawls's stance might be justified if it could be shown that a reliance on political values could assist us in managing political disagreement. Kent Greenawalt has taken up precisely this question.[19] Greenawalt is for the most part sympathetic with political liberalism's insistence on a shared public language. He argues that citizens who wish to act consistently with liberal norms should when possible agree to follow "shared forms of reasoning" and "adhere to those forms at least insofar as they give clear answers," since "that degree of commitment to a common method of discourse and thought is owed to others of diverse convictions in a pluralist society" (1988, 204). He is therefore concerned with determining which kinds of reasoning are compatible with this shared method of reasoning—in other words, which kinds of reasoning are "publicly accessible" to all citizens generally speaking.

With respect to "religious morality and religiously grounded moral judgments," Greenawalt stresses that they are unacceptable candidates for public reasoning, since "some of the crucial premises that underlie such judgments are not the subject of general acceptance or of persuasive demonstration by publicly accessible reasons" (1988, 69). It is highly unlikely, he observes, that reason alone will ever be able to settle questions of religious truth conclusively. And given the present and ever-increasing religious diversity characterizing American society, it is doubtful that anything remotely approaching a consensus now exists or could conceivably come to exist concerning the validity of religious propositions (74–76). Like judgments based on personal intuition or experience (other examples Greenawalt cites of "nonaccessible" premises), religious judgments must in an important respect remain subpolitical; at least they cannot be *publicly* authoritative in helping to resolve policy debates.

These presuppositions largely parallel political liberalism's stance on religion and public reason. That is, while political liberalism makes room for the presentation of religious viewpoints in public life, it is with the assumption that these viewpoints should never be determinate in resolving any particular political disagreement. While they can offer support for an argument we present with political values, we are never justified in giving the impression that the religious component of our comprehensive doctrine is in fact the crucial linchpin of our political position. As Rawls makes clear, the political conception we rely upon in our public reasoning must be regarded as "complete"—it "should express principles, standards, and ideals, along with guidelines of inquiry, such that the values specified by it can be suitably ordered or otherwise united so that *those values alone* give a reasonable answer to all, or nearly all, questions involving constitutional essentials and matters of basic justice" (1997, 777, my emphasis). We must steadfastly dispel any suggestion that political values are "puppets manipulated from behind the scenes by comprehensive doctrines" (777). So, for instance, when Rawls discusses the use of the "Good Samaritan" story in public discourse, he is clear that it is fully allowable, *as long as* we justify the political proposal we are arguing for "in terms of proper political values" (778). The process of *justification* in the public realm happens by the use of political values alone. Whatever religious claims are offered are of secondary, and indeed ultimately peripheral, significance and Rawls's proviso ensures that the shape of our public discourse will reflect this.

Considering Greenawalt's concurrence with political liberalism's privileging of political values, however, it is remarkable that he ends up *defending* the right of citizens to employ their "nonaccessible" convictions in making up their minds and voting on troublesome political issues—even of the most fundamental kind.[20] He justifies his argument by drawing on the results of a painstaking analysis of a number of policy issues such as abortion, animal rights, and military policy. After trying to determine whether shared premises and publicly accessible reasons can help us forge a consensus on how to approach these issues, Greenawalt ultimately concludes that they cannot. In each case, our stock of shared premises falls short at the most crucial points of each debate. Thus, with regard to abortion, Greenawalt notes that "our society lacks any shared decisive moral principle that establishes when an entity that will grow into any ordinary human being deserves protection, and rational thought may be incapable of settling upon one among the plausible candidates" (1988, 126). In situations like this one, Greenawalt argues, religious citizens can be expected to rely on their particular beliefs to assist them in determining an appropriate position to take, *even if* in doing so they are moving outside the bounds of publicly accessible reasons. "The religious believer has a powerful argument that he should be able to rely on his religiously informed bases for judgment if others are relying on other bases of judgment that reach beyond common premises and forms of reasoning" (137). If publicly accessible norms cannot determine a conclusive response to an issue, why shouldn't citizens be able to draw upon their most fundamental convictions, religious or nonreligious, in helping them arrive at an intellectually satisfying way to approach it?

Yet despite his well-articulated concerns about the limitations of secular political values when it comes to resolving political disputes, Greenawalt nevertheless is unwilling to abandon his advocacy of secular discourse as the language by which we *publicly defend* our political choices. He accepts as axiomatic the core liberal notion that "citizens of extremely diverse religious views can build principles of political order and social justice that do not depend on particular religious beliefs," and therefore he insists that citizens have a responsibility to justify their positions before one another in publicly accessible terms. They must realize that the "common currency of political discourse [in a liberal society] is nonreligious argument about human welfare" (1988, 216–217).[21] This defense of a secular model of public reason certainly appears much weaker, however, given the extent to which Greenawalt has challenged its ability to resolve many of our core moral disagreements.

One can grant that there are plenty of issues and occasions for which a secular means of discourse is perfectly appropriate. A debate over the merit of a public works project, for example, would not seem to be the kind of issue that would inevitably entail the invocation of religious premises to help us sort it out. But if we are dealing with matters such as abortion, euthanasia, or the morality of our foreign policy, questions that run to the heart of our understanding of human life, why should we regard it as necessary or proper to restrict access to the resources our religious traditions can bring to bear in coming to terms with them? Once it is established that public reason is by itself incapable of resolving these matters, we would seem to have a persuasive warrant to open up public discourse to any resources that might assist us.

In fact, there are occasions in which Rawls himself acknowledges the limitations of relying on political values alone. He suggests that there are situations in which, contrary to political liberalism's own impulses, "we may eventually have to assert at least certain aspects of our own comprehensive religious or philosophical doctrine"—as, for instance, when a citizen comes forward to argue that "certain questions are so fundamental that to insure their being rightly settled justifies civil strife" (1996, 152). If this argument is based on a religious conception, such as the idea that the "religious salvation of those holding a particular religion, or indeed the salvation of a whole people, may be said to depend on it," Rawls says that "we may have no alternative but to deny this, or to imply its denial and hence to maintain the kind of thing we had hoped to avoid" (152). Here political liberals are obligated to affirm their superordinate commitment to civic peace and hence to deny the legitimacy of any attempt to jeopardize that good on the basis of any particular comprehensive doctrine's understanding of religious truth. As Rawls acknowledges, this sort of a claim involves going beyond the realm of political values, since it is an assertion precisely about whether temporal peace is a superior good to some varieties of religious conceptions of social order, and this can in no way be stated without making at least an implicit claim about the nature of religion itself.[22] Similarly, Rawls argues that if a particular religious community maintains that its convictions "are open to and can be fully established by reason," with the correlative assumption that "the fact of reasonable pluralism" is denied, political liberals must here too respond that this community's claim is "mistaken" (152–153). In these cases, in which an exclusive reliance upon political values seems ineffectual, Rawls leaves room for political liberals to present their deeper comprehensive commitments to support their political positions.

Rawls is somewhat less forthcoming in conceding the limitations of public reason when he discusses the abortion question. In seeking to show that political values can be used to frame this issue so that we might approach it responsibly in public discourse, Rawls proposes three values for guiding our deliberation: "the due respect for human life, the ordered reproduction of political society over time, including the family in some form, and finally the equality of women as equal citizens" (1996, 243). He then presents his own view as holding that "any reasonable balance of these three values will give a woman a duly qualified right to decide whether or not to end her pregnancy during the first trimester." How does he explain this conclusion? "At this early stage of pregnancy the political value of the equality of women is overriding, and this right is required to give it substance and force. Other political values, if tallied in, would not, I think, affect this conclusion" (243). A careful consideration of Rawls's claim here reveals some serious concerns. Can Rawls be right in asserting that *any* reasonable balance of the three political values he provides would automatically lead to a right to first-trimester abortions? Certainly the official teaching of the Catholic Church, in giving a great deal of weight to "due respect for human life," would deny this right precisely on that basis. Is Rawls then implicitly declaring the church's position on abortion to be unreasonable? He seems to suggest as much when he says that "any comprehensive doctrine that leads to a balance of political values excluding that duly qualified right in the first trimester is to that extent unreasonable" (243).

Even assuming that we were able to agree on the aptness of Rawls's three political values in framing the abortion question, it still seems likely that our approach in balancing them would be unavoidably shaped by our position on other, more fundamental norms. Yet Rawls seems unwilling to come to terms with this. Surely the Catholic Church does not deny the validity of women's status as equal citizens; it simply does not assign this consideration an overriding value when measuring it against the church's understanding of what it means to demonstrate "due respect for human life." Rawls's contrary position would seem to be similarly shaped by his own way of balancing the values; he places a great deal more weight on his particular interpretation of women's rights as citizens. Both positions would thus be directly derived from their undergirding metaphysical and philosophical commitments, rather than proceeding from the political values themselves, which are after all simply markers of sorts for the convictions supporting them.[23]

Once we recognize that a reliance upon political values in public discourse is often an incomplete characterization of the real points at issue in a particular debate, we would seem to have a strong justification for introducing into the discussion the premises that more fully explain the substance of the disagreement. In fact, doing so would conceivably be consistent with one reading of political liberalism's goal of fostering a demystified politics and civic friendship. By allowing our fellow citizens access to the principles motivating our political activity, we could renounce the attempt to smuggle our core convictions into politics under the guise of some other (less obviously controversial) political stance. In addition, by openly presenting our substantive views, we would be expressing our trust in our fellow citizens' rationality, by being willing to offer our full positions for their consideration.

In insisting that in the interests of maintaining a viable conception of public reason we ought *not* be forthcoming in this way, Rawls thus reveals public reason to be less a device of clarification than an attempt to obfuscate our moral disagreements. As Rawls explains it, political liberalism requires us to be content with introducing political values to justify our positions, recognizing that "of course the plurality of reasonable comprehensive doctrines held by citizens is thought by them to provide further and often transcendent backing for those values" (1996, 243). Yet as we have seen with regard to Rawls's treatment of the abortion question, our more comprehensive convictions are crucial to the way in which we sort out the competing goods that are at stake in the most troubling public policy debates. And in this case, it indeed seems as though Rawls's own fundamental convictions effectively determine his perspective on which positions on abortion are to be considered reasonable and which are violations of public reason. Is it really preferable to confine the bulk of our reflection on these matters to the nonpublic sphere, only then emerging with a truncated argument when we enter the political domain, potentially resulting in a confusing or misleading articulation of our position?

Given the inability of public reason to make our most vexing policy debates more tractable, and the difficulties with a model of public discourse that restricts our exploration of the most fundamental bases of our moral disagreements, political liberalism would seem to require a more compelling justification for the constraints it places on public dialogue. As I suggested above, there is nothing intrinsic to the idea of disclosing our comprehensive convictions to one another that suggests it would violate either a commitment to reciprocity or a willingness to engage in social cooperation on equal terms with other citizens. As Rawls puts it, "insofar as we are reasonable, we are ready to work out the framework for the public social world, a framework it is reasonable to expect everyone to endorse and act on, provided others can be relied on to do the same" (1996, 53–54). Why must our comprehensive views be viewed as extraneous or inessential to this process?

I will suggest here that much of the justification political liberalism requires for its ideal of public reason is ultimately derived from its reliance on a particular interpretation of the liberal narrative—one that is used to great rhetorical effect. Within many contemporary liberal writings, we find a common thread: the insistence that liberalism arose from, and continues to protect against, the dangers of religious conflict. This is less a position explicitly argued for than an undergirding set of assumptions that are appealed to at various junctures.[24] These assumptions play an essential role, however, as it is only with this understanding of the liberal project that regulating the presentation of religious appeals in the public realm can remain a convincing political imperative.

Earlier in this chapter we observed that Rawls identifies the advent of liberalism in the effort to bring an end to the wars of religion of the sixteenth and seventeenth centuries. Liberalism's challenge was to devise a way to secure the autonomy of the political realm in the face of the usurpations of aggressive religious communities, each asserting a divine justification for its political vision. "During the wars of religion people were not in doubt about the nature of the highest good, or the basis of moral obligation in divine law. These things they thought they knew with the certainty of faith, as here their moral theology gave them complete guidance. The problem was rather: How is society even possible between those of different faiths?" (1996, xxv–xxvi). The strategy liberalism chose was to require religious truth-claims to recede from the political realm, thereby freeing it so that it could be governed by a political morality. And over time, once the liberal solution was in place, it became clear that "a reasonably harmonious and stable pluralist society" could be a reality. Society no longer needed to be regulated by "a general and comprehensive religious, philosophical, or moral doctrine" (xxvii). Given the character of this narrative, it becomes evident why political liberalism requires the fair terms of social cooperation to include a restriction on the kinds of arguments that can be legitimately put forward in the public forum. Unless it were presented in the proper context, and with the appropriate invocation of "political values," any publicly voiced theological appeal (or any contestable comprehensive philosophical claim, for that matter) could be construed as a refusal to acknowledge the autonomy of the political realm and, therefore, as a violation of the foundational framework that makes social peace possible.

Although this narrative has been used powerfully as a justification for the liberal project, it can be challenged. As William Cavanaugh has argued, it masks the ways in which the "wars of religion" were as much about consolidating the power of the nascent modern state, and the autonomy of the political sphere required for that consolidation, as they were the result of doctrinal zealotry. Rather than seeking merely to restore peace in the face of religious hostility, political elites were in fact *reconstituting* the political order, and they relied upon new conceptualizations to assist them in that process.

> To call these "wars of religion" is anachronistic, for what was at stake in these wars was the very creation of "religion" as a universal impulse essentially separate from an activity called "politics." The resulting appearance of the plural "religions" is said to make the secular state necessary, but in fact there is nothing inherently violent in religious

> pluralism and theological politics *unless* one assumes that politics means the totalizing practice of the state. (1998, 5, emphasis in original)[25]

Similarly, John Milbank stresses that the notion of the secular in this narrative is itself a construct brought about through the "new science of politics" inaugurated by thinkers such as Hugo Grotius, Thomas Hobbes, and Baruch Spinoza, in which the political could be envisioned as an autonomous realm independent of the influence or control of theology (1990, 10). On these accounts, the role of the secular state vis-à-vis religious communities is much less benign, and much more aggressively partisan.[26]

Even were we to assume for the sake of argument the validity of political liberalism's wars of religion narrative as a historical rendering of liberalism's origins, we would still be justified in questioning whether it should continue to govern our understanding of the relationship between comprehensive doctrines and political life in the contemporary era. It does not seem implausible to argue, for instance, that at least in the American context the liberal project, combined with propitious social and cultural developments, has demonstrably secured the conditions of political stability to the point that we need no longer fear that the introduction of controversial theological or philosophical perspectives in political life will threaten incipient civil unrest.[27] In any event, why should we continue to rely on a narrative that essentially ends once the liberal solution is put in place, thereby neglecting any inquiry into the experience of diverse religious communities and their relationship with the political order during the centuries that liberalism has regulated Western political arrangements? The fact that Rawls does not expand his account beyond the wars of religion context thus gives his treatment of religious diversity a rather anachronistic flavor. As Rawls sees it, public debate that centers on religious claims risks a high degree of social tension, as citizens guided by competing and utterly incommensurable comprehensive views struggle to "exercise their coercive political power over one another" by imposing their particular convictions on the rest of society (1996, 217).[28] Rawls's reading of the contemporary state of political discourse thus at times seems to resemble a society just emerging from a state of deep civil conflict, in which any claim made on the basis of a particular moral tradition is seen as nothing less than an attempt to (re-)colonize the public sphere.

Of course, Rawls is not incorrect in noting that there are plenty of coercive appeals made these days in public discourse. But it does not thereby follow that comprehensive doctrines pose the central danger or that religious doctrines are particularly prone to this impulse. The history of the United States is filled with instances of coercive legislation justified and carried out by drawing solely on "political values." A good example is the Americanization movement of the early twentieth century, which through a range of policies sought to ensure that newly arrived immigrant populations would be unswervingly loyal to the United States. From restricting the teaching of foreign languages to stifling labor radicalism to abolishing parochial schools, Americanizers were determined to inculcate an appreciation for "American values" and improve the quality of "democratic citizenship." Although there was a strong racist impulse contributing to the fervor of this movement, the majority of the public arguments used to justify it were concerned with seeking a secure basis for national unity and civic virtue, and thus they were perfectly compatible with political values as political liberals understand them.[29]

Nor should we assume that religious doctrines have peculiar qualities that render them particularly susceptible to coercive political temptations. In a way that is sometimes lost on political liberals, comprehensive views of life differ radically from one another, not only in terms of their secular and religious content but also in the social and political forms they take. Some are more totalizing than others, and some are more willing than others to pursue aggressive political strategies. But there does not appear to be a strong correlation between the religiosity of a comprehensive doctrine and its propensity for coercion in political life. At least in the twentieth century, secular ideologies showed themselves capable of equaling, if not surpassing, the oppressive proclivities of religious doctrines, as Nazism and Soviet Communism demonstrated. By drawing so much of its animating thrust from the wars of religion narrative, therefore, political liberalism ends up providing a distortive characterization of public discourse, one that singles out religious communities as particular threats to civil order and envisions comprehensive doctrines unidimensionally, as invariably oriented toward controlling the public sphere. Neither generalization is of significant value in determining how we should approach public discourse in a morally diverse polity.

An especially problematic aspect of this narrative is its tendentiousness. Political liberals invoke the specter of moral discord and antagonism when it is required to support their claim that controversial views about the good are a danger to public life. Yet at the same time, they insist that the conditions of moral conflict do not prevent the attainment of a consensus around *political* values. So whereas, when dealing with the reasons why comprehensive views should give way in political life, we are reminded of the incommensurability of our moral worldviews, when considering the prospects of an overlapping consensus on principles of justice we are told that "most people's religious, philosophical, and moral doctrines are not seen by them as fully general and comprehensive, and these aspects admit of variations of degree. There is lots of slippage, so to speak, many ways for liberal principles of justice to cohere loosely with those (partially) comprehensive views, and many ways within the limits of political principles of justice to allow for the pursuit of different (partially) comprehensive doctrines" (Rawls 1996, 160).

Rawls clearly does not believe that our incommensurable moral doctrines preclude us from taking part in stable political arrangements, and he expects that the presence of an overlapping consensus will over time bring comprehensive convictions into harmony with it (1996, 246). Yet this contention is problematic. For if there is nothing so sacrosanct about people's comprehensive doctrines that they cannot be justifiably altered or adjusted to support principles of justice, why must we stop there and dismiss the possibility that our views on other issues could also converge, at least on a provisional basis? Might we not remain hopeful that a more open-ended public discourse can involve more than the clashing of wills and that we need not therefore insist upon a confining conception of public reason in order to keep from imposing our ideals upon one another?

That Rawls and other political liberals either explicitly or implicitly dismiss these possibilities suggests that the wars of religion narrative has in fact indelibly shaped political liberalism's conception of the proper ends of public discourse. Where religion comes to be seen as an inherently threatening and divisive social force, doing whatever is necessary to ensure that it plays as small a role in political life as possible appears the only defensible course of action. The ultimate consequence, then, of political liberalism's fear of public religion is a telos of a well-constituted liberal order that necessarily involves a gradual transition to a purely secular means of discourse. This might at first seem paradoxical, given Rawls's and other political liberals' efforts to deny that their conception of public reason is fundamentally secularist. Yet a closer consideration of how Rawls characterizes the function of religious arguments in public life is revealing.

Rawls readily acknowledges that there are "positive" reasons for introducing religious arguments in public debate (1997, 784). These fall into two main categories. One has to do with how religious claims can be used to generate support for an overlapping consensus that is either lacking or still in a nascent stage. To illustrate this, Rawls focuses on two classic cases of religion's involvement in political life: the efforts of the nineteenth-century abolitionists and the civil rights activists who fought segregation in the 1950s and 60s. As Rawls acknowledges, those involved in these struggles invoked explicitly theological premises in making their claims. And it is clear that the issues they addressed were centrally concerned with basic justice and constitutional norms. Rawls insists, however, that both cases support, rather than challenge, his argument for public reason.[30] His contention is based on the idea that the overtly religious appeals made in each case could be viewed as necessary in order to help bring a society troubled by "profound division about constitutional essentials" into a more perfect state of justice. The participants in these struggles realized that by drawing upon a theological language that most Americans would find congenial, they could remind their fellow citizens of the great significance of the political values of freedom and equality, thereby calling them to bring their political practices in line with the fundamental ideals of the political order (1996, 251). On this reading, the religious character of the public language used by the abolitionists and civil rights leaders served a largely instrumental purpose, as it allowed them to "strengthen the ideal of public reason itself" (247).[31] Rawls suggests hypothetically that the abolitionists "could have seen their actions as the best way to bring about a well-ordered and just society in which the ideal of public reason could eventually be honored" and that the same could be said for leaders of the civil rights movement such as Martin Luther King Jr. "The abolitionists and King would not have been unreasonable in these conjectured beliefs if the political forces they led were among the necessary historical conditions to establish political justice, as does indeed seem plausible in their situation" (250–251).

As I will argue further in chapter 5, the possibility Rawls does not consider in analyzing these two historical episodes is that those involved in the struggles did not see their religious comprehensive doctrines as providing mere ornamentation for the "political values" they sought to defend. If that were the case, it would raise significant difficulties for Rawls's conception, which demands that citizens be able to separate for political purposes their endorsement of political values from their more contestable, comprehensive views. Citizens who advance their religious convictions with the understanding that they are *decisive* in determining the right course of action on a particular political issue, or who see their "political values" as being inseparable from their wider convictions, have violated the demands of public reason, for they no longer honor the fair terms of social cooperation as political liberalism defines them. These citizens would be challenging the "completeness" of the overlapping consensus by suggesting that their comprehensive doctrines play an essential role in determining the shape of public principles or ideals (1997, 777–778).

The second positive reason Rawls provides for citizens using religious arguments in public life is that it allows them to alleviate other citizens' distrust and suspicion that their comprehensive doctrines may be unreasonable. Rawls suggests that when controversial issues arise in public discourse, it is likely that citizens will "come to doubt one another's allegiance to basic constitutional and political values" and that in light of this it is wise "for all sides to introduce their comprehensive doctrines, whether religious or secular, so as to open the way for them to explain to one another how their views do indeed support those basic political values" (1997, 785). The goal of this form of discourse is to reassure other citizens that the foundation on which an overlapping consensus is built is solid and not likely to be split apart by the sudden emergence of unreasonable comprehensive doctrines that might seek to challenge some aspect of liberal justice (786). It serves a defensive purpose, in other words: Rawls clearly does not envision this mode of engagement as involving a process of *discovery,* in which new understandings of public norms might emerge from public discourse, or of *critique,* in which currently accepted formulations might be vigorously challenged. Rather, he presupposes the existence of a stable, self-evident set of political values, on behalf of which various kinds of comprehensive doctrines should merely be aligned in support. Religion cannot be justified in playing a transformational purpose in public discourse; it is always constrained by whatever norms are currently in place.

What the forgoing discussion suggests is that as a political liberal society progresses to a more perfect state of justice, the need for any reliance upon public religious appeals is expected to diminish, since their appropriate functions are limited to shoring up support for freestanding political values and playing a prophylactic role in stemming political divisiveness. Hence Rawls says that in a fully well-ordered society with an overlapping consensus firmly in place, in which "the values of the political conception are familiar and citizens honor the ideal of public reason . . . they have no great interest in introducing other considerations: their fundamental rights are already guaranteed and there are no basic injustices they feel bound to protest." In such a context, "invoking only political values is the obvious and the most direct way for citizens to honor the ideal of public reason and to meet their duty of civility" (1996, 248). It thus seems fair to say that the telos animating political liberalism entails the attempt to achieve a society in which religion eventually comes to have no significant role to play in shaping the norms of the political order. Until we reach that point, it may be tolerated in a functional sense as a necessary evil of sorts, but only if it ultimately serves to work toward the cause of its own public irrelevance, by pointing to the adequacy of purely political values. Herein lies the fundamental secularity of Rawlsian public reason.

Seen in this light, Rawls's claim that public reason can be neatly distinguished from "secular reason and secular values" is unconvincing. Rawls's argument turns on the notion that political liberalism's political values "are not moral doctrines" and that they thus can refrain from taking sides either for or against religion (1997, 775). But if in fact there are deeply entrenched suspicions within political liberalism that mandate regulating the public realm in order to ensure that religious viewpoints are unable to disrupt the proper functioning of the public sphere, suspicions derived from a contestable narrative of religious conflict, can we be so certain that there is not in fact a more fundamental set of convictions at work in political liberalism's conception of the public sphere? Is the demand that the public sphere should be governed by a logic *completely independent* of that of revealed religion capable of being defended as a "political" viewpoint that does not itself rely upon particular premises concerning the nature of truth, rationality, and the appropriate ends of political life? If political liberalism is indeed implicated in these larger questions, as I have argued, Rawls cannot in the end persuasively claim to stay above the fray when seeking to define the terms of public discourse. The privileging of the secular as a way to structure the public realm remains essential to political liberalism's core purposes.[32]

The implications of this privileging of secular reason go beyond whether religion in the abstract is welcomed in political life. They have to do with whether religious citizens are truly invited *as citizens* into a public realm regulated by political liberalism. To say nothing about how "unreasonable" religious citizens are to fare under this conception of politics, we must consider the message that is sent to all religious communities when they are told that their most fundamental convictions are at best politically irrelevant and at worst politically destructive to the cause of a just society. These citizens will learn that there is a time and a place for their religious insights—namely, during debate over less essential political matters, in less politically significant public contexts. To the extent that we value a dynamic democratic politics in which citizens are encouraged to bring their entire selves into public life, these implications seem unfortunate indeed.

Moving beyond Secular Public Reason

If we are guided by the assumption that justice requires carefully managing the presentation of potentially divisive comprehensive views in public life, we will of course be inclined to accept a conception of politics in which religious claims are bound to serve at most a functional purpose—a supplement to the shared and primary political language we agree ultimately to use in structuring our common life. But as I have argued, a singular, shared public language is precisely what we lack.[33] While there may at times be provisional convergences in political life and vocabularies that resonate with many citizens (for instance, rhetorical commonplaces such as "family values," "equal opportunity," and so forth), these vocabularies will always be subject to reformulations, and these reformulations will inevitably be influenced and informed by citizens' more fundamental commitments. Rather than denying this plurality of public languages or seeking to limit their political potential, we would be better served by acknowledging them and looking for political agreements (or, conversely, discovering those points of irreconcilability that may exist) by engaging them directly.

This kind of approach will be more sensitive to the ways in which public meanings are created and challenged continuously, both emerging and being reshaped in the play of diverse moral languages that occupy public space at any given time. Determining what counts as a public or nonpublic argument, on this view, is only something that can be done by considering the particular context in which it is presented. We cannot presume in advance to demarcate a definitive range of political values before the conversation has begun, as it were. Cordoning off particular viewpoints appears in this light to be an invidious and unhelpful attempt to limit artificially the range of public disagreement. Once this is recognized, we are no longer obligated to be wary of nonsecular moral languages that seek, alongside other perspectives, to take part in the ongoing effort to configure public space and the norms that regulate it.

For instance, freed of the overly inflexible and compartmentalized framework offered by political liberals, we can better conceptualize the kind of prophetic witness that African American churches have historically offered in addressing questions of social justice, which I will discuss at length in chapter 5. Prophetic discourse disrupts political liberalism's typology because, while it most commonly involves an explicit denial of the autonomy of the political realm, insisting on the continual need for scrutinizing the purposes of the state in the light of biblical justice, it does not entail an attempt to colonize the public sphere with a particular comprehensive vision of the good. Instead, it seeks to hold the political community accountable by offering an alternative vision of the just society with which to critique and challenge prevailing political reality.[34] A more fluid and nuanced view of discourse is required to come to terms with modes of expression, like that of the prophetic, that do not fit neatly into a framework in which every public utterance is assumed to be either a support for freestanding, autonomous political values or an attempt to impose a comprehensive doctrine on the polity.

True, acknowledging the absence of a universally recognized public perspective from which to guide public life places more, not less, responsibility on participants in public discourse. If public meanings are continuously in the process of being formulated and reformulated, political life is subject to a significant degree of indeterminacy and contestability. There is accordingly a fragility to political life that we must be cognizant of in our political activity. Recognizing this should, however, lead us to work toward an *ethics* of discourse rather than a doctrine of public reason that sorts out acceptable and unacceptable public arguments on the basis of foreordained criteria. While the content of our arguments is important, it is just as important to consider the spirit in which our viewpoints are expressed, as well as the way in which we engage other perspectives. What we require, then, are practices and dispositions that enable us to take seriously the difficulty of pursuing common ends in a morally diverse society and to do so in a way that recognizes, rather than obviates, our particularity.

CHAPTER 4

Approaching the Theological

Re-thinking Public Discourse

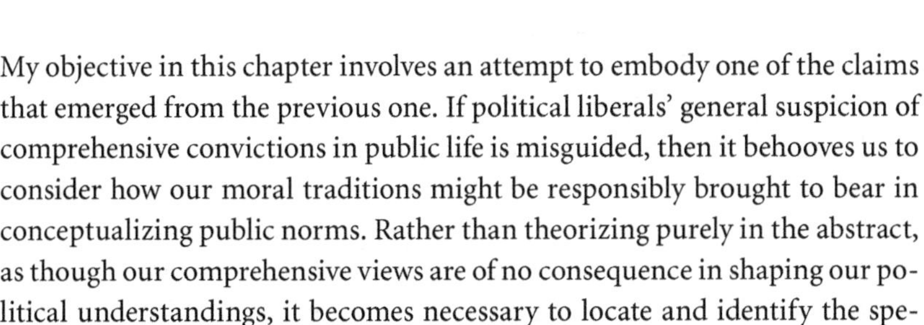

My objective in this chapter involves an attempt to embody one of the claims that emerged from the previous one. If political liberals' general suspicion of comprehensive convictions in public life is misguided, then it behooves us to consider how our moral traditions might be responsibly brought to bear in conceptualizing public norms. Rather than theorizing purely in the abstract, as though our comprehensive views are of no consequence in shaping our political understandings, it becomes necessary to locate and identify the specific normative resources from which we fashion our particular political positions. And by acknowledging those resources openly, we might thereby contribute toward a robust process of moral negotiation and democratic engagement in the quest for desirable public ends.

In this chapter I explore three theological perspectives on public discourse. Each of the thinkers I am considering works within the Christian tradition. Although there are important differences among them (as will become evident), they share this basic orientation. This is not adventitious. My concern in this chapter and the ones to follow is to illustrate the unavoidability of moral particularity in our reflection on, and pursuit of, public norms. As a Lutheran, I see the Christian tradition as a foundational source of reflection when I consider the proper aims of political life. I have thus sought to take this tradition seriously as I attempt to reconsider public discourse from a nonsecular perspective. As I will argue more fully later, I do not view moral particularity as posing an insurmountable obstacle to the seeking of shared ends. I am convinced, however, that it is the place where we must begin in approaching moral diversity responsibly.

David Tracy: The Christian "Classic" as Public Resource

One of today's preeminent Catholic theologians, David Tracy has throughout his vast body of work defended what he views as the positive gains of modernity, as well as a distinctive conception of the role theology might play in the public sphere. Tracy's qualified endorsement of modernity shares much in common with that of Jürgen Habermas.[1] Tracy celebrates modernity's emancipation of the individual and the use of reason in challenging oppressive economic and social structures that continue to stand in the way of "human liberation on a personal and societal scale" (Tracy 1975, 13). While embracing modernity's emancipatory possibilities, however, Tracy laments the manner in which instrumental rationality, suitable for regulating the "techno-economic" sphere in which "the organization and allocation of goods and services" is carried out, has gradually come to exert a hegemonic influence over all other spheres of life, to the extent that other modes of truth are systematically obscured or privatized (1981a, 7–9). As a result, it has become increasingly implausible that noninstrumental or non-technicized forms of rationality can be relied upon any longer for ordering or making sense of the public dimensions of our existence. Tracy thus sees the fate of religion in the modern era as being directly related to the marginalization of art. Just as the notion of art as disclosing "a truth about our common human condition often strikes both artists and the general public as counterintuitive," so too does religion come to be seen as a phenomenon without genuine public insights to offer (12).

> Where art is marginalized, religion is privatized. Indeed, religion suffers even greater losses than art by being the single subject about which many intellectuals can feel free to be ignorant. Often abetted by the churches, they need not study religion, for "everybody" already knows what religion is: It is a private consumer product that some people seem to need. Its former social role was poisonous. Its present

privatization is harmless enough to wish it well from a civilized distance. Religion seems to be the sort of thing one likes "if that's the sort of thing one likes." (13)

For Tracy, the privatization of religion poses a grave challenge that must be confronted by any theologian convinced that monotheistic religion has truths it can indeed offer to all human beings. "No Christian or Jewish theologian alert to the radical theocentrism at the heart of theology can rest content with the fatal social view that religious convictions are purely 'personal preferences' or 'private options'" (1981b, 350–351). Tracy thus seeks to resist those elements of the Enlightenment project that would threaten the integrity of theology as a distinctive means by which human truths can be revealed. He makes it clear, however, that his overall ambition is not merely to defend theology from the more harmful legacies of the Enlightenment, but in fact to demonstrate the ways in which a properly conceived theological project can affirm and effectively further the most salutary ends of modernity. It is not from a defensive stance that Tracy critiques instrumental reason, but rather from a more assertive position: Tracy seeks a way for theology to contribute toward the creation of a properly constituted public realm. His diagnosis of modernity's ills and his understanding of the nature of public theology are therefore intimately connected.

Theology, Tracy argues, can provide the public realm with symbolic resources that can prevent it from being subsumed beneath technicized and bureaucratic rationality, thereby enabling it to serve as a site where genuine societal transformation can take place. This is possible because every "major" religious tradition discloses "in its symbols and in its reflections upon those symbols (i.e., its theologies) some fundamental vision of the meaning of individual and communal existence providing disclosive and transformative possibilities for the whole society" (1992, 27; 1981a, 12).[2] To withhold these symbolic disclosures, allowing the public realm to be governed by an independent, technocratic logic, is to ensure the moral impoverishment of political life within modern liberal societies. Theologians thus have a particular responsibility to resist being confined to a "reservation of the spirit" where they can, from within the confines of their particular religious community, remain comfortably oblivious to the public implications of their isolation (1994, 211).

Central to Tracy's understanding of the task facing the public theologian is the idea that theology, like any other discipline, can claim a truly public role only if it is able to validate its truths at the bar of a common rationality.

> In a pluralist culture, it is important to know what will and will not count as public, that is, what resources are available to all intelligent, reasonable, and responsible members of that culture despite their otherwise crucial differences in belief and practice. In the liberal tradition, the existence of a public realm assumes that there is the possibility of discussion (argument, conversation) among various participants. The only hope for such discussion in a radically pluralist liberal culture is one based on reason. (1994, 199)

Tracy's commitment to public rationality is reflected in his division of theology into three branches, or "subdisciplines." Fundamental theology addresses foundational issues regarding the cognitive truth-claims of religion and is centrally concerned with trying to articulate these in a manner accessible to all persons. Systematic theology chiefly entails a hermeneutical attempt to better understand the revelational truths emerging from within a particular religious tradition. And the third branch, practical theology, is concerned primarily with developing effective ways to apply theologically derived truths to concrete social and political struggles (1981a, 54–58).[3] Each of these subdisciplines has a primary audience or "public" associated with it, so that the kind of language theology will speak will vary somewhat depending upon the context in which it is making its claims. Hence fundamental theology, which is situated principally in the domain of the academy, will address a different public and adopt a different approach to "publicness" from systematic theology and practical theology, which are intended to address the publics of "church" and "society," respectively (1981b, 352).[4] Nevertheless, in all cases, Christian theologians have a responsibility to be attentive to the task of bringing their insights to bear in such a way that they manage to illuminate our shared reality, taking seriously the necessity of fostering "authentically public discourse" (1981a, 28–31).

In his work on fundamental and systematic theology, Tracy explores the ways in which this commitment to illuminate shared truths should shape theology as a discipline and condition its contributions to the public realm. *Blessed Rage for Order,* his volume on fundamental theology, attempts to delineate the "religious dimension" present in everyday experience and language, as well as in the methodologies of scientific inquiry. Tracy contends that at the heart of all human experience is the recognition, at either an implicitly or explicitly reflective level, of an "objective ground in reality" that makes possible our existence and gives it its value. We are forced to confront this "ground" as God, the "objective referent" that allows us to have a "fundamental trust" in reality itself (1975, 119, 155). Tracy develops this argument by way of an extensive phenomenological investigation into our "common human experience" and a hermeneutical inquiry into the Christian scriptures. He characterizes this approach as one of establishing a "critical correlation" between those meanings phenomenology or hermeneutics may reveal about our common experience and those that emerge from the Christian tradition. In this way, theology does not stand alone in providing a secure avenue to truth but is brought into contact with other scholarly disciplines in order to determine shared "criteria of adequacy" that can be used to measure the validity of Christian theistic truth claims (44).[5] Through this approach, Tracy is confident that he can defend the appropriateness of Christian language in pointing to the reality of God in a way that does not presuppose a particular faith commitment for its plausibility and thus passes the test of "publicness" within the community of the contemporary academy.

Tracy's more recent work on systematic theology displays a similar commitment to ensuring that theology's truths are spoken in a publicly accessible language. Since systematic theology is more explicitly located within a particular faith tradition, it is less subject to the restrictions against the reliance upon "personal faith and beliefs" for its evidentiary warrants than is fundamental theology, which must meet the most rigorous test in appealing to "strictly public grounds" in defending its claims (1981a, 64). Tracy is confident, however, that the particularity of Christian texts and symbols does not preclude their being relied upon as candidates for truth in the public realm. To develop this idea, Tracy presents a theory of the religious "classic." At its core is the notion that within every culture, certain expressions—be they events, texts, images, symbols, or particular persons—present a claim that we are compelled to recognize as a disclosure of truth (102). When we confront a classic, we "find something valuable, something 'important'; some disclosure of reality in a moment that must be called one of 'recognition' which surprises, provokes, challenges, shocks and eventually transforms us; an experience that upsets conventional opinions and expands the sense of the possible; indeed a realized experience of that which is essential, that which endures" (108). This "experience of the classic" is in fact a "permanent feature of any human being's cultural experience." Grounded in our common humanity, this experience is intrinsically "communicable, shareable, public" (1981a, 108; 1994, 203). Even the most particularistic religious classic, insofar as it addresses and reflects human beings' struggle to come to terms with "those authentic, indeed inevitable fundamental questions about the meaning of the whole," manages to speak to all of us, and thus has a public import that is far from obviated merely because it originates in the experience of a particular tradition (1981a, 155).[6]

With this vision of public theology, Tracy seeks to move beyond a confining conception of the public realm that places restrictions upon religious contributions, by showing that in fact these contributions are essential if we are to avoid the dire prospect of an overly technicized, bureaucratized public sphere, where purposive discourse concerning the public good is impossible. Rather than doing away with the idea of liberal public reason, then, Tracy points toward a more expansive conception:

> It is not the case . . . that our only alternatives are a positivist and instrumentalist definition of the public realm or a sheer chaos, a multiplicity of positions on publicness, meaning, and truth sliding into the abyss of "power-politics" amidst competing interest-groups. It is the case that reason itself, however particular in origin and expression, is public in effect. Reason itself is comprehensive enough to include *both* argument on the conditions for the possibility of our common, shared, public discourse (including *de facto* transcendental arguments on "communicative reason") *and* conversation with all the classic expressions in the culture (including the religious classics of the culture). Such a scenario suggests the fuller meaning of an authentically public realm where argument and conversation are demanded of all participants. (1994, 204, emphasis in original)

Tracy's understanding of public discourse poses a significant challenge to conceptualizations of the public realm, like that of political liberalism, that presuppose that a legitimate politics must be one in which religious truths are by and large exiled to the margins. Tracy furthermore effectively points to the dangers inherent in a vision of public reason that can all too readily treat noninstrumental goods as being intrinsically private in nature. And the notion of a conversation with classics present in his more recent work suggests interesting possibilities that move beyond a narrow conception of public discourse in which only formal arguments are regarded as publicly adequate and in which particularity might be welcomed and engaged rather than feared as intrinsically harmful to public life (1994, 207).

Tracy's conception is not without its difficulties, however. In certain key respects, Tracy's understanding of the preconditions of public discourse closely parallels the assumptions that animate political liberalism's conception of public reason. This results not in expanding but rather in constraining the kinds of claims religious communities can make in political life, to the point that the possibility of theology having a truly distinctive voice in public life is essentially discounted. Tracy's parallels with political liberalism can be seen in two main areas: Tracy's presupposition that commonality is required for substantive public discourse and his conception of moral diversity, which lacks any significant communal dimension.

Tracy's tripartite framework of the "public," in which theology is understood to communicate its truths differently within different social contexts, would appear to offer some promise in moving beyond political liberalism's less nuanced public/nonpublic distinction. Yet throughout Tracy's work, there is the expectation that ultimately we should agree on a particular understanding of what constitutes a legitimately public utterance. This is evident in an obvious sense when we see Tracy insisting upon the need for theologically derived claims to be conveyed "in a manner that can be disclosive and transformative for any intelligent, reasonable, responsible human being" (1981b, 351). For Tracy, this is not merely a descriptive account of what happens when a theological claim is presented in public; it is a normative requirement. Theologians "of every radically monotheistic religion realize that its fundamental commitment to God demands that we express that theistic belief in ways that will *render it public not merely to ourselves or our particular religious group*" (350, my emphasis). This means that some kinds of theological expressions simply cannot be regarded as having public validity in a pluralistic society. Hence Tracy is suspicious of theologies which have at their core an "exclusivist christology" centered on the notion that "only and solely God's 'special revelation' in Jesus Christ is meaningful for a proper human self-understanding" (1975, 206).[7] He is particularly disdainful of "the deceptively 'public' gospel of the 'Moral Majority,'" which is ultimately merely "coercive theological nonsense" (1981b, 353). Thus while Tracy emphatically rejects the idea that theology has no business in public life, the idea of the "reasonable" person that is a recurrent theme in his work allows him to make the same sorts of distinctions that we find in political liberalism between public and nonpublic claims. In Tracy's case, however, the criteria of "publicness" have now been widened so as to allow the distinction between publicly legitimate and illegitimate *theological* claims.

Tracy takes this path because he is convinced that, despite the differences that divide us, we nevertheless share access to a singular public realm that allows us to intelligibly identify certain core experiences and convictions that are intrinsically human and thus capable of being discursively validated. Hence as we observed above, Tracy is insistent that there is an identifiable "religious dimension" that is common to our human experience and can thus serve as an uncontested fund of resources for public discourse, for the believer and nonbeliever alike.[8] Also common to the religious and nonreligious person is what Tracy describes as the "faith of secularity"—"that fundamental attitude which affirms the ultimate significance and final worth of our lives, our thoughts, and actions, here and now, in nature and in history" (1975, 8).[9] In this sense, the theologian's contribution to public life is not predicated upon an attempt to appeal across a normative or epistemic divide to those outside his or her community of faith. Rather, it consists merely in providing a different articulation of beliefs already shared in common:

> The revisionist theologian's fundamental claim is not that he happens to be Christian or that he personally finds attractive the Christian symbols as imaginative understandings of our common destiny. Rather, his claim is that nothing less than a proper understanding of those central beliefs—in "revelation," in "God," in "Jesus Christ"—can provide an adequate understanding, a correct "reflective inventory," or an existentially appropriate symbolic representation of the fundamental faith of secularity. Indeed such theologians believe that they can provide evidence to fair-minded critics inside and outside Christianity for the meaning and truth of the central Christian symbols. (9)

Tracy is confident that when all is said and done we share enough of a moral horizon to allow for a substantive discussion of different "meanings" and "possibilities of existence" that can be revealed through religious classics.

In this way, even the "most determinedly secularist consciousness" must acknowledge the moment of truth contained in those expressions (1981a, 195). Hence while Tracy follows Rawls in predicating a viable public discourse upon locating a fund of shared dialogical resources, he departs sharply from him in his insistence that our stock of shared beliefs can justifiably include appeals to a metaphysically derived "secular faith" and a common desire to find a compelling understanding of our existential situation. Given these presuppositions, Tracy moves to claim, in a way that political liberals would not, that we essentially share a common culture. As a society, we constitute a "community of interpreters," able to converse with one another in exploring the disclosures of truth provided by "our" (American) religious classics (1994, 210).

This vision of commonality exists in a good deal of tension with Tracy's desire to open up the public sphere to other voices not always included in the American cultural mainstream. Tracy stresses the need to admit as "candidates for the status of religious and artistic classics" contributions from Native American, African American, feminist, Catholic, Jewish, "Southern," and radical perspectives (1994, 210; 1981a, 38). He does not, however, see the presence of these disparate voices as challenging his understanding of a singular culture and "community of interpreters" responsible for retrieving and evaluating the truths disclosed by these sources. In fact, a more plausible rendering of this plurality points to the possibility of the American polity being constituted by a number of interpretive communities, each of which has its own traditions and conventions for determining what does or does not count as a "classic." If this characterization is accurate, it gives us reason to wonder whether Tracy's expectation that a text like the New Testament can be properly understood as an *American* cultural possession is justified. Do we really share enough by way of a common worldview and foundational beliefs to be able to be collectively transformed by such a text, as Tracy insists? And what would that transformation look like?

For a religious classic to have the kind of shared, fully public impact Tracy hopes for, we would have to abandon the idea that theology's contribution to public discourse might consist in presenting a distinctive, even counter-cultural set of norms that could call its hearers to a radically different set of normative commitments. This is ironic, considering Tracy's fondness for the "utopian visions" religion can provide as possibilities for societal change (1994, 208; 1975, 242–244). But his overriding desire to locate a public language equally accessible to both the believer and the nonbeliever does inevitably place limits on the kind of discourse theology can appropriately pursue. For instance, while Tracy respects the contributions of liberation theologians, particularly their ability to "retrieve the societal and political, not merely existentialist-individualist, meaning inherent in the symbols of Judaism and Christianity," he faults them for their uncritical reliance on orthodox theological concepts. This theological naivete, insofar as it is unable to move beyond a belief "in the omnipotent, all-knowing, and unrelated God of classical theism and, at the same time, in an exclusivist understanding of revelation and christology," comes to threaten "the ultimate value and meaning of that basic secular faith shared by all those committed to the contemporary struggle for liberation" (1975, 243, 245). Tracy's hope for a harmonious public realm, delineated by the boundaries of our "common" convictions, precludes him from welcoming into public discourse those participants who may be unwilling to jettison their "sectarian" or "exclusivist" presuppositions as the price to be paid for a shared discourse.

The second respect in which Tracy's understanding of public discourse parallels that of political liberalism lies in its noncommunal conception of moral diversity. This is evident in Tracy's neglect of ecclesiology—the study of the role of the church as sociological entity, shaping and giving life to the truths theology develops. Moral diversity for Tracy is not primarily exhibited as a plurality of moral communities, but rather in the multiplicity of "meanings" and "possibilities of existence" that emerge from the various religious traditions that happen to be present within a society.[10] This is not to say that Tracy simply ignores the role of the church in providing the context within which the theologian operates, particularly in the case of systematic theology.[11] But rarely does Tracy give us a glimpse of the way in which the "meanings" at the core of a religious tradition are embodied in the fullest sense only when they are part of a living community, where those truths are embraced as authoritative, and on that basis allowed to shape and transform the members of that community. Instead, Tracy gives us the impression that religious truths can be encountered and evaluated by anyone, in a rather straightforward and unproblematic sense. We simply need to allow a religious classic to make a "claim" on us. Tracy thus does not pursue the idea that *some* kinds of religious truths may not be adequately grasped by those outside a particular religious community—that *conversion* might actually be necessary before one comes to "understand rightly." Of course, it is the desire to witness to the Other that has historically been the strongest impulse for Christians to risk taking on a public voice in approaching those outside their communities. But this rationale for engaging in public discourse is largely absent in Tracy's corpus, and it would in any case seem unnecessary when the essential truths (that is, those that have been purged of "exclusivity") of each religious tradition are readily accessible and capable of being possessed by all "intelligent, reasonable, and responsible" individuals. For Tracy, we are *all* members of the community of interpreters responsible for appropriating religion's truths. The boundaries between moral communities, to the extent they remain at all, are entirely porous.

This understanding of religion, in which religion's chief function is to articulate symbolic meanings or possibilities of existence that can be appropriated and embraced by all suitably disposed interpreters, stands in opposition to the "cultural-linguistic" model advanced by George Lindbeck (1984). Lindbeck finds Tracy's "experiential-expressive" conception of religion inadequate, as it understands religion to be fundamentally a symbolic *representation* of primary human experiences rather than the *source* of those experiences themselves. Tracy assumes a certain bedrock of experience that all humans share in common. On this view, our religious differences can be construed as involving contrasting attempts to explain that experience. As Lindbeck notes, this way of characterizing religion's significance is in accord with some pervasive tendencies within contemporary American religion, in which

> increasing numbers of people regard all religions as possible sources of symbols to be used eclectically in articulating, clarifying, and organizing the experiences of the inner self. Religions are seen as multiple suppliers of different forms of a single commodity needed for transcendent self-expression and self-realization. Theologians, ministers, and perhaps above all teachers of religion in colleges and universities whose job it is to meet the demand are under great pressure in these circumstances to emphasize the experiential-expressive aspects of religion. It is thus that they can most easily market it. (1984, 22)

To regard this way of understanding religion as reflecting a universal condition, however, as opposed to a particular social or cultural pattern, would be a mistake, Lindbeck argues. Certainly this understanding is less pervasive within religious communities standing outside mainline Protestantism. Many non-Christian faiths as well, such as Islam, would be seriously mischaracterized by this view. In coming to terms with those traditions that are less able or willing to embrace a modernist religious sensibility, then, Lindbeck's "cultural-linguistic" model may be a more apt framework. Here religion is more appropriately understood as

> above all an external word, a *verbum externum,* that molds and shapes the self and its world, rather than an expression or thematization of a preexisting self or of preconceptual experience. The *verbum internum* (traditionally equated by Christians with the action of the Holy Spirit) is also crucially important, but it would be understood in a theological use of the model as a capacity for hearing and accepting the true religion, the true external word, rather than (as experiential-expressivism would have it) as a common experience diversely articulated in different religions. (34)

On this view, a particular religious understanding can only be truly acquired by engaging in a communal set of practices, in which "one learns how to feel, act, and think in conformity with a religious tradition that is, in its inner structure, far richer and more subtle than can be explicitly articulated. The primary knowledge is not *about* the religion, nor *that* the religion teaches such and such, but rather *how* to be religious in such and such ways" (1984, 35, emphasis in original). Before we can adequately embrace religious concepts as indeed *truths,* we must first become acclimated to their usage within a particular religious community. In contrast to Tracy's assertion that Christian theologians can, by framing their propositions in an appropriate manner, allow Christian symbols to illuminate the shared reality of believer and nonbeliever alike, Lindbeck maintains that "those unskilled in the language of faith" can neither affirm nor reject a proposition such as "Jesus is Lord." This is because in coming to terms with a religion "one must have some skill in *how* to use its language and practice its way of life before the propositional meaning of its affirmations becomes determinate enough to be rejected [or affirmed]" (68). This suggests that religious truths are not simply "out there" waiting to be discovered by sympathetic observers. Rather, as they are located within particular practices and social contexts, they can only be retrieved by those willing to undergo the extensive process of engagement whereby different practices can be experienced and evaluated to some extent "from within."[12]

Lindbeck's analysis points to the way in which the boundaries of moral communities must be taken seriously if we are to arrive at a plausible conception of public discourse. Importantly, this does not mean that discourse between communities with different foundational beliefs and practices is unnecessary or impossible. We should, however, be wary of requiring diverse communities to adopt a predetermined approach to discourse or refrain from offering their distinctive perspectives on the grounds that there is in fact one definitive, truly public language at our disposal. Such a strategy can only result in an illusory semblance of commonality. Tracy's insistence that commonality is required to undergird public discourse is thus of a piece with his problematic characterization of moral diversity, in which our differences are seen as largely superficial and insubstantial, merely different ways of expressing what is after all a common experience.

Tracy envisions a widely accessible public realm where the terms of engagement are presumed to be already established, and the language we use to interpret our religious "classics" is universally shared. Theology's role is thus clearly defined and defended, but its assertions are also delimited, constrained in a manner designed to ensure that theology can only support and reaffirm this preconceived vision of the public realm. There is a price to be paid for a theology that can only reinforce shared norms, however. As Jeffrey Stout argues in discussing Tracy's project, "there is no more certain way for theology to lose its voice than to imitate that of another" (1988, 165). If theology is forced to speak a language not its own, there is no guarantee that it will have anything interesting to say.

Richard John Neuhaus: Judeo-Christian Religion as Cultural Foundation for Democracy

One of the more prominent figures among contemporary neoconservatives, Richard John Neuhaus defends a Tocquevillian conception of liberal democracy and capitalism that draws on religion for its justification. Following Tocqueville, Neuhaus considers it essential that a thriving democratic society have a secure moral foundation. Only with sound mores shared in common can liberal democracy maintain a sense of the common good and resist collapsing into rampant individualism or political tyranny. For Neuhaus, in American society this foundation is provided by "Judeo-Christian" values.

Neuhaus stresses, however, that he does not seek a "sacralization" of the polity. Religion's proper function is not to seize control of the state but merely to keep it in its proper place, something that can only be done if religion effectively permeates the general culture. In this manner religion "clothes" the public square in transcendent values, as citizens draw upon these values in directing their political activity. This ensures that the public realm will not become a moral vacuum waiting to be filled with destructive "ersatz" religions that refuse to recognize the transcendent authority sustaining all properly ordered political communities (1984, 79–93; 1991, 141).[13]

Neuhaus also follows Tocqueville in his understanding of the way "mediating structures" preserve liberal democracy. By maintaining a plenitude of diverse associations, democratic citizens can help ensure that the state will be unable to colonize spheres of life that are beyond its effective competence. Voluntary associations, if given the space they need to pursue their distinctive missions, contribute in their own way toward the public good and can foster localized solutions to public problems the state may be ill-equipped to solve. Neuhaus considers churches to be a paradigmatic example of institutions that can fill this role, but only if they are unhindered by the government agencies and courts that frequently threaten their autonomy.[14]

Like Tracy, Neuhaus soundly rejects any theory of politics that declares religion to be irrelevant or harmful to political life, insisting that religion has an indispensable role to play in the public realm. Neuhaus differs from Tracy, however, in envisioning a more concrete political role for religion. Rather than exploring the various symbolic resources religion might provide the emancipatory project of modernity, Neuhaus instead points to religion as a sociological entity that serves the polity by playing a demonstrable social function. In effect, religious morality produces good democratic citizens and keeps the state within its legitimate sphere. Nor does Neuhaus have any stake in the liberal theological project of helping disenchanted secularists appreciate religion's transformational potential. In fact, he is sharply critical of liberal theology, which he views as an "accommodationist" strategy that militates against the church's responsibility to present its truths with authenticity (1984, 213–225). Hence Neuhaus's approach is less encumbered with some of the more problematic aspects of Tracy's work, wherein religion must be shaped and adapted to render it amenable to a particular conception of modernity. Instead, Neuhaus is freed to consider the various ways in which religious communities approach political life and to pursue a more historically grounded account of the role theology has played in the public realm.

Nevertheless, upon consideration of Neuhaus's normative project, it becomes clear that he shares with Tracy the presupposition that a properly ordered public realm must be built upon commonality. While Tracy finds this commonality within human experience itself, Neuhaus finds it within the dominant strands of American culture. It is the Judeo-Christian tradition that has provided us with our common moral vocabulary, and it is this tradition that must continue to serve as the basis for a viable public philosophy capable of guiding our polity. Neuhaus's presupposition that such a public philosophy is the only way in which a sound political order might be maintained thus leads him to advocate a particular public role for religion, one that is inherently culturally conservative. In a manner similar to what we observed with Tracy, therefore, Neuhaus's established assumptions about the nature of the public realm serve to constrain the role of religion in public, so that it is required to carry a particular social burden. For Tracy, that burden is to further the cause of modernity; for Neuhaus, it is to preserve a homogeneous democratic culture.

In *The Naked Public Square,* Neuhaus's most influential treatment of religion and public discourse, he describes what he sees as the crisis currently facing American democracy. This crisis is intimately connected, it turns out, with the declining fortunes of American mainline Protestantism. Throughout most of American history, those denominations at the core of the mainline—namely, the Methodist, Episcopalian, Presbyterian, and Congregationalist churches—had exerted pervasive influence as the dominant "culture-shaping force" in American life. They gave American democracy its "moral legitimacy," ensuring that American public purposes would be guided by a shared constellation of transcendent ideals (1984, vii, 202–225). That Neuhaus considers such guidance indispensable to any flourishing democracy is clear.

> Moral legitimation means providing a meaning and a purpose, and therefore a framework within which the violation of that meaning and purpose can be criticized. The vision that is required cannot be produced by the political process itself. Politics derives its directions from the ethos, from the cultural sensibilities that are the context of

> political action. The cultural context is shaped by our moral judgments and intuitions about how the world is and how it ought to be. (60)

And as Neuhaus goes on to argue, "for the great majority of Americans such moral judgments and intuitions are inseparable from religious belief" (60). The widely diffused cultural foundation provided by mainstream American religion was thus able to support the purposes of American democracy and ensure that those purposes would be consistent with God's will. In a manner exemplified most poignantly by the social gospel movement during the late nineteenth and early twentieth centuries, the assumption that Protestant Christianity's mission is to sanctify and redeem the American nation was once an unquestioned hallmark of mainline religion (213–215).

Yet as Neuhaus observes, cultural and intellectual elites both within and outside the churches began to reconsider the plausibility and desirability of this framework as early as the mid-nineteenth century, and the legacy of the social gospellers helped cement the fate of mainline religion. On Neuhaus's reading, the social gospel movement represented the last ardent effort to forge a synthesis among "Protestant Christianity, civilization, and America" (1984, 214). As it gradually dawned on the social gospellers and others in the mainline that they were "no longer needed or wanted" in the realm of ideas and culture, they found themselves in a tenuous position. They refused to assume a resigned posture, however. Intending to hold on at all costs to their well-established pattern of serving as America's moral compass even as their influence was waning, the mainline churches sought to accommodate themselves to the prevailing developments within science and the academy, so that they might still be able to play a supporting role in the social and political struggles of their day. The result, however, was ultimately an attenuated public presence, as the voice of the mainline churches had been rendered hollow and ineffectual. As Neuhaus explains: "The 'prophets' of what might more accurately be called the Great Accommodation were for the most part honorable, and often courageous, men. Yet they now appear to have been less prophets than pacifiers. They were prepared to accept nature's laws as promulgated by science, and to allow no exceptions for God. Their God was reliable, he would not embarrass anybody by challenging the 'realities' determined by prestige opinion" (215, 216).

As Neuhaus sees it, the price to be paid for this accommodation was that the mainline churches had essentially contributed to the creation of a secularized public realm that no longer needed them. Mainline Protestantism "had succeeded in making itself dispensable. It would be permitted to tag along on the continuing journey, to help out with odd jobs and, for old times' sake, to offer an invocation when appropriate, but it must not make a nuisance of itself" (1984, 243).[15] Many within the mainline churches came to accept this new role, offering support where possible to various extant political or social efforts (commonly under the auspices of the liberal wing of the Democratic Party), while others became more ambivalent, retreating to the cultural margins to assume a "prophetic" strategy that would mistake the noble-sounding social statements produced by churchwide assemblies for real political change. In neither case would the mainline churches any longer be willing to come forward to resume their historical culture-forming role in order to preserve a properly ordered public realm.

As Neuhaus observes, however, the fact that the mainline denominations have abandoned this task does not mean that others are unwilling to give it a try by, ironically, drawing on the same impulses that originally motivated the mainline churches. "Politically militant" evangelicals and fundamentalists, alarmed by the cultural and legal developments set in motion during the 1960s and 70s, have aggressively sought to "reclothe" the public square with a biblical vision, thereby retrieving a transcendent purpose for America that the mainline was all too willing to cede to secular forces (1984, vii). Neuhaus is largely sympathetic with the concerns animating the religious right (or "moral majoritarians," as he typically refers to them), as they seek to resist a secularizing culture and a politics that increasingly divorces questions of the good from public policy debate. He sees their emergence as confirming his thesis that the "public square will not and cannot remain naked"—transcendent ideals will be provided somehow, the only question is who will furnish them (vii). Yet for Neuhaus those on the religious right clearly present a dilemma. Their approach to public discourse does not honor the need to present publicly accessible insights but is instead based merely on the assertion of their own perspective. "Those fundamentalist forces which are most insistent that religiously grounded values should have a stronger bearing upon public life are also most insistent that those values are not subject to public discourse and debate. This latter insistence only reinforces the prejudice among otherwise thoughtful citizens that religion is an irrational or subrational 'vulgarization' that dare not be allowed to impinge upon the realm of the 'authentically political'" (158).

If religious communities are to take part in reestablishing a truly shared moral framework, a "transcendent or religious point of reference" that can render policy conflicts more tractable and less contentious, they must be willing to "'translate' those values into terms that are as accessible as possible to those who do not share the same religious grounding" (1984, 110, 125). The problem posed by the political activity of Christian fundamentalists, then, is not that religion is being made public; it is that it is being made public in the wrong way. The fundamentalists' central objective, to reclaim a transcendent purpose for America, is one Neuhaus wishes to honor. Hence he warns that, for those on the liberal end of American Christianity, to simply dismiss or demonize the moral majoritarians would be a grave error. "Our quarrel is primarily theological. Unless that quarrel is transformed into an engagement that moves toward dialogue, we will continue to collaborate, knowingly or not, in discrediting the public responsibility of religion. We will discredit it by finding ourselves in awkward support of those who would exclude religion from the public square" (19). For Neuhaus, then, the situation we confront should be viewed as an opportunity for all religious citizens to join forces, cooperating in working toward a properly constituted public realm, with a common religious heritage acknowledged as its foundation and a commitment to liberal democracy as its purpose.

Neuhaus's project presents a provocative alternative to political liberalism's attempt to secure a legitimate politics by pushing religion to the margins of public life. Neuhaus argues compellingly that those concerned about the future of liberal democracy cannot simply ignore the question of what religious forces might either threaten or support liberal political arrangements. We must not, in Neuhaus's view, isolate the political realm from nonpublic cultural elements. He insists rather that "politics is in large part a function of culture" (1984, 27). What this suggests is that it is only by attending to historical questions about the way religion has functioned politically in the American polity that we can hope to arrive at an adequate understanding of what normative foundations support American political arrangements.[16] In addition, by considering religion as a socially embodied phenomenon, Neuhaus is able to avoid the excessive abstraction that plagues Tracy's analysis of public theology, and he is better able to appreciate the role that particular religious communities can play in social and political life. Neuhaus is not content to have religion merely provide symbolic support for causes determined by other social forces; he seeks a way for religious communities to bring a distinctive perspective to bear on political life. "Against the slogan, 'The world sets the agenda for the church,' we must insist that God sets the agenda for the church. While the church sympathetically understands the felt needs and the questions of the world, a faithful and courageous Christian witness redefines the felt needs and throws into question the questions of the world" (1991, 146). Neuhaus thus gestures toward a vision of public discourse in which the particular perspectives of various moral communities and traditions can helpfully illuminate pressing public concerns.

Despite its strengths, Neuhaus's project exhibits some fundamental tensions that cast doubt on the desirability of its normative aims. First, Neuhaus shifts his ground uneasily between acknowledging the moral diversity that has become increasingly evident as the veneer of consensus provided by mainline Protestantism has eroded and insisting that we share a common religious heritage. Hence, while "we are indeed a more pluralistic society in the sense of including people of various national, racial, and cultural experiences," it is nevertheless the case that "over ninety percent of the American people say they believe in God and think the Judeo-Christian tradition is somehow morally normative for personal and public life" (1984, 145). Elsewhere he makes the case even more assertively: "One suspects . . . that there is among Americans a deep and widespread uneasiness about the denial of the obvious. The obvious is that, in some significant sense, this is, as the Supreme Court said in 1931, a Christian people" (81–82). A generous reading of Neuhaus here might concede that, empirically speaking, more Americans do in fact identify themselves as being Christian than any other particular faith. But this is not enough to demonstrate that "Judeo-Christian religion" provides an authoritative source of common moral values for the American people. Yet that is what Neuhaus often claims. The "sacred canopy" that provides refuge for all Americans, regardless of belief or creed, "is that to which Judeo-Christian religion points. Religion bears witness to it but our religion is not to be equated with it. On the other hand, the canopy is a canopy, it is not mere 'emptiness.' It is generally describable in terms of the promises and judgments revealed in the biblical story. It is not Hinduism or Taoism. Historically and in present democratic judgment, it is the biblical story" (122–123). Those religious traditions that are unable to endorse the idea of a transcendent "sacred canopy" linking God's purposes with those of the state—a subset that includes not only non-Western faiths but also dissenting Christian traditions, such as the Mennonite or Anabaptist faiths—are assigned a rather tenuous status within this framework. Neuhaus's desire to find a common moral foundation for American democracy thus leads him to subsume moral diversity beneath a reading of American history that sees the "biblical story" as America's definitive narrative.

Second, aside from insisting that the biblical story provides our "transcendent point of reference," Neuhaus rarely discusses with any specificity the content of the story itself and the way it can be expected to shape political life. Clearly he intends for it to be more than simply a vague, amorphous set of platitudes or symbols. He insists that Judeo-Christian religion is "brand-name" religion (1984, 190). Yet Neuhaus also contends that for such a thing truly to serve as a point of reference for all Americans, or even only those Americans with religious commitments, it must avoid resting upon particularistic premises that could fail to build commonality. Neuhaus does, after all, desire a struggle in which religious Americans of all persuasions come together to resist those who seek to keep the public square barren of transcendent ideals. It is hard to see how this struggle can be waged if the "biblical story" that is to animate it is defined with any specificity. For surely there are many important, fundamental differences separating various Christian traditions' readings of that story, not to mention the implications drawn from those disparate readings. And of course, to insist upon a singular "Judeo-Christian" reading of the biblical narrative makes little sense when Jewish perspectives are taken into account (a concern that Neuhaus largely sidesteps).

Neuhaus is thus caught between, on the one hand, defending a role for a shared religious perspective that is truly "religious" in some fundamental sense and thus capable of serving as a meaningful alternative to a secularist politics and, on the other, wanting to make room within this perspective for all well-meaning citizens irrespective of their particular religious convictions. It is not at all clear that he can have it both ways. If a religious perspective that emerges from a particular faith community is to serve as the unifying cultural force Neuhaus envisions, it will have to abandon much of its particularity and distinctiveness, thereby failing to remain "brand-name" religion. If, on the other hand, it retains its particularity, it will have to abandon its role as the "sacred canopy" serving as a shared value orientation for all religious Americans, many of whom will likely fail to speak its faith-language.

Finally, we are confronted with the difficulty that lies at the core of Neuhaus's vision of public discourse: the requirement that religious communities present their claims in a way that also honors a commitment to a predetermined conception of public purposes. As we observed above, Neuhaus's project can be differentiated from Tracy's in part by his insistence that public religion should reflect the particular insights of actual religious communities as they engage politics by drawing on distinctive resources. Rather than subordinating its witness to an externally defined agenda, the church is to identify from within its own tradition its authentic social mission. Neuhaus's comments addressing the failures of the mainline denominations to pursue an effective public stance as "servant church" are pertinent here:

> For the idea to be effective, the church must be clear about the service it has to render. It can in a modest way offer money, prestige, and some recruits for the causes that it believes signal God's work in the world. But such an approach means drawing upon declining capital. The capital was created by a community of faith gathered by distinctive truth claims; it can only be replenished by proclamation and faith's response. This means recovering the metaphor of "the church militant," a metaphor almost entirely absent from mainline religious thought today. Against the world for the world; the church's significant contribution is to significantly challenge. The challenge is not significant when the church merely endorses existing positions that challenge other existing positions. Significant challenge means throwing all positions into question. (1984, 224–225)

This oppositional stance is an important one, crucial to any conception of public theology that does not view religion as simply a functional support mechanism for existing social or political arrangements. It contrasts sharply, however, with Neuhaus's predominant concern to show that public religious arguments, appropriately presented, will necessarily serve to support the "sacred canopy" that is intended to provide moral legitimation to the polity (188). For as we saw above, there are limits to the extent to which particularistic truths can be offered in public discourse if they are to remain accessible to everyone. It is this concern that fuels Neuhaus's dislike of the rhetorical strategies favored by moral majoritarians, precisely as those strategies work to undermine the sense that we share a public language in which religious propositions can be meaningfully evaluated and challenged in terms acceptable to all.

The implications of Neuhaus's stance here go far beyond the religious right, however. Any religious perspective that questions whether we do in fact share the same moral horizon or that seeks to disrupt rather than affirm "shared" public norms would from this perspective have to be regarded as uncivil and publicly illegitimate. Despite his ostensible intent to defend an oppositional role for the church, then, Neuhaus's aim to maintain moral commonality and political stability leaves little room for such a role in public discourse.

Indeed, rarely in Neuhaus's work are we shown instances in which religious communities have posed a threat to accepted understandings of civility or good citizenship (aside from the oft-cited example of the moral majoritarians). Instead, Neuhaus maintains that when the church is performing its role appropriately, it will always cultivate "the human capacity for civil righteousness, thus making an invaluable contribution to the peace, justice, and good order of the polis" (1991, 144). This seems too simple. From within the perspective of their own religious traditions, citizens have often acted in ways consistent with what they thought would be conducive to peace, justice, and good order, only to experience the wrath of their neighbors for allegedly violating those very same ends.[17] What Neuhaus's account obscures is the extent to which the practices and convictions that constitute "civil righteousness," as well as the kinds of discourse appropriately considered public, are always contested at some level, as different communities struggle to reconcile the truths derived from their particular traditions with those that happen to be operative in the public realm. Any plausible "transcendent point of reference," then, can only be regarded as a provisional convergence, never a static position that can be used to wall off some voices as being inherently nonpublic. Acknowledging with Neuhaus that the public square cannot remain "naked" does not require us to suppose that it can only be clothed with a single garment. Rather than persisting in a vision of public discourse in which commonality is presupposed, we will be better served by acknowledging the public realm as a site of shifting meanings and truth-claims. Neuhaus's invocation of a common "Judeo-Christian tradition" will not help us here.

Neuhaus shares with Tracy and political liberals an understanding of the public realm in which the boundaries of acceptable discourse are, and must be, clearly delineated. They differ, of course, in where they locate those boundaries, particularly with respect to public religion, but they exhibit few reservations as to whether widely shared standards can be discovered for making these kinds of distinctions. My contention is that we should be considerably more guarded about the prospects of finding such standards. The myriad disagreements that Americans have with one another concerning fundamental moral questions suggest that even if we do have in common Neuhaus's transcendent orientation to political life, it is not accomplishing very much. Given this state of affairs, to continue to insist upon a particular public language on the grounds that *only* that language can properly honor a commitment to the public good would likely lead to a distorted understanding of our political situation and a confining, monological approach to discourse that would only result in obscuring our differences. We need not dismiss the value of the search for commonality. But if it is to be obtained, and we are convinced that our agreements should be genuine, we ought to look for a more expansive approach to public discourse that is better able to account for our particularity. It is with these concerns in mind that I turn to the work of John Howard Yoder.

John Howard Yoder: The Church as Alternative Polity

Of the three theological perspectives I am considering, Yoder's stands in sharpest contrast to the presuppositions animating political liberalism, particularly the notion that in the search for public purposes we can or should adopt a common public language. A Mennonite theologian who spent several years teaching at the University of Notre Dame before his death in 1997, Yoder worked within the "radical reformation" theological tradition. He viewed this tradition as a viable, ongoing source of renewal and critique, one not limited to those of Anabaptist denominational heritage but rather one that "honest theologians from any tradition can affirm in the pursuit of their own vocation," in an effort to reclaim an understanding of the church and its practices faithful to the example set forth in the New Testament (1984, 1–5). In contrast to Tracy and Neuhaus, Yoder was relatively uninterested in demonstrating ways in which religion might be shown to be compatible with the project of modernity or supportive of liberal democracy. Instead, Yoder's chief aim was simply to explicate the distinctiveness of the Christian ethos and to point to the reality of the church, understood as a visible community of believers, as itself constituting a "polity" that exists simultaneously both within and apart from whatever larger political community it happens to inhabit at any point in time.[18]

Throughout Yoder's work, what is primary and central to the church's identity is its faithfulness to the concrete ethical example of Jesus, and its orientation to the political realm must therefore be determined solely in view of that standard.[19] From Yoder's perspective, any assumption that in order to have public relevance theology must be done by seeking a correspondence between the church's traditions and the values of modernity, or those of liberalism, can only be regarded as an imposition that threatens the church's allegiance to the lordship of Christ.

Yoder's approach to theological ethics would be sufficient in many circles to earn him a "sectarian" label. His insistence upon the church's responsibility for being an alternative society, maintaining a critical distance between itself and the greater political community, reveals him to have a highly qualified understanding of the church's public responsibility. This stance, combined with his ardent conviction that the church must be steadfastly pacifist, places Yoder within the "Christ Against Culture" rubric presented by H. Richard Niebuhr in his seminal *Christ and Culture* (1951). Niebuhr characterizes this position, which he finds to be "the typical attitude of the first Christians," as requiring a "withdrawal" from and "renunciation" of the realm of culture, thus impugning the value of the church working within society to effect social change, or "transform" culture (45, 68).[20]

While Yoder recognizes the influence Niebuhr's characterization has had in defining the sectarian "type" for a vast readership both inside and outside academic theological circles, he adamantly rejects its validity. What Niebuhr's typology suggests, Yoder argues, is that the church must either wholly affirm or reject culture—as though it were monolithic and autonomous, something "out there" that is given and that the church must respond to in some uniform fashion (1996a, 54–55).[21] As Yoder sees it, things are not that simple. Culture is not an undifferentiated mass; it is complex and variegated. What is required, then, is for the church to engage in an ongoing process of discernment, whereby those elements of culture that are consistent with the church's ethos are celebrated and enthusiastically participated in, while others are conditionally accepted and still others are categorically rejected. There are no ahistorical or universal cultural "patterns" that can be substituted for the actual decision making of the church community itself in making these determinations. Thus the distance required of the church vis-à-vis the greater community does not signify a withdrawal from or renunciation of that community; rather, it is an attempt for the church to come to terms with the various concrete situations it faces and to decide how to act in a faithful manner in response to those situations, on a case-by-case basis (69–70, 73–74).[22]

Far from constituting a refusal to serve the greater society, then, this option does indeed represent an ethic of service. But it is not an ethic that the church simply takes as given by the greater political community, as though the church had nothing of its own to offer. Instead, the church's public activity is determined by both a concrete awareness of its location within a particular polity in particular historical circumstances and its distinctive calling as a community directed to witness to the reality of the kingdom of God. The church's political task thus becomes figuring out how to address injustices and remedy social evils, as they arise, by offering its own moral resources in a way consistent with its calling. This process can include drawing selectively on the normative resources the larger polity may offer for that purpose, but it must also involve the concrete lived pattern of existence exemplified by the church community itself.

It is this insistence on the primacy and particularity of the church's identity that constitutes Yoder's most potent challenge to the competing approaches of Tracy and Neuhaus. In keeping with the long-standing view of the Anabaptist tradition, Yoder defends the "believers' church" ideal, which emphasizes a shared discipline, as opposed to the "people's church" model he associates with the dominant Christian traditions that fail to differentiate themselves from the prevailing norms of the wider society. The churches in the mainstream of the Protestant Reformation, for all their radicalism in other respects, still clung to the vestiges of the established Christianity of their day. Not only did they persist in infant baptism, a practice that effectively "identified an entire population with the church," they also "retained (or rather established more strongly than before) the control of the church by civil authority. They retained the compulsory membership in the church of all but Jews, and retained as well the approbation of the violence of civil government within the doctrine of the just war" (1984, 106–107). Only the most radical wing of the Reformation was willing to insist upon and cultivate a "minority ethic" for the church, whereby the "Constantinian" presuppositions animating the church throughout Christendom could finally be renounced. No longer would it be necessary to assume that the church's political responsibility involved trying to steer the ship of state. No longer would the church have to deny the strangeness of its way of life in the interest of providing an ethical vision for the entire society.[23] Reclaiming the perspective that guided the early Christian churches, where the church understood itself to be a community of outsiders without power, the church would now be freed to "provide a training ground for cultivating the concrete expectation that things will usually be seen inadequately by those who read events from a posture of control or seeking to control. Thus we educate ourselves in the reasonable expectation that when we see things differently from others, we will often be seeing them more truly" (95). The church's minority vision entails a distinctive reading of history itself, in which "history is borne not by kings and empires but by the church herself" (1964, 16–17). Through this "counter-history" the church locates itself in a cosmic unfolding of events that grounds and legitimates its existence.[24]

What ultimately sustains the church's distinctive narrative is its embodiment within the practices of the community. The collective working out of the church's ethic gives shape and force to the church's claim to be considered "a political entity, a polis" (1964, 18). Commenting on the work of Christian ethicist John C. Bennett, Yoder argues that "if the things the church wants to help Christians do in the wider society, and to help the wider society to do for itself, are to have direction and integrity, there must be an empirical body of people who help one another define and fulfill the concrete social meaning of their loyalty to Jesus Christ" (1984, 91). The process of mutual discernment, whereby the church determines its particular response to its social or cultural situation, is essential to this process:

> The knowledge of the meaning for today of participation in the work of Christ is mediated ecclesiastically. The bridge between the words of Jesus or of the apostolic writings and obedience in the present is not a strictly conceptual operation, which could be carried out by a single scholar at his desk, needing only an adequate dictionary and an adequate description of the available action options. The promise of the presence of Christ to actualize a definition of his will in a given future circumstance (i.e., future to Jesus or to the apostolic writers) was given not to professional exegetes but to the community which would be gathered in his name. (117)

It is precisely because the church is a historical entity, located within ever-changing cultural, social, and political circumstances, that its ethic must be discovered and rediscovered by the community as it encounters those realities. "Each setting, each event, each relationship will open for us a set of options or challenges, where we shall need to decide how to love our enemies, how to feed the hungry, how to keep our promises, how to make the earth be fruitful, how to celebrate community, how to remember our heritage" (1996a, 89).

Yoder's convictions concerning the communal nature of moral reasoning within the church inform his understanding of the possibilities of inter-community discourse more generally. Yoder emphatically denies any account of self-evidently natural or public truth-claims that are said to stand apart from or precede the claims that emerge from concrete, historically embodied communities. While he stresses that his position "does not discount public comprehensibility nor the appeal to outside audiences," he makes it clear that these criteria cannot be determined in advance, by appealing to some universal or nonparticular source. "The reason I do not trust claims to 'natural insight' is that the dominant moral views of any *known* world are oppressive, provincial, or (to say it theologically) 'fallen.' This is true even if the terrain of the provincialism is large or if the majority holding those views is great. There is no 'public' that is not just another particular province" (1984, 40, emphasis in original). For Yoder, the notion that we lack a universal point of view from which to approach public discourse is not in itself problematic. In fact, Yoder reads the Babel narrative in Genesis as revealing a God who scattered humankind and proliferated their languages not to confuse and punish them, but to restore benevolently a state of affairs that was divinely sanctioned to begin with. This scattering only appears as "confusion" if it is "measured pejoratively against the simplicity of imperially enforced uniformity, or when forced by considerations from beyond the text into the picture of an angry, controlling, and retributive God" (1996b, 127).[25]

Yoder thus accepts the community-bound aspect of moral rationality as an ineliminable feature of public discourse. At the same time, however, he stresses that this condition need not be seen as an obstacle to different moral communities productively engaging one another. He notes that both the Jewish and the Christian communities have over time demonstrated a willingness to adopt and utilize other languages and moral rhetorics to assist them in engaging other cultures. What their efforts share in common is not an attempt first to seek a shared moral foundation or language but rather a willingness to "enter concretely into the other community (that is, one *particular* other community at a time) long enough, deeply enough, vulnerably enough" to be able to articulate their own convictions in the words of the people they encountered (1996b, 132, emphasis in original).[26] It is only by meeting one another in our particularity, then, that inter-community discourse can properly be attempted. This approach can be embraced by those who have given up the "point of view of established religion," whereby "the triune correlation seems logical between finding a vocabulary for public discourse, affirming the reliability of nonparticular sources of moral insight, and knowing that 'reason' and 'nature' or 'creation' are the names for the same." Once we have moved beyond this framework, we need no longer see our particularity as a hindrance to discourse but instead see it as an opportunity for genuine engagement to take place.

> To say that *all* communities of moral insight are provincial, that there exists no nonprovincial general community with clear language, and that therefore we must converse at every border, is in actuality a more optimistic and more fruitful affirmation of the marketplace of ideas than to project a hypothetically general insight which we feel reassured to resort to, when our own particularity embarrasses us, but which is not substantial after all when we seek to define it. (1984, 41, emphasis in original)

We can indeed come to understand and even respect one another, Yoder argues, but not by requiring our fellow interlocutors first to adopt our language, under the assumption that we have somehow arrived at a uniquely public perspective. "The way to affirm our respect for others is to respect their particularity and learn their languages, not to project in their absence a claim that we see the truth of things with an authority unvitiated by our particularity" (1984, 42). The church therefore advances its claims to truth boldly, but not in a hegemonic fashion. The recognition of the distance that separates the church's ethos from those of other moral communities, or the social order in general, must always be maintained. For Yoder, the church can and must ultimately maintain that its story is true. But this insistence must always be accompanied by the awareness that others do not accept it and could only come to accept it were they to be genuinely persuaded of its truth.[27]

The conditions of moral particularity do not simply create challenges for the church's ability to convey its message to others, however. They also provide opportunities for the church to learn from those it engages. This is a vital but often under-appreciated aspect of Yoder's thought. Yoder's ecclesiology, with its emphasis on the embodiment of the church within contingent and shifting social and historical contexts, entails a recognition that Christianity is not a closed box, with its truths safely secured and permanently established. Rather, it resembles "a project: i.e., a goal-oriented movement through time" (1984, 3). Instead of knowing all at once, or maintaining a "finished pattern," the church is continually discovering new truths and insights that enable it to critique and reform its practices (2001, 59). And one of the ways in which the church takes part in this learning process, this means of discovery, is through listening to what other communities have to say. The church must be willing to extend its process of discernment beyond its own confines, to hear the neighbor and even the adversary. The adversary too "is part of my truth-finding process"—and can reveal new understandings so as to challenge and bring the church to a fuller grasp of what God has in store for it (69). Because "modern pluralism is not a setback but a providential occasion for clarification," the church can bravely seek opportunities both to speak *and* to listen to others, knowing that God is at work in those encounters (1996b, 135). Hence Yoder affirms that "it was thanks to the loner Tolstoy and the outsider Gandhi that the churchman Martin Luther King Jr. with his Boston personalist education was able to bring Jesus' word on violence back into the churches. It was partly the outsider Marx who has enabled liberation theologians to restate what the Law and the Prophets had been saying for centuries, largely unheard, about God's partisanship for the poor" (1997, 93). Similarly, it was only through the agency of the Enlightenment and its criticisms of Christianity that the church was able to appreciate fully the value of religious liberty and democracy (1984, 23). Yoder thus offers a vivid depiction of a church that, rather than assuming an imperial, domineering posture toward others, practices humility in engaging the communities with which it comes into contact.

When we consider Yoder's robust insistence upon the particularity of all communities, and by extension all moral and political languages, the extent of his departure from political liberalism's core presuppositions emerges clearly. Yoder denies the autonomy of the political, claiming that the state exists "for the sake of the work of the church," as part of a providential ordering. Rather than subordinating the church's witness to a preconceived doctrine of publicity, Yoder maintains that "the Christian church knows why the state exists—knows, in fact, better than the state itself," and he argues that "this understanding provides both the justification for her speaking and the standards which she will apply in evaluating the way in which the authorities exercise their function" (1964, 36, 16). There is no "ethic for the state" that can stand alone (31). Yet it does not thereby follow for Yoder that the church is to implement its vision coercively, as Rawls might suppose. Indeed, it is precisely Yoder's acute recognition of the particularity of the church's worldview that leads him to insist that its discourse must always acknowledge, and come to terms with, the divergent perspectives of those in other communities. Yoder thus turns the logic of political liberalism on its head, suggesting that it is not the denial of universality that leads to coercive political strategies but rather the denial of our *particularity.* "We must abandon the chimerical vision of a set of semantic or definitional moves which would transcend the limits of one's own identity, rationally coercing assent, without taking account of a particular interlocutor or a specific dialogical setting. We must relinquish the dream of a set of social moves which would find or construct a 'world' so big as to enclose everyone else" (1992, 290).

Given the inherent provinciality of moral reasoning, then, any engagement between members of different moral communities must entail a careful attempt to bridge the boundaries that separate them. Yoder accordingly stresses the value of "middle axioms" or "semantic frames," mediating languages that can be used to shape Christian truth-claims so as to take into account the moral presuppositions of those outside the Christian community.[28] But he does not follow Rawls in assuming that such a strategy would lead to a more authentically public point of view, as though it involved moving to a greater degree of impartiality. For Yoder, particularity always remains; it can never be fully abridged. Indeed, as Yoder sees it, the process of finding a suitable mediating language is to originate within the moral reasoning of the Christian community itself and to be informed by its perspective. It is not to take place by simply adopting a neutral standpoint (as though that were possible) that makes irrelevant the source of the claims being made. Even when the church makes use of the "nonparticular" languages that may exist in the public sphere, it does so to offer its own vision of the good. So for instance, if the church in a given society has at its disposal democratic justificatory language, it can utilize this language to hold governing elites accountable and to reduce instances of unjustified coercion (1984, 158). But in doing so, the church is not validating political ends separate from its own vision of a properly ordered polity. Rather, it is using the means at its disposal to bring about a realm more properly aligned with God's purposes.[29]

Even in its boldest moments, however, it is crucial that the church's witness take place via concrete engagement with others. Here is where we find a crucial dimension of the *vulnerability* of Yoder's ethic—and further glimpse its variance from political liberalism's renunciation of particularity. Yoder insists that the church's public witness is evangelical in a social sense. That is, it is based on the notion "that the good news announced to the world has to do with the reign of God among men in all their interpersonal relations, and not solely with the forgiveness of sins or the regeneration of individuals" (1964, 23). But how that message will be received will vary depending upon the social context in which it is uttered and who is being addressed. It cannot simply be claimed as true or claimed as intrinsically public. It must be validated (if indeed it is to be validated) *within the process of engagement itself.* This means that in order for the church to proclaim its message responsibly, it must submit that message to the language of the community that it is engaging. The criteria that would allow its message to be embraced by its hearers are by necessity only "present in the intrasubjective communication setting, by virtue of the fact that the newsbearers have entered the scene, submitting to the language of the host culture, articulating and incarnating their values in the neighbors' terms. That vulnerability to the host community's criteria is the courage of the witness" (1992, 292). As bold as the church's proclamations may be, they cannot be *established* in the way that political liberalism establishes its public values as uncontestable truths. They can only be offered for others to consider and grapple with, and ultimately either to accept or reject.

There is one additional respect in which Yoder's conception of the church's witness offers an alternative to political liberalism's understanding of discourse. Rawls tends to envision public discourse as involving a struggle to present the best, or most convincing, argument in the quest to shape public policy directly. As we observed above, this assumption fuels Rawls's concerns about the dangers of comprehensive doctrines in public life. In this light, one of the most significant implications of Yoder's conception of the church's minority ethic is that the general thrust of its political involvement *does not* involve an attempt to dictate public policy or control the terms of public debate. Rather, the church is called to offer its insights precisely as a community on the margins of public life—as an alternative polity. Viewed from the perspective of mainline Protestantism, such a posture can only be regarded as one of weakness, of ceding the public realm to forces willing to exercise control over it. But from Yoder's perspective, this stance in fact gives the church a better opportunity to remain faithful to its own ethos. And under these conditions, it is able to do more than offer "arguments" in public debate—it can present genuinely enacted social possibilities rooted in the actual life of the Christian community itself. The church in this manner functions to carry out "social experiments" that it can undertake precisely because of its distance from the sites of power in the larger community. Yoder points to, among other things, popular education, institutionalized medicine, and dialogical democracy as ideas and practices that originated within Christian communities and came eventually to transform social and political life in ways beyond the expectations of those originally responsible for them (1984, 92–94; 1964, 19–21).[30] The church in its practices can attempt to embody "utopian visions" that serve as "a foretaste of the peace for which the world was made," reminding the greater society in concrete ways that there are transcendent goods that obviate the need for violence (1984, 94). In a sense, then, independently of what the church "says," the life it exemplifies is itself its most powerful public "expression": "The church represents a pedestal or a subculture in which some truths are more evidently meaningful and some lines of logic can be more clearly spelled out than in society as a whole. The credibility and the comprehensibility of an alternative vision which does not always convince on the part of an individual original or 'prophetic' person, is enormously more credible and comprehensible if it is tested, confirmed, and practiced by a community" (1984, 93). By gesturing beyond a conception of public discourse narrowly understood, Yoder thus opens opportunities for considering ways in which recognizing our particularity can in fact facilitate, rather than threaten, a vibrant process of inter-community engagement.

Considered alongside the options presented by Tracy and Neuhaus, Yoder's conception of public discourse offers both opportunities and challenges. In his willingness to abandon the attempt to obtain a uniquely public standpoint that can be validated independently of any particular moral tradition, Yoder avoids the difficulties that burden Tracy's project, which hinges on the presupposition that our religious differences are merely different ways of expressing what is essentially a common layer of human experience. Nor is Yoder compelled to show, with Neuhaus, that we share a Judeo-Christian religious heritage that renders public religion supportive of the civic realm. Both Tracy and Neuhaus seek to counter a secularist vision of the public sphere by demonstrating that religion, rather than being politically divisive, is in fact essential to the pursuit of public purposes. Yoder in his own way concurs, but from a radically different standpoint and a fundamentally different understanding of the nature of the public itself. Yoder rejects the notion that we can define a particular conception of the public realm, with particular normative content that can be used to adjudicate fairly the "publicness" of different claims, because this assumes that we can know what is or is not public before the process of engagement begins. He suggests, in contrast, that a society composed of different moral traditions will be subject to shifting public understandings, understandings that will be fashioned and refashioned through the various efforts that diverse moral communities bring to bear in shaping the public realm. Any community that advances a vision of the good, therefore, regardless of the moral foundation on which its assertions rest, can legitimately take part in that engagement, that struggle to find common ends.

Yoder's approach does require us to give up any expectation that a seamless political unity can be attained through discourse. But in acknowledging this, moral communities of diverse kinds are then freed to imagine and construct social and political possibilities that might not otherwise come into being. It may be thought that in emphasizing the barriers to a shared public rationality, Yoder deprives his project of resources that might help him conceptualize the kind of inter-community political cooperation needed to make shared political goals and movements possible. There is some truth to this, but this criticism does not take into account the benefits that can be gained by relativizing the claims of public reason. Once the provisionality of the public sphere is taken into account, we are able to assume a new flexibility in pursuing political goals on a more ad hoc or pragmatic basis. There is thus a kind of experimental approach to the political sphere that emerges from Yoder's insights into the limits of the political.[31]

A community that has renounced the goal of transforming the public realm wholesale, in the image of a particular ethical paradigm or a particular comprehensive blueprint of the political order, has a different orientation toward political responsibility, in a manner consistent with Yoder's "minority ethic":

> We have always been taught to understand the nature of power in society so as to expect that the way to get useful things done is to find a place at the command posts of the state. . . . The creativity of the "pilot project" or of the critic is more significant for a social change than is the coercive power that generalizes a new idea. Those who are at the "top" of society are occupied largely with the routine tasks of keeping in position and keeping balance in society. The dominant group in any society is the one that provides its judges and lawyers, teachers and prelates—their effort is largely committed to keeping things as they are. This busyness of rulers with routine gives an exceptional leverage to the creative minority, sometimes because it can tip the scales between two power blocs and sometimes because it can pioneer a new idea. In every rapidly changing society a disproportionate share of leadership is carried by cultural, racial, and religious minorities. (1998, 215)[32]

Hence while Yoder's vision does acknowledge many of the difficulties inherent in approaching political life in the midst of moral diversity, it also holds out the possibility of finding novel solutions to political problems. Once we are no longer obligated to subordinate our political activity to an overarching and confining political rationality, we are able to consider a wider range of approaches to politics itself, including those offered by particular communities that may otherwise stand at the margins of prevailing cultural or political reality.

In addition to its advantages, Yoder's project does pose potential difficulties. On the one hand, Yoder's uncompromising fidelity to the Christian narrative allows him to develop a vision of the church that is a welcome alternative to public theologies that simply seek to harmonize the claims of faith with the demands of the civic order. If religious communities are to make genuine contributions to public life, they should do so by drawing from the resources of their own traditions, rather than merely aligning themselves with whatever political forces happen to hold sway at any given moment. In this respect, Yoder's minority ethic indeed has much to offer. Moral particularity is not something to be afraid of; it is the place where we must begin in our moral and ethical reasoning. On the other hand, Yoder may in some respects be drawing the boundaries of moral particularity too defensively. For instance, while Yoder frequently discusses the various ways the church can engage and transform its surrounding community, he is more reluctant to explore situations in which the church might have its own understandings and practices beneficially transformed through the process of that interaction. Of the examples of the latter that Yoder does discuss, typically these involve moments of clarification in which the church's own ideals are refined or improved upon, rather than radically revised. This is evident in some of the examples of inter-community learning mentioned earlier, in which we saw Tolstoy and Gandhi catalyzing Martin Luther King Jr.'s understanding of nonviolence, and Marx spurring liberation theologians to rediscover the Old Testament prophets' condemnation of inequality. Yoder's ethic of inter-community discourse, whereby we seek to "run the risk of entrusting ourselves and what we claim to believe to the language of a moral community other than our own," is provocative in its implications, and it would seem to entail not only the possibility of the church expanding its boundaries but also the prospect that it will be radically changed in the process of that expansion (1996b, 134). Yoder's reluctance to pursue this dimension of discourse does place some limits on his ability to envision common aims emerging from the process of inter-community engagement.

Another difficulty with Yoder's perhaps too-jealous guarding of the church's narrative lies in his characterization of moral diversity, which leaves little room for overlapping community boundaries. While there is much merit in Yoder's depiction of our moral situation as involving a plurality of moral traditions and communities (as opposed to the more individualistic understanding of moral diversity we find in political liberalism, for example), most of us do find ourselves shaped and constituted by different communities. (Since I am a Lutheran who also happens to be an American citizen and a political theorist, at least three communities have helped make me who I am.) And while in some respects this condition makes things more complicated, insofar as there is a great deal to be sorted out, it also can be seen as providing more opportunities for convergences and seeing things from a shared vantage point. At least there are good reasons for resisting some of Yoder's more pessimistic characterizations of our moral diversity, wherein we are seen as inhabiting entirely distinct and separate moral worlds. As we will see in the next chapter, the strategies relied upon by religious communities in political life have sometimes involved making creative use of the resources provided by multiple traditions and languages in making their public appeals. Our diverse allegiances may be complex and at times ethically daunting, but they may also provide novel opportunities for redefining public purposes.

My own ethics of discourse, then, while drawing deeply from Yoder's project, will place a greater emphasis on the search for shared aims in political life. Yoder is right to remind us that we must not lose sight of the fundamental reality of moral particularity. But I would suggest that the crucial goal before us is to consider ways in which we might hold in tension both the need for particular communities to maintain their distinctive moral and ethical vision *and* the political necessity of forming (and contesting) public norms. Citizens who recognize a primary constitutive narrative (such as that provided by a religious or ethnic community, for instance) may still come to recognize the value of other stories, and it may be in the interaction among these various narratives and their accompanying languages that much of what animates politics is to be found.

If politics is not to be considered simply as a settled, harmonious realm of shared values or as a site of incommensurable conflict but instead as a process whereby multiple communities and traditions come into contact in a joint effort to make sense of our public space, then what are needed are political practices that can assist us in carrying out this enterprise. Before providing a fuller articulation and defense of these practices, however, I will consider the resources to be drawn from one of the twentieth century's most striking episodes of political transformation.

CHAPTER 5

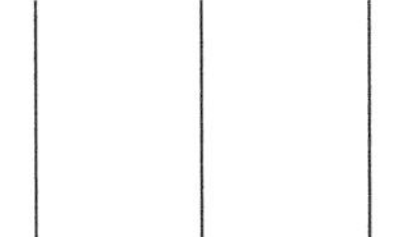

Envisioning a Politics of Moral Engagement

Glimpses from the Civil Rights Struggle

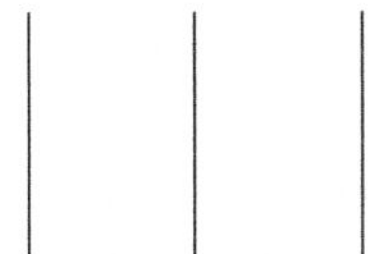

As we observed earlier, one of the historical examples Rawls points to in order to demonstrate the merits of political liberalism's approach to politics is the American civil rights movement.[1] Although this was, as Rawls acknowledges, a movement that based its public arguments on religious grounds, he finds its political activity to be fully in accord with the requirements of public reason. Rawls contends that since the struggle was waged on behalf of equality and justice, the arguments offered supported the conclusions of public reason and therefore could be seen as necessary for helping to bring about a more well-ordered and just society consistent with political liberalism's core purposes (1996, 249–251).

If Rawls is correct in this characterization, it would certainly help insulate him from the charge that his approach to liberal politics remains insufficiently attentive to the positive dynamics of religion in public life. For as exemplified in the thought and public witness of leaders such as Martin Luther King Jr., as well as the efforts of the many hundreds and thousands who joined him in sacrificing and toiling for racial justice, the struggle for civil rights was one of the most remarkable instances of a religiously inspired social movement in American history. Without the biblical vision of the beloved community that animated King's witness and the role of the black church in spiritually nurturing the women and men who gave life to it, the movement could not have succeeded as it did.

A sustained examination of the movement is needed in order to appreciate fully its distinctive contribution to American public life. It is important that we not succumb to the temptation of viewing the progress of civil rights as something automatic or inevitable, as though it were a fulfillment of a foreordained national destiny. Doing so can lead us to lose sight of the precariousness of the struggle and the great risks that accompanied it. Civil rights had to be obtained, at every step of the way, for a price. And their achievement required a fundamental transformation of the way most Americans understood racial justice. How that transformation took place, via the courageous agency of a marginalized and ostracized community, is the subject of this chapter.

My purpose here is twofold. First, I will provide a detailed, contextualized examination of the civil rights movement and its political strategies, from which I will later draw in elucidating my constructive argument for a post-secular public ethics in chapter 6. Second, I will use this account to shed light on Rawls's own view of the civil rights struggle. I argue that Rawls's treatment of the episode is inadequate and that in fact the movement's witness gestures beyond the limitations of political liberalism's framework.

The Black Church as Moral Community

To begin to place the civil rights struggle in context, it is essential to have an adequate conception of the black church and its worldview.[2] During the eras of slavery and segregation, the black church was the one institution black Americans could exercise complete sovereignty over. Most fundamentally, it was, as James Cone puts it, "a haven, a place where blacks could be free of white folks, free of Jim Crow, free of everything that demeaned and humiliated them" (1991, 25). In a world in which oppression was constant, the church provided a refuge in which blacks could exercise collective autonomy and achieve a personal and communal sense of identity. Moreover, the church provided the only space in which blacks could effectively engage in community building, broadly understood. The church served as a vital resource for cultural development, education, economic cooperation, and political activity.[3]

The political dynamics of the church were particularly important. Richard Lischer argues that due to blacks' exclusion from American politics, "the church became the *polis* for its members" (1997, 20). Thus, even though blacks were disenfranchised, they had abundant opportunities to experience political life.

> Excluded from the mainstream electoral process, black people voted and chose their leaders in their churches, selecting pastors, bishops, trustees, deacons and deaconesses, the presidents of the conventions, women's auxiliaries, and the like. This surrogate politics carried on in the Black Church became an intensive training ground of political experience with all of the triumphs and disappointments of which the political process is capable. It was the one area of social life where leadership skills and talents could be honed and tested, and it was the only area for most African Americans where the struggle for power and leadership could be satisfied. (Lincoln and Mamiya 1990, 205–206)

The democratic dispositions and practices cultivated within the politics of the black church could be easily transferred to extra-ecclesial settings once the opportunity arose. Blacks gained a taste of self-governance through their experience in the church, and this was a contributing factor in the development of their ability and willingness to envision themselves as citizens once the civil rights struggle was underway.

The centrality of the church in the black community meant that firm distinctions between the religious sphere and the spheres of economics, culture, and politics simply didn't evolve. Black pastors were never regarded as "merely" religious figures; they were community leaders in the fullest sense and were expected to address pressing issues facing the community, particularly when they concerned race (Lincoln and Mamiya 1990, 207).[4] They could legitimately involve themselves in whatever was required for community building. It was not uncommon, for instance, for black clergy to be regarded as highly for their economic leadership as for their preaching ability.[5] Even when broad-based civil rights organizations were started, such as the National Association for the Advancement of Colored People (NAACP) and the National Urban League, their leadership ranks were often comprised of black pastors (Lincoln and Mamiya 1990, 208). The cohesiveness and strength of the black church had always ensured that it would serve as the most indispensable source of leadership and guidance in the black community, both in religious and "nonreligious" spheres.

The black church's ability to permeate all areas of black community life is related in large part to its distinctive worldview. This worldview has several core features. First, at the heart of the black church's understanding of the cosmos is a God who grants freedom to the oppressed. The Exodus story, wherein God frees the Israelites from their captivity at the hands of the Egyptians, is one of the foundational narratives of the black church. It provides a vivid glimpse of God's identity: "By delivering this people from Egyptian bondage and inaugurating the covenant on the basis of that historical event, God reveals that he is the God of the oppressed, involved in their history, liberating them from human bondage" (Cone 1970, 18–19). Since this is a God who *liberates,* moreover, there is an especially powerful resonance in the idea of freedom itself. To a people in bondage, the yearning for freedom understandably becomes paramount. Freedom has had numerous meanings in the black church: during the time of slavery it was understood most directly in opposition to physical bondage, while after emancipation and during the civil rights struggle it came to be associated with economic and political liberties. The term does have an irreducibly theological significance, however, as it connotes the "absence of any restraint which might compromise one's responsibility to God," suggesting an intrinsic connection between civic freedom and spiritual freedom (Lincoln and Mamiya 1990, 4).

The second core feature of this worldview is the significance of the incarnation of Christ—that is, the reality of the Son of God as suffering servant, who bore the cross for the salvation of humankind. As opposed to an abstract conception of Jesus as a purveyor of moral precepts or as the representative of an impersonal God, such as may be found within some versions of liberal theology, the black church's understanding of Jesus is dramatically real and concrete, and is intimately associated with his kinship with the oppressed (Lincoln and Mamiya, 1990, 4). Because Jesus suffered with the oppressed, his victory over death means that they too will triumph. As Cone articulates it, Jesus' death "is the revelation of the freedom of God, taking upon himself the totality of human oppression; his resurrection is the disclosure that God is not defeated by oppression but transforms it into the possibility of freedom" (1970, 210–211). This understanding of redemption is not simply an otherworldly hope of a life without suffering in heaven. It is informed by an awareness that Jesus has made possible a new life *now,* for those who trust in him. "To live as if death has the last word is to be enslaved and thus controlled by the forces of destruction. The free man is the oppressed man who says No to oppressors, in spite of the threat of death, because God has said Yes to him, thereby placing him in a state of freedom" (211). For the black church, then, Jesus embodies the suffering that God's people must endure, but it is ultimately a suffering that leads to victory over all forces that separate humans from God and from one another.

The third core feature of the black church's worldview is intrinsically related to this understanding of Jesus' mission and is aimed at the restoration of human community. Because Jesus has triumphed over sin and oppression, the church is able to recognize the equal humanity and dignity of all people and thus provide a glimpse of the kingdom of God, where all are honored regardless of their skin color or social station. The black church's telos is thus to work at eradicating any injustices that stand in the way of revealing this new foundation for community. The various struggles for freedom that the black church has waged throughout its history—including the early slave revolts, abolitionism, and the fight against segregation—have all had a dual emphasis. In addition to seeking freedom for blacks in particular, these efforts have always involved a broader attempt to work toward a just society in which all forces of oppression would be eliminated and thus all people could come to regard one another as equals. As Peter Paris describes it, the black church exists to embody a theologically rooted "anthropological principle"—the equality of all human beings in their relation to God—and this principle has always provided its orientation to political life (1985, 17).

As an institution committed both to the survival of the black community and societal transformation, the black church has throughout its history been poised to undertake creative and courageous efforts to alter the contours of the public sphere in the aim of seeking justice. It has done so, moreover, as a direct reflection of its most essential theological convictions. In this respect, the civil rights struggle provides only one example in a long-established pattern. Where it stands out, however, is in the extraordinary visibility it generated, because of both the national news media that covered the crucial events of the movement and the unique efforts of Martin Luther King Jr. In his brilliant ability to conceptualize and present the aims of the movement before a national audience, King was able to lead a struggle that was both grounded in faith and politically transformative, leaving a profound impact on the nature of American public life.

Martin Luther King Jr.: The Civil Rights Movement's Visionary and Communicator

A Son of the Black Church

After completing his residence requirements for his PhD in philosophy of religion at Boston University, King was faced with a pressing choice. He had long wished to assume a tranquil and comfortable existence as a professor of theology, yet he also felt a strong pull in another direction. As both his father and grandfather had been pastors, there were expectations that King would continue this lineage. But most important, as he recounted in *Stride Toward Freedom,* he and his wife, Coretta, "had the feeling that something remarkable was unfolding in the South, and we wanted to be on hand to witness it. The region had marvelous possibilities, and once it came to itself and removed the blight of racial segregation, it would experience a moral, political and economic boom hardly paralleled by any other section of the country." For that reason, he decided to return to the South and become a pastor, finishing his dissertation in the process, with the expectation that somewhere down the road he would be able to pursue a second career as a scholar (King [1958b] 1986, 422). King thus implies that it was a budding desire to take part in social change that ultimately led him to take a job as pastor of Dexter Avenue Baptist in Montgomery, Alabama.

King may have been embellishing his history a bit here, as his life to that point had hardly been consumed with concerns of racial injustice or an abiding passion to become a crusader against segregation. King was a fairly apolitical student at Crozer Seminary and then at Boston, and he devoted very little attention to race issues in his academic work (Branch 1988, 93–94).[6] While he had experienced a number of painful instances of discrimination as a youth, these were not in themselves sufficient to lead him away from his more intellectually oriented ambitions. It therefore seems plausible to speculate, as Cone does, that King's decision to become a pastor and delay his academic calling ultimately turned on his loyalty to his parents and to his church, the feeling that "he had to return and pay his debt to the Negro community that nurtured his social, educational, and religious development." King knew that he was a product of the black church. It had given him his outlook on the world and provided the "spiritual center for his life," and he had talents that he could offer it (Cone 1991, 32).

The black church was not the sole influence on King's personal and intellectual development, but it was the most important one.[7] The church shaped his ideas on the injustice of racism, ideas that were reinforced by his own experience as a black youth in segregated Atlanta. The church was also the place where King learned what it meant to love one's enemies and where he first encountered Jesus the suffering servant. Not only did the church shape his general worldview, but, just as important, it showed him strategic possibilities "for ministry in a hostile land," as Lischer puts it. As one of Atlanta's most prominent black churches, Ebenezer Baptist regularly hosted some of the era's preeminent black preachers in its pulpit, leaders who were "living proponents of the linkage between religion and racial justice" (Lischer 1997, 29, 33). And King's father and grandfather, as pastors at Ebenezer, had carried out their own experiments with fighting racism. When King was six his father had helped lead a voting rights march, and his grandfather had years earlier successfully boycotted a racist newspaper (Miller 1992, 58). King's formative years in the church thus gave him a deep exposure to the pastor's role as both the shepherd and prophet of his people. The black preachers King encountered "fought for the kingdom of God every day of the week and then celebrated it ecstatically, even poetically, on Sundays," and King would be able to draw on their example as he continued that tradition (Lischer 1997, 3).

The influence of the black church in shaping King's identity is also revealed in the ways in which he absorbed and appropriated other political and religious resources. For most of his life, King expressed a great appreciation of American civic ideals, particularly the ideal of equality as expressed in the Declaration of Independence. In describing the Declaration, King asserted that "never has a sociopolitical document proclaimed more profoundly and eloquently the sacredness of human personality" ([1962] 1986, 119). King was determined to help Americans live up to their highest principles, even when they evinced little desire to do so. Yet ultimately King's patriotism, deep as it was, was shaped and tempered by his primary vision of the beloved community, a vision he first acquired in the black church. King's conception of the beloved community, rooted in the black church's understanding of the kingdom of God, was one that transcended national boundaries and pointed toward a much wider kind of human reconciliation. This would ultimately lead him to become one of the most outspoken critics of the Vietnam War, which he viewed as a violation of the Christian's imperative to seek "a world-wide fellowship that lifts neighborly concern beyond one's tribe, race, class and nation" (King [1967a] 1986, 242).

Similarly, while King underwent an extensive immersion in liberal theology during his graduate education, it was not enough to turn him into a full-fledged theological liberal. King did enjoy the intellectual challenges he faced at Crozer Seminary and at Boston, and he pursued a serious engagement with the writings of the major figures of the liberal theological tradition. These ranged from Walter Rauschenbusch, whose *Christianity and the Social Crisis* is commonly credited with giving birth to the social gospel movement, to Reinhold Niebuhr, whose "Christian realism" as advanced in *Moral Man and Immoral Society* challenged King's appreciation of Rauschenbusch and gave him new questions to consider about the relationship between Christian social ethics and political power.[8] Just as important were the famous liberal preachers, such as Harry Emerson Fosdick and George Buttrick, from whose sermons King borrowed heavily throughout his life.[9] These influences certainly left an imprint on King's rhetorical style and approach to the pulpit. But the worldview of the black church always conditioned his ability to embrace liberal theology's core presuppositions. Lischer expresses this well:

> No matter how many times he repeated the liberal platitudes about the laws of human nature, morality, and history, King could not *be* a liberal because liberalism's Enlightenment vision of the harmony of humanity, nature, and God skips a step that is essential to the development of black identity. It has little experience of the evil and suffering borne by enslaved and segregated people in America.... [King] represented a race that had collectively bypassed the Enlightenment and that consequently knew nothing of the ideal of individual autonomy but a great deal about the freedom of a people delivered at the Red Sea and redeemed by the blood of Jesus. (1997, 53, emphasis in original)

What liberal theology gave King, in the end, was "a new language with which to rationalize his more original religious instincts," rather than a new worldview that supplanted the old (53).

As we will see, King's ability to make use of the different languages that shaped him would contribute to his rhetorical power as a public representative of the civil rights movement. It allowed him to adapt to the widely diverse audiences he faced: whether addressing a small rural black church in a Sunday sermon, a predominantly white congregation at Fosdick's famous Riverside Church in New York City, or a national audience on the mall in Washington, DC, King would be able to offer his core insights in a way that could resonate with all but the most hostile white conservatives and black power activists. It allowed him to make his vision of the beloved community, as Keith Miller puts it, "a mainstream American idea" (1992, 85). Yet throughout his speeches and writings, King's primary language of the black church remained the touchstone that oriented his use of these other supplementary languages. And toward the later years of his life, when his frustration with the fate of the movement and the extent of injustice in America began to set in, it was this language that he came to rely on most heavily.

The Movement's Visionary

King's leadership role in the civil rights movement was twofold. First, he inspired and motivated those on the front lines of the struggle, helping them to see their actions as consistent with God's purposes in liberating the oppressed. And second, he presented the message of the movement to a wider world, enlisting support for the cause from those already sympathetic and seeking to persuade those not yet convinced. These roles were not entirely separable, since King sometimes addressed audiences that included both allies and adversaries. Moreover, King was aware that in most cases anything he said could potentially be made known to a national audience through the news media. But King did face a different set of challenges and imperatives when addressing Northern audiences removed from the heat of the battle than when he was working on particular campaigns in the deep South, where men and women regularly faced severe hardship and even death for their activism. In the former context, King's role was the movement's communicator; in the latter, he was its visionary.

When individual campaigns against segregation and Jim Crow laws were underway, beginning with the Montgomery bus boycott in 1955, King would regularly address black congregations both in Sunday worship services and during the mass meetings that would be held throughout the duration of each campaign. In these situations King, along with other prominent leaders of the movement, would give direction and guidance to those waging the struggle. King's crucial responsibility here was to *make sense of* the struggle, to provide an interpretive framework that would give his hearers confidence in knowing that they were engaged not merely in a local dispute with racist county officials or businessmen but in a momentous quest for justice with national implications, one in which God was directly involved. For most of those taking part in the boycotts, demonstrations, and marches, the struggle was an unprecedented and often frightening undertaking. Accustomed to being regarded as second-class citizens or worse and therefore as wholly unwelcome in the public sphere of white society, these men and women were boldly seizing the public stage, in a manner that was virtually certain to arouse the wrath of preservers of the status quo. Great courage would be needed for such an effort, and King drew on the resources of his church tradition to inspire it in his hearers.

There were two key themes in King's messages to these audiences. He would stress the nature of the struggle and why it had to be waged nonviolently, and he would point to God's unfailing presence in the movement. King saw the movement as a quest for the beloved community, not merely as a way to gain equal status for blacks in American life. As King announced in a speech soon after the end of the successful Montgomery boycott in 1956:

> We have before us the glorious opportunity to inject a new dimension of love into the veins of our civilization. There is still a voice crying out in terms that echo across the generations, saying: Love your enemies, bless them that curse you, pray for them that despitefully use you, that you may be the children of your Father which is in Heaven. This love might well be the salvation of our civilization. . . . It is true that as we struggle for freedom in America we will have to boycott at times. . . . But the end is reconciliation; the end is redemption; the end is the creation of the beloved community. It is this type of spirit and this type of love that can transform opposers into friends. ([1956a] 1986, 139–140)

It was precisely because the movement was based on love, King insisted, that it had to involve a renunciation of violence. Because reconciliation between all people was the aim and purpose of the movement, violence would contradict everything it stood for. It is often observed that King's convictions regarding nonviolent disobedience were influenced by his exposure to the thought of Mahatma Gandhi. King was himself eager to acknowledge this debt, noting that he had enthusiastically read much of Gandhi's work and that he had overcome his doubts about nonviolence as a social strategy largely by considering the merits of Gandhi's approach ([1960] 1986, 38). There was also a good deal of indirect influence provided through some of King's key advisors, such as Bayard Rustin, Harris Wofford, and James Lawson, whose commitment to Gandhian philosophy was far more extensive than King's.[10] When addressing black churches on the subject of nonviolence, however, King's emphasis was always on Jesus, the suffering servant, whose exemplification of *agape* was immediately familiar to his hearers in a way that Gandhian *Satyagraha* was not. Jesus pointed the way to the beloved community because he was willing to undergo suffering voluntarily, loving his enemies rather than fighting them. As King would later remark in reflecting on the movement's origins:

> From the beginning a basic philosophy guided the movement. This guiding principle has since been referred to variously as nonviolent resistance, noncooperation, and passive resistance. But in the first days of the protest none of these expressions was mentioned; the phrase most often heard was "Christian love." It was the Sermon on the Mount, rather than a doctrine of passive resistance, that initially inspired the Negroes of Montgomery to dignified social action. It was Jesus of Nazareth that stirred the Negroes to protest with the creative weapon of love. ([1958b] 1986, 447)

In addition to grounding the movement's actions in Jesus' example of nonviolent love, King stressed God's constant presence in the struggle. It was only through God's persistent intervention in each crucial event that the movement would ultimately be enabled to triumph. In seeking to illustrate God's workings in this fashion, King explicitly assumed the mantle of prophet to his people: he could perceive the significance of the "ordinary" and see the divine within it. Prior to a pivotal march from Selma to Montgomery in 1965, King knelt on the road and prayed, "Thou has sent us to fight, not just for ourselves, but to fight for this nation so that democracy might exist here for the whole world." King was thereby allowing those on the march to see the fuller significance of their actions, and to understand them as consistent with God's own redemptive purposes (Lischer 1997, 122).

The Exodus story pervaded King's sermons and speeches; God's liberation of his people was taking place in a tangible, forceful way. An apt example is a sermon King gave in Atlanta during a particularly bleak period in the movement, shortly following the assassination of John F. Kennedy and a particularly horrible church bombing in Birmingham. Acknowledging the despair all in the congregation were feeling, King reminded them of God's delivering their ancestors out of the bondage of slavery, and he extended the Exodus narrative by declaring boldly that God would continue to guide them toward the promised land. Reciting with the congregation the last stanza of James Weldon Johnson's great Negro spiritual, "Lift Every Voice and Sing," King declared in emphatic terms that God would not abandon his people (Branch 1998, 182–183).[11] King was fond of saying that the movement enjoyed "cosmic companionship" and that each campaign in the movement was a "proving ground" in which God was revealing his purposes through the efforts of those taking part in the struggle.[12] In this way, as Lischer points out, King left no room for granting these "secular" events "a life of their own outside the terms and framework of the biblical world" (Lischer 1997, 203). With his ability to draw the life of the movement into the world of the Bible, King could assure his audiences that they were truly part of a "Word-of-God movement" (220).

Both of King's dominant themes were evident in a particularly pivotal speech that he delivered at the outset of the Montgomery bus boycott. The speech took place during an evening mass meeting at the Holt Street Baptist Church, and in it King framed the purposes of the boycott and gave the packed church an appreciation of the magnitude of their decision to pursue justice. As this was King's first official address as leader of the Montgomery Improvement Association, the hastily formed group entrusted with organizing and maintaining the boycott, it lacked some of the sophistication and nuance of King's later movement speeches.[13] Nevertheless, most of the essential ingredients that would characterize King's more mature speeches were already present. King began by acknowledging the group's citizenship under the Constitution: "We are here in a general sense, because first and foremost—we are American citizens—and we are determined to apply our citizenship—to the fullness of its means" (Branch 1988, 138–139). He stressed that the protest was therefore intended not to violate but to uphold the true meaning of the Constitution (Lischer 1997, 86).

King then went on to characterize the situation facing Montgomery blacks, beginning with a description of Rosa Parks, whose courageous decision to refuse to give up her seat on a segregated bus was the catalyst of the boycott. King honored Parks for "the depth of her Christian commitment and devotion to the teaching of Jesus," making it all the more appalling that she was arrested merely for resisting an unjust ordinance (Lischer 1997, 86). He proceeded to point to the community's collective suffering of injustice, saying, "And you know, my friends, there comes a time . . . when people get *tired* of being trampled over by the iron feet of oppression," and he launched into a refrain on this theme that prompted the congregation to explode into a tumult lasting three minutes (87, emphasis in original). Perhaps sensing the danger of raising the crowd's spirits to a boiling point, King was then careful to stress the deeper identity of the congregation. "I want it to be known throughout Montgomery and throughout this nation that we are Christian people. . . . We believe in the teachings of Jesus." Consequently, the protest would be utterly nonviolent: "There will be no crosses burned at any bus stops in Montgomery. There will be no white persons pulled out of their homes and taken out on some distant road and murdered. . . . We are not . . . advocating violence. We have overcome that" (86).

King reminded the congregation that God's own authority would sustain the movement, in a manner consistent with the best purposes of American democracy. "If we are wrong, the Supreme Court of this nation is wrong. If we are wrong, the Constitution of the United States is wrong. If we are wrong, God Almighty is wrong. If we are wrong, Jesus of Nazareth was merely a utopian dreamer and never came down to earth. . . . We are determined . . . to fight until 'justice runs down like water and righteousness like a mighty stream'" (Lischer 1997, 87–88). By moving from the authority of the nation's highest judicial body to God's own authority, King placed the movement in a context that both presupposed the legitimacy of the American civic tradition and gestured beyond it to God's sovereignty, a rhetorical move that was given greater emphasis through King's use of the words of the prophet Amos. Near the conclusion of the speech King went further, again appealing to God's authority, this time in an even rawer, more forceful tone. While God is a God of love, King exclaimed, "He's also the God that standeth before the nations and says, 'Be still and know that I am God—and if you don't obey Me I'm gonna break the backbone of your power'" (Branch 1988, 141). It was this God of love *and* justice who would assure the Montgomery blacks their place in history as a "race of people, of black people . . . who had the moral courage to stand up for their rights" (Lischer 1997, 88).

In his movement speeches and sermons, King was able to take blacks' struggle for justice and present its significance as consistent not only with the best of America's civic ideals but ultimately with God's own justice and redemptive purposes. The Holt Street speech is a particularly good example of King's skill at interweaving civic resources with biblical ones, leaving his audience convinced that the struggle for American democracy and equality was merely a part of a much larger spiritual reality, one that the black church was chosen to be a part of as a result of its kinship with Christ. In this way the movement sought to claim and transform the public sphere—nonviolently, persuasively—with a vision of justice culled from the church's own narrative of liberation and quest for the beloved community.

The Movement's Communicator

King's ability to merge languages from different sources became even more vital when he addressed diverse audiences in his effort to maintain support for the movement and keep it at the forefront of the nation's consciousness. As the most widely recognized leader and symbol of the movement, King endured a grueling schedule of almost nonstop speaking engagements, fundraising rallies, and sermons in a wide range of settings throughout the country.[14] Many of these addresses took place on the well-worn "pulpit circuit" that had been traveled by pastor-theologians such as Rauschenbusch, Fosdick, and Niebuhr in their own day, and that brought King into contact with large audiences of mainly supportive whites. In addition, King was able to publish hundreds of columns and essays in various periodicals, as well as five books through Harper & Row, one of the leading publishers of liberal Protestant thinkers (Miller 1992, 68, 69–70). And finally, King held the rapt attention of national news media and television, which gave him an instant audience through programs such as *The Tonight Show* and *Meet the Press* (Lischer 1997, 142). These diverse forums gave King abundant opportunities to define and defend the aims of the movement, and while his rhetorical task became more complex in these settings, King's prophetic voice remained prominent.

The challenge before King, particularly as he understood it in the early years of the movement, was to forge a supportive coalition in favor of civil rights by appealing to moderate and liberal whites, while at the same time keeping committed blacks on board. Toward this end, King made heavy use of a distinctive interpretation of American civil religion, whereby he could draw from the well of American civic ideals and liberalism's vision of progress while offering a prophetic critique gesturing beyond the limits of that tradition. This involved identifying the goals of the movement with the Constitutional tradition and then connecting that tradition to God's providence. As Lischer argues, before King could "confront white America with its betrayals of its own ideals, he first had to establish that 'these truths' are woven into God's truth and therefore belong to all people. They are transcendent truths and therefore apply even to those who have been traditionally excluded from their blessings" (Lischer 1997, 151). King would frequently place the wisdom of the Declaration and the Constitution, as well as civic heroes such as Thomas Jefferson and Abraham Lincoln, alongside biblical references and figures in a way that fused the American political tradition with God's purposes in the movement.

> It may be that the salvation of the world lies in the hands of the maladjusted. The challenge to us is to be maladjusted—as maladjusted as the prophet Amos, who in the midst of the injustices of his day, could cry out in words that echo across the centuries, "Let judgment run down like waters and righteousness like a mighty stream"; as maladjusted as Lincoln, who had the vision to see that this nation could not survive half slave and half free; as maladjusted as Jefferson, who in the midst of an age amazingly adjusted to slavery could cry out in words lifted to cosmic proportions, "All men are created equal, and are endowed by their Creator with certain unalienable rights, that among these are Life, Liberty and the pursuit of Happiness"; as maladjusted as Jesus who could say to the men and women of his generation, "Love your enemies, bless them that curse you, do good to them that hate you, and pray for them that despitefully use you." (King [1958a] 1986, 89–90)

King also relied upon the liberal theological tradition he encountered during his graduate education. This tradition gave him a language that was purged of the theological specificity that permeated discourse in the black church and therefore allowed him to paint in broad strokes a vision of history in which progress was inevitable. For instance, King could try to appeal to those across the theological divide, as it were, by stating that

> I am quite aware of the fact that there are persons who believe firmly in nonviolence who do not believe in a personal God, but I think every person who believes in nonviolent resistance believes somehow that the universe in some form is on the side of justice. That there is something unfolding in the universe whether one speaks of it as an unconscious process, or whether one speaks of it as some unmoved mover, or whether someone speaks of it as a personal God. (King [1957b] 1986, 13–14)

King could similarly appeal to liberal theological commonplaces such as "the Brotherhood of Man and the Fatherhood of God" and "the arc of the moral universe is long, but it bends toward justice" and refer to the "ethical insights of our Judeo-Christian heritage" to couch his claims in terms that he knew would resonate with white liberal audiences (Lischer 1997, 148; Miller 1992, 154; Lischer 1997, 180).

In his use of civil religion and liberal theological concepts and terminology, King was pursuing what Lischer calls an "identification" strategy, an attempt to achieve the "merger of black aspirations into the American dream" (Lischer 1997, 142). King's conviction that American democracy could be redeemed meant that his use of these languages was sincere; it was not merely a tactical approach. Nevertheless, they remained supplementary languages, enabling King to express his more particular convictions to a wider range of audiences. King always envisioned the God he first encountered in the black church as the ultimate authority underlying his other kinds of appeals. In fact, it was King's confidence that God permeates all areas of life that allowed him to merge these various languages so boldly. As Michael Eric Dyson argues, King's "acts of translation were driven by the belief that the universe belongs to God, that truth is not trapped in church sanctuaries, and that God transmutes hostile powers to achieve the divine will" (2000, 128). Or as he says elsewhere: "Since the world belongs to God, and the powers that exist, even if evil intentioned, may have good consequences in the eyes of faith, God can use whatever forum necessary to deliver divine gift or judgment. . . . For black Christians, God is the original and ultimate polyglot" (1993, 306). King could thus be assured that, as long as the languages he used were consistent with God's redeeming purposes, God would be able to work through them to effectuate justice. This confidence also allowed him, when it was necessary, to assume a more radical prophetic stance, challenging political and social reality in a more forceful language not mediated by these civil and liberal theological traditions.

Two of the most powerful examples of King's ability to merge languages in addresses intended for broad audiences are his "Letter from Birmingham City Jail," written during King's imprisonment for his role in the Birmingham demonstrations of early 1963, and his "I Have a Dream" speech, delivered as the keynote address of the March on Washington later that year. King wrote his "Letter" as a response to eight moderate clergy who had, through an open letter, criticized the civil disobedience of the movement, urging instead that the campaign for justice be pursued chiefly through the courts.[15] King was aware that the letter would ultimately reach an audience well beyond those eight, however. A few years earlier the liberal Protestant magazine *Christian Century* had invited King and its other editors-at-large to submit letters that, while addressed to particular individuals, could be published for the benefit of the magazine's readership. King's letter was eventually published not only in *Christian Century* but in two other liberal Protestant periodicals, *Liberation* and *Christianity and Crisis,* as well as pamphlets distributed by the Fellowship of Reconciliation and the American Friends Service Committee (Miller 1992, 162–163).[16] Thus while King was addressing an ostensible audience of clergymen, he was at the same time crafting a message he knew would be read by liberal and moderate white Protestants generally.

King's effort to articulate and defend the movement's strategy of nonviolent civil disobedience involved placing that strategy in a broader theological and civic context, revealing the movement to be not a local eruption of civil unrest but a reflection and extension of principles at the heart of both the biblical and the American civic traditions. King assumes a clear prophetic role in the letter, explaining that

> I am in Birmingham because injustice is here. Just as the eighth century prophets left their little villages and carried their "thus saith the Lord" far beyond the boundaries of their hometowns; and just as the Apostle Paul left his little village of Tarsus and carried the gospel of Jesus Christ to practically every hamlet and city of the Graeco-Roman world, I too am compelled to carry the gospel of freedom beyond my particular hometown. Like Paul, I must constantly respond to the Macedonian call for aid. ([1963b] 1986, 290)

King's reference to Paul is particularly significant, in that it links him to a figure who was similarly called to preach truth and justice despite the personal trials and sufferings that accompanied that task; Paul wrote some of his epistles while imprisoned. King is thus able to claim a kinship with the church's chief apostle and prisoner (Lischer 1997, 184–185). For those not yet convinced of King's continuation of Paul's legacy, however, he offers another justification for his witness, based on the idea that we are "caught in an inescapable network of mutuality." Here King borrows a liberal theological commonplace from Harry Emerson Fosdick to point to the way in which all Americans are affected by one another's actions. There are no "outsiders" in the United States who can afford to be unconcerned about injustice (Miller 1992, 166).[17]

King also employs a number of different argumentative strategies for convincing his readers of the rightness of nonviolent civil disobedience. In response to the inevitable question "How can you advocate breaking some laws and obeying others?" King offers a number of replies. He begins with an Augustinian theological justification. There are both just and unjust laws; what distinguishes the two is that a "just law is a man-made code that squares with the moral law or the law of God. An unjust law is a code that is out of harmony with the moral law." He then provides a more general response rooted in a liberal theological worldview. "Any law that degrades human personality is unjust," and thus "all segregation statutes are unjust because segregation distorts the soul and damages the personality" (King [1963b] 1986, 293–294).[18] And finally, King moves away from the theological terrain altogether and offers a different kind of argument. An unjust law "is a code that a majority inflicts on a minority that is not binding on itself," which is essentially "difference made legal." Similarly, because just laws are ones enacted by democratically elected legislatures, Alabama's segregation laws are illegitimate because blacks had no ability to choose the legislators who passed them (294).

King's argumentative flexibility here is noteworthy, but his real brilliance lies in his ability to frame the movement in terms that are true to both his vision of the church and his understanding of America's highest purposes. King's ultimate target in the letter is not Southern segregationists but rather those moderate white Christians who refuse to join the struggle for civil rights alongside their black brothers and sisters.

> I have almost reached the regrettable conclusion that the Negro's great stumbling block in the stride toward freedom is not the White Citizen's Counciler or the Ku Klux Klanner, but the white moderate who is more devoted to "order" than to justice; who prefers a negative peace which is the absence of tension to a positive peace which is the presence of justice; who constantly says "I agree with you in the goal you seek, but I can't agree with your methods of direct action"; who paternalistically feels that he can set the timetable for another man's freedom; who lives by the myth of time and who constantly advised the Negro to wait until a "more convenient season." (King [1963b] 1986, 295)

These attitudes are particularly offensive when they are rooted in the church, King argues, because the church is by its very nature an alternative society willing to challenge injustice, with urgency, wherever it is found.

> There was a time when the church was very powerful. It was during that period when the early Christians rejoiced when they were deemed worthy to suffer for what they believed. In those days the church was not merely a thermometer that recorded the ideas and principles of popular opinion; it was a thermostat that transformed the mores of society. Wherever the early Christians entered a town the power structure got disturbed and immediately sought to convict them for being "disturbers of the peace" and "outside agitators." But they went on with the conviction that they were a "colony of heaven," and had to obey God rather than man. (300)

King's purpose here is thus twofold: to hold up the example of the black church as an exemplar of the kind of public witness the church at its best has always engaged in, while at the same time admonishing those who, despite their Christian convictions, would choose to rationalize their noninvolvement in challenging injustice.

What the mainstream defenders of moderate change fail to see, King stresses, is that it is precisely through the efforts of this beleaguered "colony of heaven" that God will call America to justice. Just as it was through the black church that the "dimension of nonviolence entered our struggle," it will be through this community and its allies that the effort to redeem a fallen nation must take place (King [1963b] 1986, 297).

> We must come to see that human progress never rolls in on wheels of inevitability. It comes through the tireless efforts and persistent work of men willing to be co-workers with God, and without this hard work time itself becomes an ally of the forces of social stagnation. We must use time creatively, and forever realize that the time is always ripe to do right. Now is the time to make real the promise of democracy, and transform our pending national elegy into a creative psalm of brotherhood. Now is the time to lift our national policy from the quicksand of racial injustice to the solid rock of human dignity. (296)

This creative minority of God's "co-workers," willing to undergo sacrifice and suffering for the sake of justice, thus joins the ranks of those "extremists" who have set forth bold visions for the edification of the greater human community, a list on which King includes Jesus, Amos, Paul, Martin Luther, John Bunyan, Abraham Lincoln, and Thomas Jefferson, in a provocative threading together of religious and civic figures (297–298). So thoroughly does King merge the biblical and civic traditions that at times the distinction between the purposes of God and those of the nation seems in danger of being blurred. This is evident, for instance, when King argues that "we will win our freedom because the sacred heritage of our nation and the eternal will of God are embodied in our echoing demands," suggesting that America's "sacredness" stands coequal with God as a guarantor of the movement's success (301).

Yet in the end, by insisting that the only way the nation could ultimately be redeemed is by the direct agency of a marginalized, God-led community, one willing to suffer in the pursuit of justice, King makes it clear that America cannot save itself. Only a faithful and courageous people could accomplish the task: "One day the South will know that when these disinherited children of God sat down at lunch counters they were in reality standing up for the best in the American dream and the most sacred values in our Judeo-Christian heritage, and thusly, carrying our whole nation back to those great wells of democracy which were dug deep by the Founding Fathers in the formulation of the Constitution and the Declaration of Independence" (302). King was perfectly willing to acknowledge the merits of American democracy and its ideals, even to go so far as to assign them a sacred status. But in boldly proclaiming his own disenfranchised and oppressed faith community as the source of America's redemption, King spoke in an uncompromising prophetic voice—announcing that God was using the humble to foil the proud and forcing America to learn from those it had excluded from its promises of freedom and justice.

In his "I Have a Dream" speech, King's deft interweaving of civic and biblical languages is again in evidence, but with an even more impassioned prophetic voice pronouncing God's justice on America. As Dyson observes, because of the selectivity with which the speech has been excerpted, it is not usually observed that "King intended that day not simply to detail a dream but to narrate a nightmare" (2000, 17). King delivered a jeremiad that lamented America's failures as much as it pointed the way to a better future, and it invoked God's presence in a more direct, immediate fashion than we find in King's "Letter."

King begins the speech by invoking Lincoln's Emancipation Proclamation, acknowledging it as "a great beacon light of hope to millions of Negro slaves who had been seared in the flames of withering injustice" (King [1963a] 1986, 217). However, "the Negro still is not free," King goes on to add. Similarly, although the Declaration of Independence issued a "promissory note," a "promise that all men, yes, black men as well as white men, would be guaranteed the unalienable rights of life, liberty, and the pursuit of happiness," America has defaulted on it (217). King reminds his audience of these failings and of blacks' increasing dissatisfaction with them, warning that the "whirlwinds of revolt will continue to shake the foundations of our nation until the bright day of justice emerges," even while stressing vigorously the movement's renunciation of violence (218). King re-emphasizes, again and again, that blacks will never be content while segregation and inequality, and the indignities that accompany them, persist.

> We can never be satisfied as long as our bodies, heavy with fatigue of travel, cannot gain lodging in the motels of the highways and the hotels of the cities. We cannot be satisfied as long as the Negro's basic mobility is from a smaller ghetto to a larger one. . . . We can never be satisfied as long as our children are stripped of their selfhood and robbed of their dignity by signs stating "for whites only." We cannot be satisfied as long as a Negro in Mississippi cannot vote and a Negro in New York believes he has nothing for which to vote. No, we are not

> satisfied, and we will not be satisfied until justice rolls down like waters and righteousness like a mighty stream. (218–219)

At this point, roughly halfway through the speech, the prophet Amos's voice emerges, as it does so often in King's addresses and sermons, to declare God's judgment on a fallen society and proclaim the possibility of it one day becoming just. The rest of the speech is a vision of a transformed America, but one in which God's active intervention is taking place. It is an eschatological vision, announcing not merely the approach of a redeemed American democracy but the kingdom of God. After King details his vision of a transfigured South, from Georgia to Mississippi to Alabama, he appeals to the even more glorious vision of the prophet Isaiah, who first was given the dream in which "one day every valley shall be exalted, every hill and mountain shall be made low, the rough places shall be made plain, and the crooked places shall be made straight and the glory of the Lord will be revealed and all flesh shall see it together" (King [1963a] 1986, 219). It is thus King's faith in God's ability to restore justice and human community that gives him confidence that "we will be able to transform the jangling discords of our nation into a beautiful symphony of brotherhood" (219).

King's concluding appeal to "let freedom ring" across America derives much of its power from the eschatological context King establishes in this last section of the speech. When King concludes his oration it is not simply a renewed American polity that is celebrated but a beatific vision of a human community that has been emancipated from the chains that had kept human beings divided from one another:

> And when we allow freedom to ring, when we let it ring from every village and hamlet, from every state and city, we will be able to speed up that day when *all of God's children*—black men and white men, Jews and Gentiles, Catholics and Protestants—will be able to join hands and to sing in the words of the old Negro spiritual, "Free at last, free at last; thank God Almighty, we are free at last" (King [1963a] 1986, 220, my emphasis)

So while King forges a link between America's purposes and those of God, it is in the interest not of sanctifying the American nation but rather of subordinating it to God's greater redemptive plan, one that will only ultimately be fulfilled once God's kingdom is finally revealed in the last days. King's vision of a restored community gathered together to sing a Negro spiritual is, of course, precisely the image of the kingdom of God King encountered in the black church—and King offers it at the end of the speech without apology.

In his "Letter" and "I Have a Dream," King endeavored to reach across the political and theological boundaries that separated him from other Americans, seeking ways to forge a shared political vision capable of sustaining the movement's arduous pursuit of justice and equality. He was thus willing to marshal various languages and rhetorical themes in an effort to meet the concerns of those who questioned whether the movement's purposes were consistent with the biblical and civic traditions with which they were familiar. But in the end, King's voice remained that of a prophet: holding out the promise of a just community, but not without first bringing God's judgment to bear on our failures. King knew that the idea of a black preacher calling the nation to repentance would not be an easy one for many Americans to embrace. But he also knew that the effort to transform America did not rest solely on his shoulders. He could count on the heroic sacrifices and faith of his brothers and sisters in the movement and the role of the black church in sustaining their struggle.

A Collective Effort to Transform Public Space: The Role of the Black Church in the Movement

Because King's presence in the movement eventually grew to such huge proportions, the importance attributed to him often overshadowed the significance of the more "ordinary" individuals whose tireless labor on behalf of the struggle often went unnoticed. We do the movement a major disservice if we neglect their contribution, because at its heart the civil rights movement was a *community-based* movement. That is, it involved typical men and women deciding collectively to claim the citizenship and equality that had been up to that point denied them. Thousands of people had to be willing to march, demonstrate, wage boycotts and strikes, engage in sit-ins, embark on freedom rides, take part in voter education/registration efforts, and suffer jailings and beatings while doing so. It was the cumulative impact of these activities that contributed to building the critical mass that, step by step, removed the barriers to desegregation and racial equality throughout the South.

This is not simply a question of historical accuracy, however. For if we neglect the dynamics of collective protest and demonstration that were at the heart of the movement, we lose sight of the way in which these efforts functioned alongside the rhetorical appeals and public arguments of King and the other civil rights leaders. As we have seen, King's claim was not merely that God was working to bring about justice in America but that God was using *the black community* and its movement to accomplish this purpose. The urgency with which King voiced his appeals was given substance because his audiences knew that, even while he spoke, campaigns were being waged in towns and cities all across the South to claim the rights of black people. Because he could appeal to the example set by the "ordinary" folk involved in these campaigns, King could impress upon his listeners or readers in vivid terms the concrete reality of the struggle in a way that he could never do if he were to rely only on abstract arguments about America's civic ideals or the nature of justice. Focusing on the collective nature of the movement's protest is therefore helpful in illuminating an important dynamic of public discourse and how it can effectuate social change.

It is worth noting that the more visible efforts to reconfigure public space were only one dimension of the overall struggle for civil rights. The NAACP engaged in prolonged and expensive legal battles and was actively involved in voter registration efforts, as were activists in the Student Nonviolent Coordinating Committee (SNCC) and the Congress of Racial Equality (CORE). Voter registration was often the most dangerous work, particularly in rural areas, where Jim Crow laws were able to keep the overwhelming majority of blacks from taking part in political life. In some counties, simply expressing an interest in registering to vote would result in persecution from local officials or white vigilante groups. Some of the most courageous individuals of the movement were those who risked their lives to build the organizational networks needed in rural communities to make blacks' citizenship a reality. These efforts were by necessity surreptitious and thus never generated the collective excitement of the mass demonstrations. They were not for that reason any less significant, however.

Furthermore, without the community building and leadership base already established by the black church, the movement would never have gotten off the ground. The role of black women was especially vital, although it was severely undervalued by the male-dominated leadership of King's Southern Christian Leadership Conference (SCLC). As one scholar of women's roles in the movement, Mary Fair Burks, points out, the Montgomery bus boycott was not started by King or his fellow preachers. It was initiated by the Women's Political Council of Montgomery, and King and the others took charge after things were already underway (Burks 1990, 71). Consistent with their historical role as "culture carriers" of the black community, women contributed the lion's share toward making sure churches could serve as the organizing centers and places of refuge for those students who traveled long distances to take part in sit-ins or do citizenship training.[19] As Dyson stresses, "national leadership of the sort King symbolized did far less than local, largely anonymous, female leaders of the nitty-gritty work of organizing poor people to take their destinies in their own hands" (2000, 299–300). It was because women had helped make the black church the center of black community life that it could effectively play its role as the strategic and inspirational center of the movement.

That the church was at the heart of the movement was clear not only to blacks but to their hostile adversaries as well. As Lincoln and Mamiya note, from 1962 to 1965 alone ninety-three churches throughout the South were burned or bombed (1990, 97). Local black churches played a twofold role in empowering the protests and demonstrations of the movement: first, they served as organizational and strategic sites for each local campaign, and second, and even more important, they were the places where those on the front lines of the struggle would come together to celebrate the successes and mourn the tragedies of the movement, and find spiritual strength to continue the fight.

The unique phenomenon of the mass meeting was indispensable for each of these roles. Beginning with the Montgomery bus boycott, whenever a local campaign was underway in a particular city, various churches would alternate as sites for these community-wide gatherings that would commonly last several hours and draw overflowing crowds. As King later recounted in *Stride Toward Freedom,* the mass meetings "accomplished on Monday and Thursday nights what the Christian church had failed to accomplish on Sunday mornings"—they brought Christians together across denominational and class lines ([1958b] 1986, 447–448). The meetings were also commonly attended by journalists, as well as undercover agents from the FBI and local law enforcement.[20] The mass meetings served an essential logistical function, as they provided the one way to ensure that all local blacks could be apprised of each day's developments and prepared for what was to come.

It was also during the mass meetings that King and the other leaders of the movement taught the importance of nonviolence and the practices needed to sustain it, and encouraged audiences to take an active role in the struggle. "Night after night the group was admonished to love rather than hate, and urged to be prepared to suffer violence if necessary but never to inflict it" (King [1958b] 1986, 448). There was a keen awareness among the leadership that only if the means employed by the movement were consistent with its ends would its witness be effective. In his "Letter from Birmingham City Jail," King emphasized the importance of "self-purification" in the struggle—the effort required by each individual to ensure that his or her actions would be characterized by *agape* love for those who might respond with violence to the protests ([1963b] 1986, 291).[21] Extensive training and workshops took place to guide participants in the tactics of nonviolence, and strict tests were applied to ensure that those who wished to take an active role as demonstrators were truly prepared to do so. During the Birmingham campaign, each participant was required to fill out a "commitment card" that indicated her or his willingness to "meditate daily on the teachings and life of Jesus," "walk and talk in the manner of love," and "refrain from the violence of fist, tongue, or heart" (King [1963c] 1986, 537). The mass meetings provided the primary opportunity for King and the other leaders of the campaign to recruit volunteers for this disciplined "army" of nonviolent protesters:

> The invitational periods at the mass meetings, when we asked for volunteers, were much like those invitational periods that occur every Sunday morning in Negro churches, when the pastor projects the call to those present to join the church. By twenties and thirties and forties, people came forward to join our army. We did not hesitate to call our movement an army. But it was a special army, with no supplies but its sincerity, no uniform but its determination, no arsenal except its faith, no currency but its conscience. . . . It was an army whose allegiance was to God and whose strategy and intelligence were the eloquently simple dictates of conscience. (536)

While they were essential for organizing campaigns and equipping participants to take part in disciplined protest, the mass meetings served an even more important function in their ability to inspire those in the movement to persist in the struggle. As King recalled in connection with the Birmingham campaign, it was through the mass meetings that "we were able to generate the power and depth which finally galvanized the entire Negro community" ([1963c] 1986, 535). A movement that was at its heart a spiritual struggle against injustice would require constant spiritual renewal and strengthening in order to continue in the face of daunting and sometimes life-threatening obstacles. Hence it was during the mass meetings that the community reminded itself of its purpose and appealed to God for continued protection. Through the preaching, singing of spirituals, prayer, and testimonials from those on the front lines, those in attendance could experience at first hand the power of a movement that was both a particular reflection of blacks' distinctive worldview and a dynamic force setting about changing the social order. As Coretta Scott King recalled about the Montgomery meetings, they sustained "the feeling that something could be done about the situation, that we could change it" (Lischer 1997, 244).

The sense of empowerment embodied in the meetings enabled the movement's participants to continue boldly, confident that their faith in the liberating God of Exodus would be rewarded. As King remarked proudly in describing the commitment displayed in the mass meetings: "In a world in which most men attempt to defend their highest values by the accumulation of weapons of destruction, it is morally refreshing to hear five thousand Negroes in Montgomery shout 'Amen' and 'Hallelujah' when they are exhorted to 'pray for those who oppose you,' or pray 'Oh Lord, give us strength of body to keep walking for freedom,' and conclude each mass meeting with: 'Let us pray that God shall give us strength to remain nonviolent though we may face death'" ([1956b] 1986, 80). The courage inspired in the meetings sustained the protesters' public witness even in the most harrowing situations. As King explained regarding the Birmingham campaign, during which children were widely included in the marches for the first time, "I have stood in a meeting with hundreds of youngsters and joined in while they sang 'Ain't Gonna Let Nobody Turn Me 'Round.' It is not just a song; it is a resolve. A few minutes later, I have seen those same youngsters refuse to turn around from the onrush of a police dog, refuse to turn around before a pugnacious Bull Connor in command of men armed with power hoses. These songs bind us together, give us courage together, help us to march together" ([1963c] 1986, 535–536).

The remarkable spirit of the meetings was often enough to astonish even disinterested observers. Pat Watters, a writer for the Atlanta *Journal* who reported on the movement from late 1961 onward, provided this poignant reflection on the power and significance of the mass meetings:

> I sit and lament anew that the movement did not reach southern whites, lament the southern proscriptions that made it impossible for whites to enter such churches, hear such eloquence, feel the southernness of those meetings, and lament as much the forces, the compulsions of American culture that prevented any serious attempt by the media (television being surely the most appropriate) to present what was said and felt by the Negro people in those meetings. Back then, even then, I understood enough to say that if ever they would just put one mass meeting on television, for however long it might take, it would all be over. (Lischer 1997, 246)

The critical mass of inspiration and courage created during the mass meetings sustained each dramatic venture into the public sphere and therefore was central to the movement's transformation of social and political life. As King articulated it, the essential purpose of the protests was the attempt to generate a sufficient amount of "constructive nonviolent tension" in the community to compel its leaders to consider dismantling the edifice of segregation ([1963b] 1986, 291). The movement was consistently successful in this endeavor; mass marches and demonstrations involving heretofore politically quiescent local blacks rarely failed to create a substantial amount of social tension. Part of the genius of the movement's leadership was its ability to anticipate the kind of public witness that would be most effective in drawing attention to its appeals.[22] Keith Miller calls this part of the movement's strategy the enactment of "medieval morality plays" in which the nonviolent resisters would face all manner of police persecution and hostility from angry white mobs, thereby demonstrating in a particularly compelling fashion the virtue of nonviolent love and the appalling evil of racially motivated violence (Miller 1992, 99–100).

The symbolism inherent in these public "performances" was indispensable to the movement's public witness. The demonstrators were seeking to present a glimpse of the just society, and through their commitment to suffer violence without resistance, they signaled to the greater society that true justice entailed the creation of the beloved community, in which all social strife and persecution would be abolished, and in which equality and fellowship among all people would become a reality. King provides a vivid characterization of this image following the mass march from Selma to Montgomery in 1965: "After the march to Montgomery, there was a delay at the airport and several thousand demonstrators waited more than five hours, crowding together on the seats, the floors and stairways of the terminal building. As I stood with them and saw white and Negro, nuns and priests, ministers and rabbis, labor organizers, lawyers, doctors, housemaids and shopworkers brimming with vitality and enjoying a rare comradeship, I knew I was seeing a microcosm of the mankind of the future in this moment of luminous and genuine brotherhood" ([1967b] 1986, 560).

Each discrete event of a campaign could provide such glimpses, as activists sought to model by their example an ideal basis for community in the midst of an oppressive society. Bus terminals were transformed into churches as racially mixed groups of freedom riders would sing freedom songs such as "We Shall Overcome," and student leaders would take turns preaching while enraged white mobs surrounded them (Branch 1988, 440–441). Mass jailings afforded additional opportunities for those in the movement to display their convictions, as prisons were converted into temporary revival meetings, despite guards' unavailing efforts to dampen the prisoners' enthusiasm (484–485). Through these displays of collective resolve, demonstrators announced that there was no realm that God would not redeem, and no system of injustice, no matter how entrenched, that God would not be able to transform into the beloved community. And as King explained, there was something about these acts of public protest that "spoke" just as effectively as formal arguments.

> The nonviolent resisters can summarize their message in the following simple terms: We will take direct action against injustice without waiting for other agencies to act. We will not obey unjust laws or submit to unjust practices. We will do this peacefully, openly, cheerfully because our aim is to persuade. We adopt the means of nonviolence because our end is a community at peace with itself. We will try to persuade with our words, *but if our words fail, we will try to persuade with our acts.* We will always be willing to talk and seek fair compromise, but we are ready to suffer when necessary and even risk our lives to become witnesses to the truth as we see it. ([1958b] 1986, 484–485, my emphasis)

It is thus clear that the movement's campaigns of nonviolent disobedience were much more than tactical attempts to force adversaries to the negotiating table. Those in the movement realized that by their "direct action" against injustice, they were *already* effectuating a transformation of public space. Rather than placing all their trust in a distant federal government that frequently seemed to view the civil rights struggle merely as an annoying distraction, or waiting for local businessmen or civic leaders to deliver on overdue promises they often had no intention of keeping, blacks stepped forward on their own to claim their status as citizens and as equals, confident that in doing so they were inaugurating a new era in American social and political life. In this way, the prophetic activity of the movement was evident not merely in King's speeches, but in the movement's public effort to present signs of what was coming to pass in the South. And as Lischer points out, the consistently hostile reactions these nonviolent actions provoked would certainly seem to suggest that local whites were well aware of what the demonstrations signaled.

> Of course, it may appear that to interpret ordinary actions like walking or eating as prophetic signs of an imminent reality is to overinflate them with symbolic or theological significance. But how *does* one explain the irrational fear and anger that a sit-in or a march engendered in white southerners? Outsiders have occasionally wondered why the authorities did not simply permit a group of Negroes to walk a few blocks to city hall without offering violent interference. What provoked these distorted grimaces and snarls on the faces of spectators, now frozen for history in old photographs and museum exhibits? Perhaps these Bible-believing southerners suspected what ancient Israel knew, that the actions of the prophets, just as surely as their words, are the signs of a new order that is rapidly approaching. (1997, 183, emphasis in original)

Because it had always refused to recognize any distinction between the sacred and the secular spheres, the black church was well equipped to undertake a struggle in which every public action became an announcement of the advent of the kingdom of God. King's discourse declared in no uncertain terms that God was guiding and sustaining the movement, and those who participated in the struggle by offering their own bodies so that its public witness might go forward did so as a visible reflection of the faith King proclaimed. In this light it becomes evident that, as important as King's leadership was, it was ultimately a *prophetic movement* that courageously offered its voice to proclaim a new possibility for human community.

Lessons from the Struggle

With this account of the civil rights movement before us, I will turn to consider the specific challenges it poses to political liberalism's framework. This will first involve assessing King's provocative rhetorical strategies, followed by an examination of the collective dynamics of the movement's activism, in order to determine what each reveals about Rawls's understanding of politics. I will argue that in both of these areas, the civil rights struggle illuminates political liberalism's propensity to obscure the ways in which political meanings are transformed through discursive engagement. Insofar as the movement exemplifies a politics in which moral communities are able to assist the process of discovering better formulations of public ideals, it points the way beyond political liberalism's conception of public life, and it suggests that a robust process of democratic engagement can play an indispensable role in altering the contours of the political sphere.

King's Quest to Transform American Justice

In analyzing King's public arguments, Rawls contends that King relied on his particular comprehensive doctrine as a way to offer support for the political values of justice and equality that he was trying to effectuate (1996, 247–251). In other words, King voiced his Christian convictions so as to make his political ideals more widely appealing. After all, in an America thoroughly shaped by Protestant Christianity, an argument for racial justice that did not take advantage of the authoritative power offered by this religious tradition might indeed be significantly weaker. Rawls thus defends King's reliance on his comprehensive ideals as the most efficacious way in which a society without an agreement on racial equality could be brought toward a closer approximation of the "well-ordered society." The dialogic strategy favored by King and other civil rights leaders would therefore be consistent with public reason, assuming that "the comprehensive reasons they appealed to were required to give sufficient strength to the political conception to be subsequently realized" (251).

To be fully convincing, Rawls's interpretation depends upon the plausibility of the notion that the "political value" of justice contains meaning that can be somehow detached from the other ideals and narratives that shape and influence our understanding of it. In King's case this is simply not possible. Justice as King conceived and articulated it was multifaceted and complex, and it cannot be reduced to a mere political value without doing violence to his ideas and denying their distinctiveness. King's vision of justice was thoroughly permeated by the ideal of human reconciliation that he had first encountered in the black church and that always served to orient his political activity. In developing this vision, King drew liberally from his core theological insights—*agape* as the way to respond nonviolently to one's enemies, the socially transformative power of suffering, God's ability to liberate the oppressed, and the beloved community—and fused them together in his leadership of the movement and his public addresses. It was through the interaction between these ideals and the American civic tradition and liberal theology that the full power of King's witness was realized. Hence when King gave his "I Have a Dream" speech, his appeal to the words of Amos was not intended to provide a rhetorical flourish, a kind of ornamentation for his other more purely "political" arguments for justice; it expressed King's understanding that God was in fact working to bring a *higher* form of justice to America. This God-inspired justice went beyond legal provisions of political or economic equality, as it would ultimately lead to a reconciliation in which all human beings could enjoy brotherhood across racial and cultural lines.

Rawls's idea that the civil rights movement was merely trying to gain support for a political value that was already in full view thus involves a misreading of the movement's unique contribution to American political life.[23] King and the other leaders of the civil rights movement knew that they had distinctive insights to offer to America's understanding of justice. The SCLC's motto, "To save the soul of America," was a direct reference to what these leaders perceived as the transformative mission of the movement (King [1967a] 1986, 233). Through offering the nation a glimpse of God's providential plan for racial reconciliation, they sought to inspire Americans to envision and bring about an understanding of justice that went substantially beyond what was imagined by the writers of America's founding documents. By bringing its own understanding of justice to the forefront of its witness, the movement thus sought to change the vocabulary with which Americans thought and spoke about justice. In the process, they transformed its meaning.

What King's example reveals, then, is the way in which our "comprehensive doctrines," far from posing a threat to political life, can in fact play a pivotal role both in bringing to light new understandings of political ideals and in informing, sustaining, and promoting those understandings.[24] For instance, the nonviolent love of the enemy that was so integral to King's public witness was not merely a verbal expression of the tactics of civil disobedience chosen by those leading the demonstrations. It was the expression of a commitment to a justice that exceeds comparatively less ambitious norms such as reciprocity or mutual respect. The hope of a justice built on *love* for one's fellow citizens is one King had encountered in the black church. In making that hope the fulcrum of his public appeals, he pointed beyond the limits of America's political tradition, toward the realization of an even more ennobling and inspiring ideal.

Rawls's ideal of public reason requires a fixed horizon of public meanings and constitutional norms that can be safely insulated from the public challenge of comprehensive doctrines. It cannot, therefore, welcome the kind of creative discovery that was exemplified by the civil rights struggle, wherein comprehensive ideals were used to confront the limits of prevailing political reality and to gesture toward new political possibilities. King's experience in the black church gave him access to a prophetic tradition that perceived that God was working actively to liberate God's people, and this gave him a distinctive critical perspective from which to examine American justice and locate its failings. Cornel West characterizes this prophetic stance as follows: although "human beings can change and be changed, both individuals and societies, yet no individual or society can fully conform to the requirements of the Christian Gospel, hence the need for endless improvement and amelioration and relentless critique" (1990, 122).[25] Only through his involvement in this tradition was it possible for King to forge a conception of justice that obtained its power and dynamism precisely as a result of the unique combination of moral languages with which it was presented. King's assertion that those in the movement were fulfilling a divinely ordained mission of "enlarging the whole society and giving it a new sense of values" thus sheds light on the way in which our particular convictions can play an indispensable function in probing the limits of current political understandings and pointing toward previously unimagined alternatives.[26] Absent this possibility of political discovery, we remain trapped in a monological political framework insulated from contestation or challenge.[27]

The Movement's Activism: The Political Significance of the "Nonpublic" Domain

Just as King's discourse challenges political liberalism's framework, so too does the way in which the movement as a whole conducted its effort to further the cause of racial justice. As we observed earlier, King's public appeals were only one component of the broader movement; the demonstrations, marches, and sit-ins were just as important in drawing local and national attention to the cause of civil rights. The fact that these elements of the struggle typically took place outside of Rawls's conception of the "public political forum" illustrates a crucial failing of political liberalism. By insisting on its inflexible public/nonpublic distinction and locating politically significant activity solely in the former realm, it is unable to recognize some of the most striking possibilities of citizenship exemplified by the movement's witness. It thus remains blinded to potential sites of democratic engagement where a more expansive vision of public discourse could be pursued.[28]

Rawls's distinction between the background culture and the public political forum presupposes that while "full and open discussion" takes place in the former domain, the content of that discussion has no bearing on the values that are to regulate the public realm, at least with respect to constitutional essentials and matters of basic justice (1997, 768). When pressing issues concerning political fundamentals arise, it is imperative that the political realm be insulated from the potentially unreasonable views that can be freely expressed in the background culture. This view entails an essentially elite-driven conception of political change. Only those citizens able to offer formal arguments in the public forum (i.e. "judges, legislators, chief executives, and other government officials, as well as candidates for public office") are entrusted with the full responsibility of adhering to public reason, since only they are properly situated to take part in crafting or revising political ideals (768–769).

When it is applied in conceptualizing the public witness of the women and men on the front lines of the civil rights struggle, this framework reveals its limitations. For what was involved in the sit-ins and marches was, properly understood, political activity in the fullest sense. It involved the presentation of an alternative vision of justice and equality, matters certainly located within Rawls's category of political fundamentals. And as we have seen, these activities were intrinsically connected with King's own more formal public arguments. Properly understood, they worked in conjunction with them, as visible manifestations of the ideal of the beloved community King articulated in his speeches and sermons.

The extensive preparation that potential demonstrators underwent before they were allowed to march reflects in an acute way King's understanding that the means undertaken by the movement would have to be consistent with its ends in order for its public witness to carry persuasive power. Demonstrators were keenly aware that their commitment to Christian nonviolence was being tested every time they were provoked and challenged to retaliate. If they gave in to violence, a national audience would behold angry blacks and whites fighting each other, and the movement's appeal to blacks' unmerited suffering would be jeopardized. Especially in the South, white media were eager for any opportunity they could find to portray blacks as rabble-rousers and agitators; it thus became especially imperative that these expectations were challenged by the character of those on the front lines of the marches and demonstrations. That those in the movement were remarkably consistent in actualizing the ideal of nonviolent love for the enemy is without question one of the most distinctive traits of the struggle, and it reflects the leadership's concerted effort to ground the movement's witness in the faith of the black church. When marchers refused to retaliate against police dogs and high-powered water hoses and accepted joyfully the taunts of jeering white mobs, they revealed in a particularly effective way the church's vision of a community of love and reconciliation.

The same commitment was evident at the conclusion of successful campaigns. After the Montgomery bus boycott ended as a result of the Supreme Court's ruling on the unconstitutionality of Alabama's bus segregation laws, leaders endeavored to ensure that the protesters would be as exemplary in their efforts to integrate the buses as they had been in staying off of them. As King described it, the prevailing theme was that "we must not take this as a victory over the white man, but as a victory for justice and democracy," and therefore triumphalism and vindictiveness were soundly rejected, even though such attitudes would have been entirely understandable under the circumstances ([1958b] 1986, 457–458). In order to prepare for the tensions that would accompany integrated buses, the mass meetings shifted their emphasis to training bus riders in ways to defuse hostile situations that would surely arise. In addition to holding teaching sessions during the mass meetings, a list of suggestions was distributed throughout the city that stressed blacks' "tremendous responsibility of maintaining, in the face of what could be some unpleasantness, a calm and loving dignity befitting good citizens and members of our race." Passengers were urged to "pray for guidance" in boarding the buses and to "be loving enough to absorb evil and understanding enough to turn an enemy into a friend" (458–459). King observed that although the movement's leadership engaged in these strenuous attempts to prepare for integrating the buses, "not a single white group would take the responsibility of preparing the white community" (459). Because the movement sought a way to achieve a reconstituted human community, it was prepared in a way that whites were not for working toward "an integration based on mutual respect" (461). It was therefore able to contribute toward a renewed public space, one in which blacks and whites could coexist on a now equal footing, without the recourse to violence that many had feared would inevitably ensue when the boycott ended.

The extraordinary effectiveness of the civil rights demonstrations challenges the adequacy of political liberalism's conceptualization of the public sphere, where meaningful political discourse is assumed to be comprised chiefly of formal arguments. In fact, the discipline of the movement helps us to see the way in which our actions can in many respects provide a more compelling kind of "argument" than other kinds of public utterances. King explains this in connection with civil disobedience. Even when whites were adamantly unwilling to listen to the movement's appeals, there was something about blacks' willingness to suffer without retaliating that exerted its own persuasive force:

> Every time one Negro school teacher is fired for believing in integration, a thousand others should be ready to take the same stand. If the oppressors bomb the home of one Negro for his protest, they must be made to realize that to press back the rising tide of the Negro's courage they will have to bomb hundreds more, and even then they will fail. . . . Faced with this dynamic unity, this amazing self-respect, this willingness to suffer, and this refusal to hit back, the oppressor will

> find, as oppressors have always found, that he is glutted with his own barbarity. Forced to stand before the world and his God splattered with the blood of his brother, he will call an end to his self-defeating massacre. ([1958b] 1986, 485)

A community's efforts at transforming political life can take many forms, and need not be limited to discourse in the formal sense. Particularly when our differences are significant and we fail to speak the same moral language, a community's actions may be a more productive form of social and political involvement than other approaches. And in addition, when we can point to our own moral community as a visible manifestation of the public arguments we do offer, as King could in his own speeches and writings, our arguments can take on greater persuasive force.

Just as the movement's activism challenges political liberalism's understanding of the *means* of discourse, it disrupts its expectations about *where* politically significant activity occurs. Those on the front lines of the movement were well aware that their actions were an essential component of the overall strategy to pursue racial reconciliation, and that their political engagement was as crucial to the transformations taking place in American public life as King's speeches. In fact in one sense, their role was even more vital. The "ordinary" men and women who risked their lives by registering to vote or facing vigilante mobs during a march were already effectuating a transformed public sphere, one in which they could take their places as equal citizens no longer held down by Jim Crow. It does the movement a major disservice, therefore, to assume, as Rawls must, that because this kind of activity did not take place in the halls of Congress or on the steps of the Lincoln Memorial it should be located within the nonpolitical "background culture."

This raises important implications for a reconceptualized ethics of public life. If politically meaningful change can be carried out by typical citizens involved in the challenges of transforming their local communities, then the dispositions and practices that characterize their activity are hardly insignificant. Once we reconsider the compartmentalization at the heart of political liberalism's background culture/public political forum distinction, it becomes clear that the sites for engagement between members of diverse moral communities are in fact abundant, and the consequences of that engagement of immense importance for defining the shape of political community, especially on a local scale. An approach to public life that is able to help citizens navigate their way through these sites of engagement will be of greater benefit than one that relies on ignoring them, on the presupposition that such engagement is not in fact politically relevant.

The civil rights struggle shows us that a more flexible and expansive understanding of the search for public purposes is needed if we are truly to welcome opportunities for political discovery. This requires a recognition that political ideals are always subject to contestation and reformulation and that the sites in which this activity takes place are numerous, located in shifting public contexts. Rather than requiring citizens to honor a particular predetermined conception of the public sphere and compartmentalize their political activity accordingly in ways that are both invidious and unhelpful, we will be better served by fostering the dispositions and practices that can allow citizens the confidence to face the challenging opportunities for democratic engagement that accompany life in a morally diverse society.

CHAPTER 6

The Promise of a Post-Secular Politics

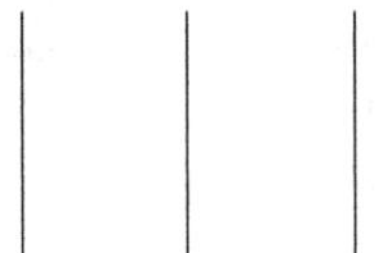

Political liberalism's goal of achieving a politics characterized by concord and mutual respect is a worthy one. Generating civic trust is an important social and political aim, one essential for a flourishing polity. Moreover, insofar as the challenges of reaching agreement on political purposes seem to mount as our moral diversity becomes more evident, the quest for a basis for political life that can be widely shared and embraced by citizens on a principled level has genuine merit. To the extent we can establish salutary political norms in a noncoercive fashion, we make it possible to pursue political aims that are both legitimate and carefully delimited, thereby also ensuring that space will exist for our differences.

My criticisms of political liberalism do not impugn its aims of fostering civil peace and mutual respect and trying to obtain agreement on political fundamentals. But they are intended to throw into question whether the most appropriate route toward these goals requires the particular categorizations at the heart of political liberalism's framework. By insisting that we use criteria such as the reasonable to cordon off religious or other kinds of particular claims as publicly invalid, or confine public purposes to political values immune to contestation by comprehensive views, political liberalism places constraints on political life that limit its attractiveness as a political vision.

Throughout this study I have focused on two central concerns that could be addressed more adequately by moving beyond political liberalism's presuppositions and normative requirements. The first of these has to do with our ability to negotiate the challenges of moral diversity, by seeking defensible solutions to conflicts in which the fundamental convictions of a moral community collide with those of the wider society, such as we encountered in the *Mozert* dispute. Political liberalism provides a ready solution for resolving such conflicts, but at the price of the flexibility and solicitude that might generate more accommodating, less divisive outcomes. In situations like these a more robust kind of engagement, one in which we forge political solutions through taking into account the comprehensive views of affected moral communities, can afford us possibilities for negotiating our differences that would not be available were we to rely solely upon an insular set of political values.

The second concern involves the role of our moral convictions in shaping and critiquing core political ideals. How can we envision a politics in which our particular perspectives, religious or otherwise, are not seen in a suspect or threatening light, but instead are welcomed as part of a process of political discovery? As we saw in chapter 5, political liberalism's vision of public discourse makes little room for the kind of transformation of public purposes that took place via the public witness of the civil rights movement. On those occasions when moral communities are not content simply to offer support for freestanding political values but instead seek to reshape or transform political ideals by drawing on their comprehensive views, political liberalism views such efforts as incompatible with the demands of public reason. Its approach to securing a widely shared standard for political life thus results in a confining framework that serves to stifle political change and creativity.

Both of these concerns point toward the need for more, rather than less, democratic engagement in public life. While there are certainly no guarantees that a robust democratic politics can lead inexorably to social stability or to an attenuation of political conflict, what such a politics does promise us is a way to pursue agreement (and locate insuperable points of disagreement) honestly and directly, without placing the kinds of constraints on citizens that are more likely to result in dampening politics than sustaining it. My contention is that a post-secular politics will be less likely to arouse ill-will and political apathy than conceptualizations of public life that rely on a vigilant monitoring of the political in order to ensure that "unreasonable" views cannot make an appearance there. Indeed, we will have more to gain by engaging each other's comprehensive convictions, even if we find other citizens' views objectionable or unjust (or they find ours objectionable or unjust!), than if we refuse to do so by relying upon contestable categorical distinctions for managing public discourse.

So while I am contending that a less restrictive political vision can be attained without neglecting the goods of civic concord and the pursuit of shared norms, it is crucial that these goods be sought in a way that recognizes and welcomes the role of our moral particularity in shaping the various dimensions of public life. Only if our "comprehensive doctrines" are perceived as having real value in probing the limits of present political arrangements can we hold open the possibility of arriving at mutually acceptable solutions to the challenges of moral diversity. There is a strong pragmatic justification for the approach to public life I am defending, since if our particular ideals are made known to one another, we can more confidently aim for public policies that are as inclusive and equitable as possible. But the justification for this approach is not merely prudential. For as the example of the civil rights struggle shows us, opportunities for political learning and discovery are made possible when moral communities rely on their particular convictions to reconfigure public space. More expansive political visions can be made available to us. And new ways of conceptualizing political purposes can be revealed.

In the first section of the chapter, I will present my account of the practices and dispositions that are needed to guide citizens' political activity if we are to pursue an ethics of public life that does not proceed by relying upon a conception of public reason or a rigid topology of the political sphere. In doing so, I will draw extensively from my earlier discussion of Yoder's thought in chapter 4 and the example of the civil rights movement in chapter 5. I will then turn to revisit the *Mozert v. Hawkins* case, in order to illustrate the advantages of my approach for coming to terms with this particular instance of moral conflict. Finally, I will consider two cases in which the merits of a post-Rawlsian approach to determining public purposes are evident: international debt relief and the abortion debate.

Four Practices of a Post-Secular Politics

If we are to pursue a conception of public life in which our particular convictions play a role in shaping the contours of political life and the norms that regulate it, it is imperative that we possess the dispositions and distinctive capacities needed for such an enterprise. What is required is, first, *sincerity,* whereby we are committed to discerning and offering with integrity those insights that our particular moral traditions can offer to the greater political community; *discipline,* which requires us to seek consistency in offering our convictions for other citizens' consideration; *dialogic creativity,* needed for a complex process of forging political ideals and solutions to policy conflicts by engaging and working with the particular languages at our disposal; and finally, *forbearance,* which enables us to approach the public sphere with humility and patience, recognizing the unavoidable difficulties and sometimes tragic outcomes that can characterize politics in a morally diverse society.

Sincerity

A vision of public life that welcomes the engagement of a wide range of particular perspectives requires moral communities to offer their distinctive views honestly and thoughtfully, without seeking to dissemble or mislead. This process entails a sustained effort to mine the resources of our particular traditions and to rely on them to ground our political activity. The only way that citizens can fairly assess and come to terms with each other's arguments is if they are expressed straightforwardly, clearly, and as a truthful representation of the convictions supporting their positions. Yoder's argument on this point is particularly forceful. He continually chides those who are eager for the church to be politically active yet are inattentive to whether its witness is genuine. For Yoder, the central question is whether what Christians say in public life is "honest and representative" (1984, 192–193).

An emphasis on sincerity does not presuppose that moral communities are homogeneous or that as individuals our worldview will be shaped by a single moral tradition. Indeed, as I stressed in chapter 4, it is increasingly unlikely that most citizens will view political reality from the perspective of only one community. The practice of sincerity, therefore, requires an ongoing process of discernment *within* moral communities as much as between them. Each moral community must seek to determine how its particular traditions can be presented honestly in political life and on which public issues it is prepared and able to offer a contribution. Individuals must similarly in their own reflection consider how best to be faithful to the various moral convictions that inform their own perspective.

Nor does the practice of sincerity require us to bare our souls each and every time we enter the public sphere. For most citizens, few occasions ever arise where they feel compelled to reveal the fundamental convictions animating their political activity. Yet being able to draw these connections is something we should be willing to do; a commitment to sincerity does entail a sense of political responsibility. When attempts to mislead or dissemble are forsworn and sincerity is regarded as a virtue, citizens can advance their views in public life with the confidence that others will regard them seriously and engage them in a spirit of mutuality.

In his willingness to draw deeply from the resources of his moral traditions to guide his political activity, King exemplified a commitment to sincerity in his public witness. He sought to lead a movement that was distinctly and thoroughly Christian in character. His public appeals to the ideal of the beloved community were derived from his faith in a God who redeems His people and works to reconcile humankind. King's reliance on these ideals, however, did not preclude him from also drawing on his convictions rooted in the American civic tradition and liberal theology. These too were genuine convictions, formed through King's experience both as an American citizen and as a scholar of Protestant theology, and given their distinctive shape in his public witness through their interaction with those bedrock insights King derived from the black church tradition.

A commitment to sincerity requires us to recognize the traditions in which we stand and make those traditions a real part of our political activity. This demands a process of ongoing reflection and discernment, as we seek to make clear to ourselves and others our distinctive vision of the common good and why it is defensible. In a way, this practice came naturally to those who congregated in the mass meetings of the civil rights campaigns. As an oppressed community of faith, those in the black church knew that their particular moral resources would be essential to their endeavor to transform politics in the direction of justice. Each night they gathered was thus a crucial opportunity to remind each other of where they stood and how they would go forward, working to bring about the beloved community in a manner consistent with their foremost convictions.

The practice of sincerity is indispensable for a politics of engagement, in which we are propelled to bring our whole selves into public life. The convictions that animate our political activity need not be hidden or treated as politically insignificant. Instead, when they are viewed as part and parcel of political life, they can be assessed and evaluated by other citizens, through the ongoing process by which we determine political purposes and pursue shared norms. In this way, civic trust and concord can be fostered, and mutual respect can be generated. When citizens are willing to present the fundamental convictions animating their political activity, they express a confidence in other citizens' political rationality. Moreover, by disavowing any intention of dissembling, they can help sustain a politics in which public deliberation can take place in a climate of goodwill.

Instead of a politics of sincerity, political liberalism offers us a politics of evasion. Rather than fostering a predisposition toward mutual engagement, it facilitates a stance of withdrawal. An overriding fear of the potentially divisive effects of comprehensive doctrines in public life leads Rawls and other political liberals to deny their political value, except when they can be offered in support of freestanding secular political norms. Thus when Rawls asserts that comprehensive doctrines "belong" to the background culture and that "it is normally desirable that the comprehensive philosophical and moral views we are wont to use in debating fundamental political issues should give way in public life," he is essentially seeking to quarantine these views so that they cannot interfere with the workings of the insular set of political values that are to regulate the public sphere (1996, 14, 10). Citizens who embrace this understanding will be especially wary of bringing their comprehensive convictions forward in public life, except in those unavoidable instances where doing so is required to assuage their fellow citizens' suspicions that their ideals might be unreasonable. Even open-ended discussion in the background culture (which political liberalism condones) could, on this view, conceivably come to have a corrosive effect on the political values regulating the political sphere, were citizens to fail to be circumspect about presenting comprehensive ideals that might not square with the values of public reason.

While this approach is ultimately intended to mitigate citizens' distrust and establish grounds for mutual respect, an insistence on a shared public language insulated from our comprehensive convictions in fact has the potential to *increase* mistrust and suspicion among citizens, because it encourages the concealment of our "nonpublic" premises. If it is the case, as I argued in chapter 3, that public reason is by itself inadequate to resolve many of our most pressing policy conflicts, then citizens and public officials will typically be making a rather significant number of political choices on the basis of comprehensive views that are not widely shared. Rather than leaving each other to wonder about the deeper sources of our political positions, why shouldn't we encourage these to be brought into the open, so as to enable one another to wrestle with our arguments in their complete form? Even were some citizens to reveal that their comprehensive ideals were clearly at odds with the balance of public views on a particular issue, having these differences out in the open would seem a preferable alternative to encouraging citizens with such perspectives to cloak their convictions or maintain the false impression of agreement.

Michael Perry notes that the assumption that citizens should refrain from revealing the convictions animating their public activity seems counterintuitive from a democratic perspective. As he argues with particular reference to elected officials:

> It is virtually axiomatic that in a liberal democratic society the truthful disclosure of all the reasons why one's representative is inclined to stand where she does is an overriding, if infrequently honored, value. I suspect that most of us citizens of a liberal democracy would be more than willing to endure some feeling of being "imposed upon" if that were the price for knowing all the reasons why our representatives stand where they do. Among other things, if we know all the reasons, we can respond more effectively—especially when our representatives are up for reelection—than if we know only some of them. (1997, 52)

Perry makes a convincing case for the idea that, since religious arguments often in fact serve to help inform legislators' (as well as citizens') political decisions, we have a strong justification for bringing these and other comprehensive arguments forward in public discourse, in order that they might be "tested" there alongside other perspectives (61).[1]

Indeed, as I suggested in chapter 3, political liberalism itself relies upon contestable presuppositions to ground its own conception of politics—presuppositions that do not remain neatly within the realm of "political values." *All* of us have deeper wellsprings from which we draw in animating our political activity; for political liberals to insist that we can or should cultivate a separation between these resources and our political positions is both artificial and tendentious, insofar as their own political framework cannot be adequately justified without reference to their deeper body of ideals and understandings. What political liberals do, then, is participate in a kind of *selective* concealment, in which they will hold their tongue during occasions of political justification when the values of political liberalism are safely secured but reveal their more fundamental truth-claims when those values come under attack. For instance, J. Judd Owen argues that political liberalism must at the end of the day rely upon a contestable "theological premise," since "it cannot take any religious prescription as authoritative for its actions," and it therefore "*in principle* denies that there are any true, politically relevant religious prescriptions" (2001, 119, emphasis in original). We have seen the way in which Rawls himself relies upon a version of this principle when he argues that political liberals are justified in denying the truth-claims of citizens who reject the burdens of judgment. On occasions such as these, "we may eventually have to assert at least certain aspects of our own comprehensive religious or philosophical doctrine" to justify refusing public status to those citizens' political arguments (1996, 152–153). But if those citizens respond in kind by offering *their* own fundamental views and the deeper presuppositions on which they rest, they will be labeled unreasonable, and their claims will be shunted aside.

This raises a serious dilemma for how the process of political justification is to be conceptualized in a democratic society. Who, after all, is to determine when "we" may venture outside the overlapping consensus to draw on "our" comprehensive doctrine to support our political choices? Are only political liberals permitted to determine the acceptable boundaries of democratic discourse? It is this hegemonic thrust to political liberalism's resistance toward full disclosure in public life that should give us pause. Patrick Neal wonders whether "each and every citizen" is truly enfranchised within Rawlsian liberalism, or if in fact the voice of the theorist is intended to prevail (1997, 125–127). Or, alternatively, is it public officials and judges who are ultimately entrusted with wielding power and managing politics, given Rawls's distinction between the background culture and public political forum?

Perhaps it is not the theorist per se, or public officials, but political liberal citizens in general who ultimately enjoy unequal power in a Rawlsian society. Citizens whose core convictions tend to harmonize neatly with political liberalism will experience very little difficulty in abiding by the constraints of the reasonable, and they will see the public realm as an accessible and inviting place. They will not experience the difficulties faced by "unreasonable" citizens in justifying their political positions. On the other hand, unreasonable citizens who are unwilling simply to alter or relinquish their core ideals will have to choose between either misrepresenting their political positions by dissembling, or presenting their most compelling justification for their position and jeopardizing their status as political equals in the process.[2] Such disparate barriers to exercising sovereignty and political power are indefensible from a democratic perspective, at least if we are to take seriously the importance of mutual respect and political equality as the touchstones of our life in common.

None of this is to deny that political divisiveness is a real possibility when we move from a managed process of discourse to a more unconstrained and open-ended politics. That said, it would still seem as though bringing our differences to the surface, provided that this is done in good faith, would be more beneficial than persisting in masking them. Even on Rawls's own terms, if our goal is a political sphere in which we can be confident that citizens' views on justice or equality are consistent with political values rightly understood, encouraging engagement rather than withdrawal would seem more conducive to seeking this assurance.[3] And of course, we should question the notion that our most divisive policy disagreements will become less divisive simply by limiting our reliance upon comprehensive convictions in public discourse. Moral disagreements are often intense because they touch on issues connected with citizens' most fundamental worldviews and convictions, and these differ in far-reaching ways. Relying solely on a freestanding set of political values to approach our moral disputes will leave the deeper bases of these disagreements untouched. For these reasons, therefore, a politics characterized by sincerity seems more desirable than political liberalism's politics of evasion.

Discipline

A politics involving democratic engagement among a wide range of comprehensive ideals demands more of us than one guided by an uncontested set of political values. There is more risk involved, as well as a greater measure of uncertainty in pursuing shared aims. A commitment to discipline in our reason giving will help us avoid the prospect of politics becoming an agonistic free-for-all without direction or purpose. This is not to say that our arguments must be muted or inoffensive; a disciplined public argument can be offered boldly and provocatively. But we should be deliberate in ensuring that whatever contributions we do make to public life are grounded in genuine insights that emerge from the moral communities of which we are a part. The public sphere should not be viewed as a site of play where anything goes. Rather, we should assume a measure of accountability whenever we seek to alter the shape of the political realm. When we can make clear to other citizens that the arguments derived from our comprehensive convictions are in fact consistent with and embodied in the life and practices of the moral communities to which we belong, we stand the best chance of allowing those arguments to play a meaningful and creative role in shaping public norms.

An important aspect of a commitment to discipline involves a reluctance to inject our perspectives into public discourse simply for the sake of doing so. We should be conscientious in identifying those resources from our moral traditions that can offer a distinctly helpful perspective in grappling with particular public problems. On some issues we may have nothing to contribute. Yoder makes this point succinctly in regard to the church's witness: "The church should speak only when she has something to say" (1964, 21). We should look for those issues that affect us most directly and that we can thus speak to with a measure of experience and authority. As Yoder stresses,

> There should be no sense of a responsibility to "cover the field" with a full gamut of statements on every kind of subject that might be of any moral significance. Only such matters as can be clearly identified by the church as presenting a clear moral challenge or abuse can justify their being given more than perfunctory attention. Speaking within the American denominational framework, it might well be that a predominantly rural church should sense a special responsibility to speak to farm problems—that here it would be worth speaking only if the Christian farmers had something to say that was distinct from the largely self-interested testimonies of agricultural lobbying; that denominations with special experiences in overseas relief might speak of the distribution of surplus commodities in a way others could not. . . . Only a church doing something about prisoner rehabilitation would have any moral right to speak—or have any good ideas—about prison conditions or parole regulations. (22)

Moral communities that are accustomed to coming forward in public discourse only when they have specific and experiential insights to offer will contribute toward a search for public purposes in a much more effective way than groups that speak out too frequently, on issues not directly connected to their core practices or way of life.

Just as it is important that we seek to draw careful connections between our communities' practices and our public arguments, we should be aware of the ways in which these practices themselves "speak" in public life. Again referring to the witness of the Christian church, Yoder suggests that

> if the church is visible in that these people keep their promises, love their enemies, enjoy their neighbors, and tell the truth, as others do not, this may communicate to the world something of the reconciling, i.e., the community-creating, love of God. If, on the other hand, those who call Christ "Lord, Lord" do whatever the situation calls for just as do their neighbors, then what is communicated about their "religion" will probably be that just like the other cultures they have preachers and Sunday gatherings and prescribed ceremonies. (1998, 81)

The extraordinary discipline of the civil rights demonstrators is illuminating in this regard. Because they were committed to nonviolence in a fundamental sense, determined not to strike back against those who provoked them, they were able to offer their witness in a remarkably powerful way. Simply put, if the black church was to make credible its vision of a reconciled community, it was imperative that its actions be wholly consistent with that vision. The mass meetings were especially valuable in this regard, as they reinforced the importance of love for the enemy among all those participating in the sit-ins and marches:

> In the Montgomery, Albany, Birmingham, and Selma meetings the preachers blessed their persecutors (police and local politicians), prayed for those who despitefully used them, and incessantly exhorted the people to love their enemies. At Saint James Baptist in Birmingham, the police recorded King's pleas that his hearers not only boycott the after-Easter sales in white department stores but do so with purity of heart: "For even ole' Bull [Connor, feared Birmingham police commissioner] is a child of God. We love ole' Bull." The preachers prayed for the sheriffs and their kin when they were sick, and on the rare

> occasions when the authorities came to the church, the marchers treated them with respect. In Birmingham, Rev. Gardner even commended the undercover detectives for their perseverance in attending so many meetings in a row. (Lischer 1997, 251)

On those rare occasions when demonstrators would retaliate against local authorities or hostile whites, the movement's leadership would call them to repentance and to a recommitment to nonviolence. Branch recounts one of these instances when Andrew Young, one of the prominent SCLC leaders, admonished a mass meeting audience in Birmingham for the rock-throwing in which some had taken part. "'We have a nonviolent movement . . . but it's not nonviolent enough. . . . We must not boo the police when they bring up the dogs. . . . We must praise them. The police don't know how to handle the situation governed by love, and the power of God. During these demonstrations we must tell the crowd to behave'" (1988, 763).

The actions of those on the front lines of the struggle exemplified and magnified the more formal public arguments of King and other movement leaders, thus giving the movement a persuasive power that would simply not have been possible otherwise. The requirement of disciplined engagement is thus not merely a burden to be borne by those who would be conscientious citizens. Through its discipline, a moral community can gain opportunities for communicating its truths to others that might be even more effective than more formal argumentation. This is particularly the case during moral disagreements in which groups' convictions differ widely. In those situations, when a moral community can offer its convictions with integrity and as an outgrowth of the community's way of life, it can contribute toward public discourse even when its arguments fail to convince its opponents. Conversely, when communities fail to display this discipline, it makes it that much more difficult for others with radically different convictions to engage their perspective.

Political liberalism does demand a certain form of discipline from citizens, although it is a much more attenuated version of dialogic discipline than what I have delineated here. As Rawls explains it in his most recent account, the context in which ordinary citizens are obligated to adhere to public reason is in their voting decisions, either when selecting their elected representatives or in registering their views on referenda when those happen to concern constitutional essentials or questions of justice (1997, 769). While this does entail that all citizens be "prepared to offer one another fair terms of cooperation according to what they consider the most reasonable conception of political justice," Rawls now seems to view the occasions in which such engagement would take place as few and far between, limited chiefly to those situations in which citizens' fidelity to public reason might be called into question by other citizens (770).

The chief difficulty with Rawls's position here is that it overlooks the ways in which moral communities can help shape the contours of political life *by their very existence.* Rawls's understanding of public reason requires the assumption that the only kind of public discourse with significant political consequences consists of those arguments that are offered by persons in positions of political responsibility, in the "public political forum." But if the background culture/politics boundary required for this assertion to hold is illusory, as I have argued, then it becomes much more difficult to maintain a strong normative distinction between the political activity of ordinary citizens and that of political professionals. On this view, the civil rights movement's protests were political activity of the first rank, even though they did not usually involve the presentation of "arguments" in the conventional sense and would be characterized by Rawls as taking place in the background culture.

What this suggests is that we cannot be oblivious to the variety of ways in which moral communities offer their convictions to the greater polity. We should not assume that since these communities are not typically lobbying on behalf of elected officials or helping to draft legislation that what they do is of little consequence. The advantage of the norm of a disciplined practice of discourse is that it alerts us to the political significance of our communities' actions and ways of life, and it reminds us of the need for care and thoughtfulness in trying to ensure that we are making an effective and responsible contribution to the search for public purposes. This does not mean, of course, that most citizens will necessarily see their political activity as stemming directly from their immersion in a particular moral community, or even perceive fully the political significance of their involvement in the life of one or more moral communities. Extraordinary moments of organized and disciplined collective witness, such as what transpired in the civil rights struggle, are indeed extraordinary. But what moments such as these do reveal is the fact that substantive political change can happen in multiple ways and that we need to be cognizant of how our moral communities are making their impact on the public sphere. This cannot be a matter of indifference.

So while a more ambitious practice of discipline does place demands on citizens, they are of a fundamentally different order than those of political liberalism. We are not required to subordinate our moral commitments to a particular understanding of liberal justice or police our "nonpublic" views to ensure that they do not contaminate our political activity. We are, however, under an obligation to make our political activity meaningful, by doing what we can to guide our political conduct in a manner that is both consistent with our fundamental convictions and able to contribute helpfully to the search for public purposes. Put somewhat differently, we should see our responsibility as entailing the willingness to present truthful visions of the good for other citizens' consideration and to help those we are engaging to perceive and understand the deeper justifications for our positions. When these stem from the life of a particular moral community, we can and should make that connection clear. If they do not, we should still be prepared to present the most thoughtful and complete articulation of our position possible, even if actual opportunities to do this are rare. A mutual commitment to integrity in our public activity will go a long way toward achieving a purposive public discourse, while at the same time avoiding the problematic distinctions between reasonable and unreasonable views, and between the background culture and politics, that so plague political liberalism's framework.

Dialogic Creativity

Once we come to terms with the inadequacy of any effort to establish a secure and uncontestable set of political values, the challenge becomes discovering how to conceive of provisional public norms emerging out of a more vigorous, but also more precarious, process of moral engagement. It is in this context that dialogic creativity becomes a pivotal practice. This requires bringing our particular moral languages forward to participate in the process of shaping and transforming public ideals, while at the same time recognizing the extent to which this process must entail a careful encounter with the particular languages of other communities. We should not seek to colonize the public sphere with our particular perspective. Rather, by offering our convictions sincerely for other citizens' consideration and grappling with their views in a serious fashion, we can facilitate the search for public meanings by taking part in a process of mutual discernment.

Dialogic creativity, as I am characterizing it, is similar to Jeffrey Stout's idea of *bricolage*—a term he borrows from Claude Lévi-Strauss to denote the process of crafting ethical and moral meanings by taking the bits and pieces of available moral languages and reconfiguring them, attempting to find a more compelling way of framing the problems we are confronted with and perhaps finding better solutions to them (1988, 74–77). Stout makes a compelling case that all moral and ethical philosophy proceeds in this fashion, and I would suggest that the best kind of political discourse must happen in this manner as well. Whenever we enter public space to offer an argument concerning the common good, we can rely on any of a number of languages to make our claim, and it is via the interaction between insights specific to our own tradition or moral community and forms of argumentation accessible to other communities that usable truth claims come about, particularly when politics concerns value-laden questions about the good.

King displayed a mastery of this approach to public discourse in his speeches and sermons. He could and did rely on the American civil religious tradition, a resource that was particularly helpful in reaching out to white Protestants, but he channeled that tradition through the particular insights of the black church, thus transforming its meaning in the process. King's radically prophetic version of civil religion led him to assume the more insistent and less compromising rhetorical voice that characterized the later years of his life, as he stepped up his protests against economic inequality and the Vietnam War. Similarly, while King would build arguments around terms such as freedom and equality, they would be given different connotations and nuances as a result of the particular theological convictions that guided King's usage of them.

King was confident that he could shed new light on America's political ideals because he was a product of the black church and thus had a well of experience and convictions he could draw upon in examining and reclaiming them. Absent this particularity, King would not have had the transformative impact he had on American public life. At the same time, the fact that King was a committed American citizen and a student of liberal theology was of vital importance in helping him craft public appeals that were able to resonate with the diverse audiences he encountered. King's creative genius was found in this ability to work with a variety of viable civic and moral languages, allowing their particular strengths to help him reconfigure the terms of public discourse in the context of an America greatly divided over the question of racial justice.

The practice of dialogic creativity presupposes an ongoing need for scrutinizing our political ideals and adapting them so as to respond to changing social, cultural, and political realities. We must always seek to measure the adequacy of our political understandings and use whatever normative resources are at our disposal to critique and refashion them when they fall short. This is a process that requires imagination and discovery, as well as flexibility and a desire to experiment with diverse political approaches. In contrast, political liberalism envisions a politics more akin to *political engineering* than to political creativity.[4] The ideal of the well-ordered society Rawls champions is one in which the most essential questions of justice and rights have been settled. While important political conflicts may remain, it is assumed that they will be addressed solely by referring to the political values contained in the overlapping consensus (1996, 248). What political liberalism offers us, therefore, is a politics that is as *inflexible* as possible: the extent to which we can perpetuate a tightly structured framework from which to approach political disagreements is a crucial indicator of how just our political arrangements are. It is in part by limiting our reliance on comprehensive doctrines in political life that we help maintain political norms that, because they can be endorsed by all reasonable citizens, are capable of solving political problems in a straightforward and self-evident fashion, or at least arriving at uncontroversial ways of determining what is at stake in each disagreement.

But as we have seen, the scope of policy dilemmas that can be effectively approached solely by drawing on political values is not as large as Rawls sometimes suggests. It is worth noting, moreover, that with the rapid increase in local and state-level ballot initiatives and referenda, citizens are gaining more opportunities for having a direct say in these contested policy disputes. While Rawls posits that the issues at stake in these contexts "are rarely fundamental questions" (1997, 769), a quick survey of state-level ballot proposals from the last few years reveals otherwise. Voters in different states have had to decide matters concerning affirmative action, medical use of marijuana, gay rights, congressional term limits, gun rights, school vouchers, and late-term abortions, all of which would fall under the constitutional essentials/questions of basic justice category. If an insular political framework will not supply ready-made solutions to these policy dilemmas, allowing citizens recourse to all of their convictions in approaching and deliberating about them seems entirely warranted.

A discourse characterized by creativity rather than political engineering also allows a deeper inquiry into the limitations of our current political norms and practices. Political liberalism's temptingly simple invocation of political values can shield us from the deficiencies of those values or the more problematic impulses that may animate them.[5] This kind of complacency is a crucial liability of political liberalism, insofar as it discourages the kind of interrogation that allows us to scrutinize all of our political ideals—even the most widely held and uncontroversial ones—in an effort to refine and improve upon our political understandings. For instance, Neal raises concerns about the way in which Rawlsian discourse, through taking matters off the political agenda, effectuates an impulse to ignore or downplay the struggles for recognition that particular groups must wage to assure their status as equal citizens (1997, 122–125).[6] A discourse emphasizing democratic engagement, in contrast, expects a continual examination of our currently accepted views, and indeed it makes that activity much more prevalent precisely through welcoming a more vigorous process of contestation through which our political ideals can be subjected to greater and more visible critique.

Rawls is correct to insist that "politics in a democratic society can never be guided by what we see as the whole truth" (1996, 243). Our moral differences are real. Taking these differences seriously dispels the illusion that we can simply legislate our convictions into public policy, absent the process of mediation and negotiation that must accompany politics in this context. But acknowledging this truth with Rawls does not require us to embrace his recommendation for an inflexible adherence to a finite set of political values. On the contrary, an appreciation of the challenges of moral diversity should lead us into engagement with one another, to seek shared norms by creatively exploring our particular perspectives and determining what they might have to offer for solving political problems. Only by learning where our fellow citizens stand, and the traditions that undergird their political activity, can we have any hope of reaching mutually acceptable negotiations of our political differences, for only in that way are we able to consider how our own body of convictions can best function in the ongoing process of creating public meanings. We can thereby better determine what is needed in public life.

Forbearance

The practice of forbearance assumes special importance once we can no longer take for granted a singular public language for guiding politics. The flexibility and creativity that are intrinsic features of the post-secular ethics of public life I am presenting here should be accompanied by a certain humility and patience when we approach fellow citizens whose convictions may stand radically opposed to our own. My effort to throw into question political liberalism's conception of the reasonable is thus intended not merely to challenge the value of a monological view of public discourse, wherein we attempt to solve all political problems with a single set of political values. I am also questioning the categorization of *citizens* into reasonable and unreasonable camps, in the expectation that by jettisoning this distinction we might work toward a more accommodating vision of public life.[7]

Yoder's assertion that *every* engagement among moral communities involves an effort of translation, a struggle to "converse at every border" given the absence of a "nonprovincial general community with clear language," serves to emphasize the need for thoughtfulness and creativity in engaging other moral and political perspectives (1984, 41). There is a certain opacity to all inter-community discourse that we should be aware of when engaging others with diverse moral convictions.[8] But there is a corollary *self*-awareness that should accompany this as well. If all perspectives are partial and provincial, then we are not permitted to assume that our own set of political norms, no matter how "general" or "public" we may regard them, are entirely adequate to withstand critique or challenge from other points of view. We cannot take for granted, in other words, the superiority of our own perspective in such a way that we negate the contributions of other moral traditions, by preemptively cordoning them off as being unreasonable or incompatible with public purposes properly understood. While it is unavoidable that particular political struggles must sometimes result in winners and losers, we would be well served to eschew the supreme self-confidence that leads us to demonize our adversaries or dismiss them peremptorily.

In addition, when we become more keenly aware of the boundaries separating moral communities, we become more cognizant of the struggle involved in *persuading* others of the merits of our perspective and the limits inherent in that process. If all efforts to create and maintain shared political norms are subject to negotiation and contestation, and we cannot assume a public standpoint that is beyond challenge, there will be numerous occasions in which agreement over political ends will not be forthcoming. In such situations, it becomes imperative that we have the fortitude to continue the search for commonality at the same time that we resist coercive political strategies that would attempt to circumvent that search. In other words, we must be prepared for those inevitable failures that will accompany political life in a morally diverse society—those moments of engagement in which we fail to bridge the normative divides separating moral communities. Such moments can have a distinctly tragic character, and coming to terms with this possibility becomes a critical challenge for any vision of public life that does not assume we can easily establish an uncontestable public perspective from which to manage our disagreements.[9]

We can look once again to King for guidance here. His commitment to maintaining a respectful and generous stance toward the opponents of desegregation was dramatically evident in the movement's nonviolent public witness. Rather than vilify his adversaries, King sought to reach out to them. He emphasized again and again that the movement did not wish to "triumph" over the white community; as the movement's goal was to create "an interracial society based on freedom for all," it would have to be based on persuasion, not coercion (King [1956b] 1986, 81). And because of the black church's status as a marginalized community, King was prepared for the tremendous perseverance needed for the attempt to bring about far-reaching changes in Americans' understanding of justice and equality. Fully aware that he could not simply assume a privileged public stance that would give his appeals presumptive validity, he could gird himself and the movement for the concrete struggles that were required to effectuate justice one step at a time, and be ready for both the victories and the defeats that followed those efforts.

Because political liberalism denies the inherent contestability of political norms and relies on its own understanding of public reason as an unproblematic public language, it depends not on forbearance, but on reasonableness—that quality which ostensibly allows us to transcend our differences altogether. Those citizens whose convictions are consistent with the reasonable, and who can perform the particular tasks accompanying this vision of citizenship, are worthy of mutual respect and are welcomed in public life. Those who cannot are not thereby denied equal status as citizens, but neither are they entitled to solicitude or having their views taken seriously. If politics is predicated on a common point of view, those unable to adopt that perspective will simply find themselves on the periphery of political life.

As is evident with Macedo's treatment of the *Mozert* case, political liberalism sometimes succumbs to a kind of aphasia when it encounters communities with convictions that lie outside its own conception of public purposes. "Public reason puts conflicting comprehensive views aside: it does not seek a compromise or balance among those wider views, and it does not furnish any sort of guide for weighing and assessing the disproportionate effects of various public laws and policies" (2000, 189). To venture onto that terrain would be to jeopardize the insularity and purity of the political perspective public reason supplies. It would complicate matters considerably to suggest that such a perspective might be insufficient to negotiate our moral disagreements and that we might therefore have to engage one another's moral views more deeply in order to secure a more accommodating public space. So instead political liberalism refuses to explore such questions, retreating to the position that insists that such concerns are extra-political: we must resolutely avoid "relying on 'private' grounds when fashioning the principles that underlie the basic political institutions of society" (189). Citizens who insist on relying on such grounds in justifying their political activity will thus find themselves denied a legitimate role in helping to define public purposes.

This self-confidence in its own political rectitude ensures that political liberalism will remain inattentive to the potentially tragic outcomes that can accompany life in a morally diverse society. These outcomes are acknowledged in a perfunctory sense, to be sure. "Political liberalism's guarantee of a formalistic neutrality seems implicitly to narrow our view and to imply a measure of real arbitrariness: some valuable ways of life (such as that of the Amish, perhaps) will suffer severe disproportionate burdens in this regime" (Macedo 2000, 190). And if prudential political considerations warrant it, we might in some circumstances be justified in recognizing the claims of particular communities for accommodations. But the possibility of actually adapting our public understandings in the face of the challenges posed by such communities is not to be seriously considered. It is always assumed that political liberalism's particular view of civic purposes is to prevail.

If, as I have suggested, the tensions surrounding moral diversity are becoming more, not less, prominent, the insularity that renders political liberalism unwilling to engage other perspectives has detrimental implications for the prospects of negotiating our moral disagreements generously and capaciously. If we cannot recognize the partiality of our own perspective, and acknowledge the way in which even the most broad and encompassing political norms such as justice or equality are in the end contestable and subject to competing interpretations, it will become more likely that we will use terms such as "the reasonable" to reinforce invidious distinctions among citizens, thus ensuring that a politics characterized by genuine mutual respect and concord will remain an elusive goal.

Locating a Politics of Engagement: Considerations of Context and Publicity

These four practices constitute a marked shift from political liberalism's understanding of the public sphere, precisely because they do not rely upon a determinate public/nonpublic distinction or a doctrine of public reason. Instead, they alert us to the way in which our dispositions and intentions are indispensable in determining how we carry out the responsibilities of democratic citizenship. Indeed, my claim is that these factors should ultimately bear much more weight in conceptualizing an ethics of public life than a preoccupation with the publicness of citizens' arguments or the appropriateness of the particular forums in which they are presented.

This is not to say, however, that we should be oblivious to the significance of the contexts in which our public arguments are offered. Although Rawls goes too far in suggesting that the public political forum can always be neatly distinguished from the wider background culture, he is right to contend that the political activity taking place there is of great significance when considering the dangers of coercive politics. Political liberals are certainly justified in warning us about the coercive power of the modern state. It is thus crucial that those with direct access to that power, such as elected representatives and judges, are exceptionally aware of the precarious yet essential effort to find justifications for policies and decisions that are as widely accessible as possible. The difficulty with seeking to erect a barrier between the political and the nonpolitical does not lie in the intuition that some public decisions are of greater consequence for questions of justice or rights than others. Rather, it is the assumption that one can best discern an individual's public responsibility in any given situation by trying to locate his or her activity in one domain or the other.

For instance, while we must certainly insist that public officials are under an obligation to represent all citizens equally, it would be going too far to assume that because of this responsibility they should never speak in a morally particular voice or reveal the fundamental convictions on which their positions are based. Sincerity in this regard is an obligation shared by all citizens, irrespective of the forums they are addressing. Undoubtedly there should be a heightened awareness of the possible *risks* involved in speaking in a particular voice as one's audiences become larger and more diverse; thus public officials will tend to bear a disproportionate burden in ensuring that they are speaking both sincerely and with an eye to inclusivity in their appeals. But this is a difference of degree rather than category.

Similarly, the political significance of the public arguments of religious leaders or political activists is not attenuated simply because they do not occupy official positions of political power. Considerations of context must inform their own claims as well. A religious leader who is giving a speech during a protest on the steps of the capitol will likely feel compelled to use a different range of expressions than she would if addressing her own congregation, just as public officials will sometimes address a national audience in different terms from those used for a local one. Here too, however, complexities emerge. What does one do, for instance, when addressing a faith community when media representatives are present and the topic concerns an issue of intense public disagreement? There will rarely be unambiguous solutions to these kinds of dilemmas. But acknowledging a more permeable boundary between the public realm and the wider culture does render us more aware of the need to consider these complexities in a way that a more rigid demarcation does not.

Just as we should not be unaware of the role context plays in our public arguments, we must not neglect the vital importance of arriving at shareable justifications for the policies we endorse. It is worth emphasizing that the central purpose of a politics of engagement is not to celebrate wild diversity over commonality but rather to pursue commonality *through* an engagement with particularity rather than by trying to circumvent or ignore it. Along these lines, we need not suppose that a healthy democratic politics must continually involve throwing any and all settled agreements on public norms into question. Although Rawls and other political liberals are wrong to insist upon a civic core of shared norms beyond contestation, we are certainly justified in championing and maintaining proven public ideals—not the least of which, of course, being those that have been instrumental in establishing the conditions under which moral diversity itself has flourished. Rights of assembly, speech, religious freedom, and political equality are not trivial goods. An insistence on the necessity of moral particularity in informing our definitions, analyses, and reformulations of such norms does not entail the assumption that we must consistently prefer disruption or critique to supporting worthy public ideals.

Here too, then, my alternative to political liberalism does not reject its core intuition as much as it challenges the way in which that intuition is actualized politically. Rawls's desire to seek shared public aims is not to be faulted. But it *is* imperative that we become more aware of the nuances and complexities that accompany that search and we refrain from characterizing arguments in public discourse as being either intrinsically public or nonpublic, based solely upon the nature of the premises invoked. Rawls relies on this move in suggesting that claims involving comprehensive views that exceed current political values are essentially non-public, while those that use political values consistent with the overlapping consensus are fully public. In contrast to Rawls's account, I would offer a more variegated conception. Our truth-claims can serve a wide variety of functions in public life: to propose novel social possibilities not yet on the public agenda; to persuade; to witness; to challenge existing political arrangements; and to offer justificatory support for our political views. The particular objective(s) a given argument is meant to accomplish, or the language used to present it, are not in themselves sufficient to allow it to be categorized as inherently public or nonpublic, but having a more complex taxonomy can help us better understand the relationship between moral particularity and publicness in a politics of engagement.

There is an essential difference, for instance, between occasions in which discourse is serving the purpose of *witnessing*, and those in which *justification* is taking place. The former involves citizens advancing their fundamental convictions in a quest to draw attention to injustices or to highlight a better approach to the public good. The latter, in contrast, involves contexts in which citizens or public officials are explaining or debating the rationale behind particular governmental policies or decisions. In witnessing, a more radically particular voice may be more appropriate (and effective), whereas in justificatory speech the pressures to locate a more widely accessible public position are (and should be) greater.[10] For example, King's discourse during his "I Have a Dream" speech was boldly and justifiably particular, even though the issues he was addressing, as well as the setting in which he delivered the speech, were undeniably public in nature. Supreme Court opinions are arguably no more inherently public in import or impact than King's more notable public addresses, but due to the justificatory purpose for which they are written, justices are obligated to rely upon a less morally particular rhetorical approach in formulating them. Here too, however, it is worth emphasizing that these are differences in degree rather than fixed category. Insisting that judges are never justified in appealing to aspects of their "comprehensive doctrine" in defending their decisions is as unacceptable as suggesting that the political speech of "ordinary" citizens need not attend to considerations of publicity or the dynamics of appealing to diverse audiences.

It is clear, then, that a politics of engagement requires a heightened sensitivity to the shifting contexts and purposes of public life. Refusing to fix these in a determinate fashion does make us more aware of the challenges of politics in a morally diverse society. It should also, however, draw our attention to the various opportunities for engagement and mutual learning that can emerge when we refuse to rely upon an inflexible topology of the public sphere.

Additional Challenges and Tensions

It is worth considering two additional concerns that may arise in connection with the four practices. First, there stands the potential for tensions among the practices themselves. While all four practices are intended to work in harmony with each other, allowing a unified approach to public life, it is not unlikely that different communities will weigh the practices differently depending upon their constitutive understandings. In some contexts, and for some citizens and communities, balancing the practices may prove difficult. Here I will focus on two points of tension in particular: between sincerity and forbearance, and between sincerity and dialogic creativity. Second, there is the matter of the practices' distinctive provenance. Relying as I have on the thought of Yoder and the political practices of King and the civil rights movement, it may be wondered whether these norms are capable of being embraced by citizens from non-Christian moral traditions. The extent to which this poses a problem for my approach must also, therefore, be addressed.

Tensions among the Practices

Sincerity, discipline, dialogic creativity, and forbearance must all be present in some form if we are to pursue a vision of public life that is welcoming of a wide array of visions of the good and at the same time characterized by patient engagement and a reluctance to dominate the public sphere with our particular convictions. A mutual commitment to sincerity not accompanied by a willingness to be disciplined in our approach to discourse might result merely in noisy exchanges that, while offering a glimpse into the range of extant moral perspectives, would provide little by way of a purposive politics. Similarly, without forbearance we might fall prey to the temptation of assuming a hegemonic stance in advancing our own perspective (even while doing so sincerely) and neglect to consider the challenges that might be raised by communities whose traditions are at odds with our own. However, while all four practices are essential, their realization in particular instances is one that requires discernment on the part of individual citizens and moral communities. Not all communities will find all four of the practices equally compelling or without impulses that pull in competing directions.

One possible point of tension will be experienced by communities that will find it difficult to draw sincerely on their own moral tradition while assuming the receptive stance toward those of other traditions that is required by forbearance. This task will be a more natural one for those moral communities that find themselves on the periphery of American public life; when you are not accustomed to having political power, the idea that your point of view is not universally shared is not a difficult one to accept. Yoder points out that this is a lesson that has been particularly hard for Christians to learn, since from the time of Constantine the assumption that Christianity should serve as *the* guiding moral language of the state was rather firmly rooted in the Christian worldview. Indeed, the view of America as a Christian nation has continued to function as a normative disposition for many Christians even in the present era of church/state separation (1984, 135–147).

We may regard Jerry Falwell's *Listen, America!* (1980) as a representative example. Falwell's Moral Majority organization was instrumental in galvanizing Christian conservatives into political action in the 1980s. Prior to that time most evangelical Protestants disdained direct political involvement, on the assumption that it would jeopardize Christians' moral integrity to take an active role in politics. Falwell's efforts helped convince legions of conservative Christians that they had a religious obligation to advance their convictions politically.[11] Falwell's rhetorical approach was on one level highly particular, emphasizing specific biblical warrants for his arguments, yet he also sought to forge a broader coalition among moral conservatives generally by casting much of his agenda as a defense of freedom and the family. Ultimately, as he put it, he sought to "rally together the people of this country who still believe in decency, the home, the family, morality, the free-enterprise system, and all the great ideals that are the cornerstone of this nation" (244).

The difficulty Falwell's argumentative strategy presents is not due to the particularity of his claims or the sincerity with which they are offered. In these respects, his public appeals are consistent with an ethics of engagement. There is even an impressive degree of creativity in Falwell's approach, as he seeks to draw connections between his moral/political positions and American civic traditions dating back to the founding period (1980, 29–50). But Falwell's arguments display little by way of forbearance. Instead, they draw lines of battle as tightly as possible between the morally righteous and those bringing America to ruin. For Falwell, feminists, gays and lesbians, "humanists," pornographers, and abortion providers are arrayed against those who would return America to its religious foundations. "When *we as a country* again acknowledge God as our Creator and Jesus Christ as the Savior of mankind, we will be able to turn this nation around economically as well as in every other way" (81, my emphasis). The conviction animating Falwell's politics is that America "was founded on a belief in God and the moral principles of the Bible," and therefore it is incumbent upon people of faith to do whatever is necessary to ensure that the nation is restored to that condition (259).

The ideal of a "Christian America" is simply not conducive to a proper recognition of the challenges accompanying moral diversity in the present-day United States—especially when that ideal is harnessed to a far-reaching legislative agenda, as it was in the case of Falwell's Moral Majority. The practice of forbearance as I have articulated it is incompatible with relying upon our particular convictions to attempt to colonize the public sphere. Rather, it requires us to acknowledge and engage respectfully the other perspectives that also occupy public space. It is worth noting, however, that the temptation of assuming a hegemonic stance toward citizens of other moral traditions is not one to which those on the Religious Right are uniquely vulnerable. It will be faced by any group accustomed to assuming a privileged place in public discourse. As we have seen, despite their protestations to the contrary, political liberals themselves are prone to excluding other voices and taking an approach to public life that has its own hegemonic thrust, because of their conviction that their political conception alone is able to provide a legitimate framework for liberal politics.

It seems inevitable that some citizens and communities will have an easier time than others of coming to terms with the consequences of their moral particularity. Those that are not accustomed to viewing their particular perspective as a provincial one will have to wrestle with the tension between a genuine presentation of their self-understandings and the need for forbearance, particularly when this kind of forbearance might be a practice foreign to their core convictions. There is no easy way to confront this challenge, except to encourage both sincerity and forbearance and expect that as citizens come to appreciate the contributions that other traditions can make to our political understandings, they will perceive the advantages to be gained from engaging those traditions more widely and generously. In addition, it seems plausible to expect that as citizens come to recognize more clearly the differences separating moral communities, they can better understand the dangerous coercive propensities entailed when these differences are ignored or shunted aside in the interests of bypassing moral engagement.

This is ultimately a tension that will confront any conception of politics that seeks to take moral particularity seriously. The main advantage that a politics of engagement offers is that the process of negotiating this tension is brought forward into political life directly, rather than circumvented, as we find in political liberalism. Political liberals view the presentation of comprehensive views and their relationship to public political values as acceptable, provided that such engagement works to reinforce a societal consensus and takes place under the safe rubric of the reasonable. But they cannot encourage such presentation when it might work to throw into question an overlapping consensus. Such an approach emphasizes preserving a veneer of commonality over an honest consideration of political differences. If political liberals find Jerry Falwell's political agenda objectionable, might it not be more productive for them to engage Falwell's ideas directly, patiently demonstrating their limitations, as opposed simply to dismissing them as unreasonable and therefore unworthy of further consideration? By welcoming a democratic engagement over the good and encouraging the sincere presentation of our disparate political positions, my own approach opens up possibilities for wrestling with these disagreements in a way that is denied us if we must submerge our differences beneath Rawls's overlapping consensus. By encouraging democratic contestation over core ideals, it becomes less likely that ostensibly shared "political values" can be used to shield our deeper commitments and obscure the true fault lines of any particular public disagreement.

Just as the practices of sincerity and forbearance may be difficult for some communities to reconcile, in some political situations the practice of sincerity may be in tension with that of dialogic creativity. That is, in our effort to have an effective impact on political life, we may be tempted to avoid presenting our convictions sincerely, choosing instead a kind of selective dissemblance when it may seem a surer route to political success. This is essentially the choice that confronted King during the latter stages of the civil rights struggle, when he was urged by many activists in the movement to discard the Christian emphasis on nonviolence and patient protest in favor of a more combative political stance. Had he fully embraced the black power wing of the movement, it is possible that King might have had more of a direct political impact at a time in which his overall influence seemed to be waning. Yet he steadfastly refused to renounce the convictions that animated the movement from the very beginning, even though it seemed to entail a significant political sacrifice. It certainly cost him the support of many of his most ambitious activists, who had grown weary of King's Christian love for the oppressor and thus focused their energies elsewhere.[12]

In cases like these a commitment to sincerity might very well necessitate political defeat. Even when the choice is not framed this starkly, however, there will be moments in our political activity when we must determine how to present our convictions in a way that is best able to contribute toward public purposes. This might in some instances lead us to attenuate our emphasis on certain elements of our traditions. For instance, disparate religious communities that are working collectively for common goals might threaten their ability to cooperate if they were to stress their religious particularity in an aggressive or insensitive way. These kinds of determinations cannot be made independently of the context of particular sites of engagement or political struggle. But it is important to recognize that communities who wish to be both responsible to the demands of sincerity and effective contributors toward shared public aims will need to wrestle with how they can adequately fulfill both practices in their political activity. A politics of engagement does not require that we reveal the full justification behind our political positions each and every time we enter the public sphere. But it is critical that we avoid intentionally disguising the nature of our positions in an attempt to deceive or gain political advantage.

Of course, if we are concerned about the dangers of dissemblance, we must note that Rawls's model is vulnerable here as well. It is certainly possible to disguise one's true motives in a political struggle by cloaking one's position in the language of the reasonable. For example, legislators whose opposition to gay marriage is based at least in part upon particular biblical passages can (and do) frame their appeals using political values such as a concern for the strength of families, the welfare of children, and so forth. The same can be done in debates over abortion, euthanasia, and many other issues where we might be tempted to defend our position by offering a tactical justification that is not in fact the principal rationale consistent with our deepest view of the matter. The crucial question is whether such strategic dissemblance would be rarer under political liberalism than under a politics of engagement. I would conjecture that the answer would have to be no. Without the language of public reason to serve as a cloak for our comprehensive convictions, it would seem that much more difficult to justify concealing them.

While they are not insignificant, these kinds of tensions do seem to be unavoidable consequences of politics in a morally diverse society. The process of negotiation and contestation through which we struggle to create viable public norms in the midst of our deep disagreements is inevitable; our obligation is to consider how to carry out that process in a responsible fashion. In this light, the challenge of reconciling the fundamental convictions that animate and sustain our political activity with those norms that regulate the public order is, as Rawls has argued, a crucial requirement of democratic citizenship. To be sure, this challenge becomes more *visible* when we refuse to characterize it as a private obligation. But in this way we can contribute toward the creation of a public realm that is less subject to obfuscation and thus perhaps more able to sustain a politics characterized by genuine mutual respect.

The Translatability of the Practices

In developing my conception of a post-secular ethics of public life, I have relied heavily on the insights of both Yoder and King. Their perspectives, as we have seen, were derived from particular theological premises, and they depended crucially on those premises for much of their integrity and power. But of course, we might then be justified in wondering whether their ideals are truly capable of serving as resources for public ethics in a society in which many citizens do not share their underlying presuppositions and commitments. To what extent are these practices translatable, capable of being endorsed and carried out by non-Christian moral communities?

This concern can be addressed in part by considering Yoder's own response to this challenge. Especially in his later work, Yoder displayed an acute interest in discerning the ways in which the practices embodied in the life of the church could be offered to the wider society as political or social norms.[13] On the one hand, he acknowledged that the Christian community is sustained by its account of who God is, and only through its distinctive identity can it carry out the arduous ethical demands required of it. To expect these practices to be *fully* embraced, in all their particularity, by communities defined by other constitutive understandings would be foolhardy. Yet at the same time, Yoder did expect the church to be able to offer glimpses of alternative social and political practices that could contribute toward fostering desirable norms in the society at large. In an especially valuable essay on this theme, "Sacrament as Social Process," Yoder explains that the distinctive characteristics of the Christian community, such as fraternal admonition and the breaking of bread of the Eucharist, insofar as they are displayed genuinely in the life of the church, can illuminate broader norms that can be taken up by others outside of the faith community. Fraternal admonition, whereby members of the church are committed to a process of mutual ethical discernment and a process of reconciliation when wrongs have been committed, can "provide models for conflict resolution, alternatives to litigation, and alternative perspectives on 'corrections.'" Similarly, the breaking of bread can be viewed as "a paradigm, not only for soup kitchens and hospitality houses, but also for social security and negative income tax," as this practice gestures toward the elimination of socioeconomic inequality (1998, 369–370).

For Yoder, although each of the church's practices are highly particular in that they reflect God's nature and purposes, because they are concretely embodied, *social* practices they can be observed and understood by others. "These forms are derived from and illuminated by reference to specific components of the faith stance of the first century's messianic synagogues, yet they are accessible to the public. People who do not share the faith or join the community can learn from them" (1998, 369). That a particular political norm or idea stems from the convictions of a particular moral community does not, therefore, disqualify it as a potential candidate for a usable truth-claim or beneficial political practice. Its intelligibility and value will emerge insofar as it is able to help make sense of our shared social reality or enable us to gain a better understanding of how to live our life in common.

We can see this dynamic in the political activity of the civil rights movement. The nonviolent disobedience through which the protesters displayed forbearance toward their adversaries was made possible and sustained through their faith that God was guiding and protecting the movement at every stage of the struggle. King was fully aware of the demanding nature of this witness, and he knew that faith was a vital resource in sustaining it. Yet it also seems hard to deny that the movement's ideals and practices have left a lasting imprint on American understandings of justice and the possibilities of nonviolent protest, in an influence extending far beyond the confines of the black church. King's idea of the beloved community resonated differently with different audiences; non-Christian listeners were not denied access to its power simply because they did not share the constitutive understandings of black Christianity. In the same way, citizens of diverse convictions have taken up the practice of nonviolent protest without needing to rely on a distinctively Christian narrative to sustain their political activity.

If, as I have argued, politics is always subject to the formation of provisional convergences in the search for shared ideals, it would stand to reason that any ethics of citizenship would be subject to a similar process, as differing viable interpretations of the demands of citizenship emerge and are sifted in public life. It seems entirely plausible to imagine overlaps forming around particular norms and practices that can guide citizenship on a societal level. A practice such as sincerity, for instance, would not seem so far removed from the commonsense expectations most citizens bring to their understanding of political life—namely, that people should speak their minds, and mean what they say. Similarly, forbearance would be another way (albeit a more demanding one) of capturing the significance of regarding one's political opponents with respect and fair-mindedness. There will always be disagreement at some level about how precisely the demands of citizenship should be understood and carried out; the fixed determinacy envisioned by Rawls's overlapping consensus is clearly unrealistic. But there can be something more substantive than a dialogical free-for-all. We can be justified in hoping that particular political visions, even if they are rooted in a particular religious worldview, can contribute meaningfully to finding shared norms of public life.

What I have tried to do with my framework is show that it is possible to draw richly on the particularity of moral traditions in developing public norms suitable for a morally diverse society. Whether and to what extent the particular practices I have defended can be embraced by a wide range of citizens and moral communities are empirical questions that I cannot take up here. I would contend that in its emphasis on the value of noncoercive and genuine political engagement, this approach to politics should appeal to many moral communities that would find it a welcome alternative to approaches in which their deepest convictions are viewed as a hindrance to political life. But in any event, the process I have carried out is intended to exemplify the dynamics of discourse I have argued for throughout this book. It is not by claiming an uncontestable public perspective that we establish the desirability of our political ideals, but by drawing on particular normative resources and developing them as creatively and compellingly as possible, in the hope that other citizens and moral communities will find them accessible and valuable. If we are to take our moral differences seriously, we cannot take any shortcuts to the process of engagement if we are to fashion public ideals that are genuinely shared, as opposed to being merely asserted as unchallengeable truths.

Negotiating Moral Diversity: *Mozert* Revisited

With the four practices in view, I will now consider how they might be used to approach contemporary political challenges, beginning with the *Mozert v. Hawkins* case first discussed in chapter 2. How might a post-secular public ethics help us approach divisive moral conflicts such as this one, where a group of religious citizens perceives its way of life to be profoundly threatened by a public school curriculum? Is there a justifiable alternative to the unfortunate outcome that seems foreordained under political liberalism, whereby the concerns of fundamentalists and other "unreasonable" citizens are deemed unworthy of serious consideration?

If we approach the conflict from the standpoint of a politics of engagement, the paramount goal would be to avoid giving the *Mozert* families the impression that there is no room in the public schools for religiously devout students and their parents. A public school system that is perceived as siding against some students because of the nature of their most fundamental convictions will stand in the way of a politics in which all citizens are encouraged to contribute to the pursuit of public purposes. And indeed, the *Mozert* parents had hoped to keep their children in the Hawkins County public schools. Once the school board ended the opt-out program, however, many felt they had little choice but to go elsewhere (Bates 1993, 176–181). Justice Boggs, who alone of the three Appeals Court judges acknowledged the tragic nature of the conflict, perceived the outcome as sending a message of exclusion to the families.[14] By deciding to end the opt-out accommodation, the school board had ultimately rejected "any effort to reach out and take in these children and their concerns" and "specifically argued that it was better for both plaintiffs' children and other children that they not be in the public schools, despite the children's obvious desire to obtain some of the benefits of public schooling" (*Mozert v. Hawkins,* 827 F.2d 1073). While insisting on the Holt readers may have appeared to "solve" the problem, it did so only by convincing many of the families that the only schools where they would be welcomed and respected were private ones.[15]

The *Mozert* families thus found their suspicions about the limitations of the public schools confirmed. As they saw it, the schools were not *genuinely* public in the sense that they as ordinary citizens were actually encouraged to take part in helping to define their mission.[16] On those occasions when they did come before the school board, they were often treated with scorn and derision.[17] School board officials assumed that since *they* could not discern any deleterious messages in the readers, the *Mozert* parents must simply have been concocting a false sense of their dangers, in an effort to stir up trouble (Bates 1993, 38–39, 65–92). And the tenor of Justice Lively's and Kennedy's opinions suggests that the parents fared little better when they came before the Appeals Court. Lively asserted that the readers "*appear to us* to contain no religious or anti-religious messages" and implied that the plaintiffs' ultimate objective was simply to alter the content of the curriculum itself in accordance with their own convictions (*Mozert v. Hawkins,* 827 F.2d 1069, 1064–1065, my emphasis). Kennedy offered additional reasons against an accommodation, citing the school board's interest in avoiding "religious divisiveness" and speculating that to grant the plaintiffs' request for an opt-out exemption would result in "a public school system impossible to administer," due to the precedent it would set for other groups to come forward and request exemptions (1072–1073). These assertions characterize the *Mozert* parents as a group of ill-mannered and disruptive troublemakers, rather than as involved parents trying to play a role in shaping their children's education. If we are concerned with ensuring that public schools should remain places of inclusion for students and families of the widest possible range of backgrounds, these dynamics should trouble us.

Nor should we overlook the likely prospect that had they remained in the public schools, the *Mozert* children (as well as their classmates) would have been able to learn some of the skills required for coexisting with those of different convictions—a crucial lesson for citizens in a society in which this is an essential feature of social and political life. If a politics of engagement is to be fostered, it will have to involve helping young citizens to appreciate the challenges of moral diversity, a goal that will be harder to achieve if we make public schools less rather than more diverse. As Stephen Bates argues:

> If we truly believe that pluralistic public education is an essential foundation of a peaceful multicultural society, then we should do what we can to keep fundamentalists (and other religious dissidents) in the public schools. Even skipping the occasional book or class, they benefit from and contribute to the democratic mission of public education. They acquire information and attitudes that they wouldn't otherwise get. . . . By their presence, fundamentalists also give other students an object lesson in diversity. We shouldn't panic when the differentness manifests itself, as when some students leave the room or read a different book. Embracing diversity but forbidding its public expression is a crabbed form of pluralism. (1993, 316)

The outcome of this conflict thus resulted in a step back from, rather than toward, a politics of engagement. Each side could take some comfort in the fact that they would no longer have to put up with the other: the school administrators were finished with the trouble of fielding the complaints of angry parents trying to negotiate alternative reading texts for their children, and the parents could take refuge in sending their children to private Christian academies that reflected a much more insular worldview.[18] But the price for this "solution" was a great deal of social turmoil, with lingering resentment and hostility, as well as a missed opportunity for mutual learning—all of which might have been avoidable had a more generous process of engagement taken place.

To consider how such an engagement might proceed, we must first take seriously the need for opening up a genuine encounter with the *Mozert* families and refraining from caricaturing them.[19] The parents found the Holt readers objectionable, first and foremost, because they prevented them from obeying what they understood as a divine mandate to shield their children from a secularizing culture determined to reduce the question of truth to a competition among value systems. They viewed the classroom setting as an important but also potentially threatening site where their children's convictions might be jeopardized by the wrong curriculum or by teachers insufficiently sensitive to the content of their children's faith. These are not unusual concerns among religious parents of a wide range of faiths, who worry that their children's experiences in the public school setting might pose difficult challenges for the continuance of their religious upbringing.[20] The *Mozert* families should not be faulted for their concerns about sustaining their children's faith convictions or for voicing those concerns in an effort to gain an exemption from the reading curriculum. The fact that they expressed these concerns from a viewpoint that from political liberalism's perspective is based on "private" premises about the truth of the Bible is what allowed them to make clear what was at issue in the dispute. Properly understood, their lack of reticence in this regard is to be welcomed in that it allows us to sort out the competing claims at stake and to try to negotiate an amicable solution to the dilemma.

Of course, recognizing the parents' more congenial attributes should not blind us to their more problematic characteristics. Most of the parents were at best ambivalent toward the Holt readers' laudable goal of fostering students' awareness of moral and cultural diversity. For many of the parents, a belief that the mission of public schools is to reinforce "love of God and country" was deeply ingrained, and they thus regarded the readers' emphasis on other cultures and worldviews with deep suspicion (Bates 1993, 68).[21] That some of the parents offered the 1830s *McGuffey's Readers* as an alternative series for their children is illustrative: these textbooks present a very different world, one permeated with biblical narratives and both culturally and ethnically homogeneous (74, 158–159, 206–218). Nor was the parents' public agitation against the readers limited to a defensive concern with preserving their own convictions. Particularly during the early days of the conflict, some of the *Mozert* parents were rather vocal in protesting what they viewed as a concerted effort by school board officials to root out "Judeo-Christian values" from the schools. Some of the parents sought to ban the Holt readers altogether, under the rationale that they were spreading "secular humanism" (Bates 1993, 117).[22]

Macedo's criticisms of the *Mozert* parents thus have some merit. Some of their objectives did involve imposing their views on the curriculum as a whole, and there are valid questions to be raised about their children's acquisition of needed citizenship skills. Indeed, from the standpoint of my own approach it is of particular concern if the *Mozert* parents desired to shield their children not merely from the dangers of secular humanism but from encounters with diversity in general. Unless citizens become attuned to the presence of our moral differences and have at least a basic appreciation of their political and social implications, it is difficult to see how they can be expected to take part in a process of mutual engagement whereby we search creatively for norms that can be widely shared among citizens with diverse convictions.

Our goal in engaging the *Mozert* families more generously should not be to overlook the significant difficulties they present, but rather to open up possibilities for seeking a less divisive outcome and try to draw them into a politics that might gradually temper some of their suspicions toward moral diversity. Continuing the opt-out accommodation would work toward these ends, whereas the families' decision to leave behind the public schools altogether, on the grounds that they felt they had been exiled from them, clearly did not. Had school officials continued the opt-out program, it would have communicated to the parents that they remained welcome participants in the larger project of public schooling. This would not provide a guarantee that they would cease their complaints about the Holt readers and their emphasis on cultural awareness. But it would likely have helped to mitigate their discontent. In contrast, by denying the accommodation, members of the school board simply fueled the families' ongoing concerns that the schools were unreservedly hostile toward God-fearing citizens.

It is significant that the parents did not see themselves as obstructionists. As far as they were concerned, their actions were merely intended to improve the overall condition of the public schools. In trying to advance what they genuinely believed to be the best interests of their children and others as well, they displayed commendable citizenship traits and a sincere commitment to the mission of public education as they perceived it. This suggests that the parents could have been welcomed into a wider dialogue over the larger direction and purpose of the public schools, one in which they would have been able to forge cooperative relationships with other concerned parents. The merits of dialogic creativity and forbearance emerge clearly here. If other parents had tried to see past their more obvious disagreements with the *Mozert* families over curricular issues, they might have been able to draw them into more positive efforts to contribute toward the betterment of the schools in areas in which they were in agreement. This in itself would likely have done a great deal to mitigate the animosity that accumulated over the Holt readers.[23]

By attending to these dynamics of the conflict, we can see that the blame for the tragic outcome must be shared by all parties involved—by the *Mozert* families and their fellow citizens as well as the school board officials.[24] Collectively, they could have averted the chain of events that led to the court case being filed. Once the conflict advanced to that level, however, the lasting damage to the Hawkins County community had already been inflicted. And a valuable opportunity for mutual learning had been lost.

Much disagreement remains in our society over how best to go about inculcating civic virtues such as tolerance and respect for differences. This is a complex and ambiguous undertaking. And it is by no means clear that the "smorgasbord" strategy of exposing students to a multiplicity of worldviews in the hopes that they will come to see them as somehow equally valid or interchangeable is the most defensible approach. There is much to be gained, then, if we are willing to see the *Mozert* controversy and similar kinds of disputes not simply as conflicts to be resolved, but as opportunities for exploring creative solutions to pressing dilemmas surrounding diversity and its political ramifications. Judge Hull, the district court judge who first heard the *Mozert* case, raised this possibility in suggesting that alternative arrangements might have been capable of meeting the aims of the Holt readers: "This great big system, isn't it big enough, broad enough, smart enough to be able to take this in. . . . All the facilities the state has, all the educators, the minds of the world, can't we take care of thirteen children over there who don't want to go to class and want to learn some other way? . . . Surely in this broad, diverse country of ours, there's more than one way of doing things, isn't there?" (Bates 1993, 243). Had the opt-out arrangements been allowed to continue, it would have been possible to gauge their value as an alternative approach to fostering respect for diversity and as a way to negotiate disputes over educational curricula that are becoming more, rather than less, common in our day.

With the forbearance, creativity, and solicitude that are integral to a politics of engagement, we can approach vexing conflicts among moral communities more confidently, as opportunities for discovery—for finding beneficial solutions that can shed light on public problems more generally. Such an approach allows us to reaffirm the importance of mutual respect and tolerance not by transcending our moral differences but by grappling with them head-on, and in that way aiming for resolutions to our disagreements that are as equitable and inclusive as possible. We can thus hold out hope for a politics that can be less inhospitable to communities at the margins of public life and for approaches to political conflicts that are less adversarial in nature.

Moral Engagement in Public Debate: Jubilee 2000 and Abortion

In addition to those moral disagreements in which we must try to negotiate a way to coexist in the midst of our divergent convictions, we face numerous public policy conflicts in which what is at issue is the way in which we conceptualize and attempt to arrive at shared solutions for public dilemmas. In this section I explore two of these. The Jubilee 2000 movement for international debt relief originated in the mid-1990s as a biblically inspired quest to impel wealthy industrialized nations to forgive the debts of the world's poorest countries. It provides a contemporary example of how a particular religious vision, when presented in public life, can stimulate political change and reshape international responses to a pivotal public policy concern. In a different context, the current debate over abortion provides another example of how particular religious ideals can play a helpful role in envisioning new approaches to public dilemmas. Here too the promise of a politics of engagement is apparent, as two recent efforts to reconceptualize the debate demonstrate.

Jubilee 2000: Leviticus as Impetus for Debt Relief

Recent years have witnessed the growing devastation experienced by many of the world's most impoverished nations as they struggle to meet the demands of crippling foreign debt. In these countries, governmental expenditures on debt repayment dwarf the amounts devoted to health care, education, and other vital social needs. One of the most heavily indebted nations, Tanzania, spends nine times more money on debt payments than on health care. In 1997 over half of Nicaragua's revenue was devoted to debt repayment (Edgar 2000). In many cases these debts are the result of loans given to corrupt regimes in the 1960s and 70s. The burden of paying the interest on these loans must now be carried by citizens who bear no responsibility for those regimes' misdeeds (Rowden 2001).

Only since the mid-1990s have serious efforts been made to expedite reducing the debt burdens of the worst-off countries. In 1996 the leaders of the G-7 nations (United States, Japan, Germany, Britain, France, Italy, and Canada), recognizing the toll debt repayment was taking on the populations of the indebted nations, launched the Debt-Relief Initiative for Heavily Indebted Poor Countries (HIPC), a program intended to finance debt relief for the forty-one poorest third-world nations (Rowden 2001).[25] Once the initiative was approved, the question became whether the G-7 countries would follow through on their commitment to it. Early signs were not promising, as only three nations were offered debt relief assistance in the first three years (Atkinson 2000).

Beginning at around the same time as the HIPC initiative, however, a somewhat unlikely movement started that sought to put the issue of debt relief on the public stage in a way that would pressure the G-7 leaders to take the problem seriously. Originally conceived by Martin Dent, a retired British economics professor, the Jubilee 2000 campaign involved a grassroots effort among churches and other international relief organizations, such as Oxfam and Bread for the World, to apply the jubilee teachings of the Old Testament to the contemporary debt crisis (Peterson 2001). Specifically, the movement focused on the provisions of chapter 25 of Leviticus, which announced that every fiftieth year would be known as a "jubilee year." During the jubilee all debts would be forgiven, slaves would be liberated, and the members of every family given back their ancestral property, if they had either sold it to cover debts or lost it due to falling into slavery.[26] The jubilee year was to signal that the Israelites possessed the land not through their own agency but as a gift from God; it was not, therefore, theirs to dispose of as they saw fit but to be used faithfully and in harmony with God's law. The radical social and economic reordering to take place in the jubilee year was thus God's way of ensuring that justice would be periodically restored among God's people.

Pope John Paul II had placed particular emphasis on the debt-relief aspect of the jubilee year in his own teaching, beginning in 1994 with an apostolic letter, *Tertio Mellenio Adveniente*:

> If in his providence God had given the earth to humanity, that meant that he had given it to everyone. Therefore the riches of creation were to be considered as a common good of the whole of humanity. Those who possessed these goods as personal property were really only stewards, ministers charged with working in the name of God, who remains the sole owner in the full sense, since it is God's will that created goods should serve everyone in a just way. The jubilee year was meant to restore this social justice. (1994)

In proclaiming the year 2000 the "Great Jubilee," the Pope declared that the church must recommit itself to carrying out its "preferential option for the poor and the outcast," and that "in the spirit of the Book of Leviticus (25:8–12), Christians will have to raise their voice on behalf of all the poor of the world, proposing the jubilee as an appropriate time to give thought, among other things, to reducing substantially, if not canceling outright, the international debt which seriously threatens the future of many nations" (1994).

The Jubilee 2000 movement embraced this challenge and, remarkably, managed to achieve its improbable goal of transforming international debate on the merits of debt relief. It did this in two crucial ways. First, it created a groundswell of grassroots political activity, as churches in Europe and America took part in letter-writing campaigns, discussion groups, and public rallies in an effort to raise awareness about the cause. The public presence of the movement was especially pronounced in Europe. In May 1998, during the G-7 summit in Birmingham, England, over fifty thousand people gathered to proclaim the need for debt forgiveness: "As President Clinton and his counterparts met in a nearby villa, church bells chimed, reggae music echoed songs of freedom and rams' horns wailed in the tradition of the biblical jubilee. The crowd snaked for more than six miles, many grasping symbolic chains of slavery" (Peterson 2001). Similar demonstrations took place during the G-7 summit in Cologne in June 1999, at the WTO meetings in Seattle in the fall of 1999, at the IMF and World Bank meetings in Washington, DC during the spring of 2000, and later that year again when the IMF and World Bank convened in Prague in September 2000. At the Prague meeting, Jubilee

2000 workers brought a petition with 24 million signatures from 166 different countries (Hoover 2001, 16). These events helped make the debt-relief issue a public concern, one that public officials could no longer sidestep.[27] The European wing of Jubilee 2000 was so noteworthy in this regard that one journalist characterized it as "comfortably the most successful mass movement of the past 25 years" (Elliott 2000).

Just as important as the public visibility it garnered was Jubilee 2000's ability to frame the issue in a compelling moral language that lent urgency to the legislative efforts needed to make debt relief a reality. The G-7 nations had agreed in Cologne to reduce an even more sizable amount of debt for the most heavily indebted countries, but the U.S. Congress was still reluctant to work toward major reform of U.S. policy toward debtor nations. It was during debates in 1999 on various foreign-aid bills with debt relief provisions that unlikely champions defending the cause began to emerge, particularly among conservative Republicans. Probably the most noteworthy of these was Spencer Bachus, a representative of Birmingham, Alabama, and chair of the House Subcommittee on Domestic and International Monetary Policy. Bachus had long been an ardent opponent of foreign-aid efforts, but he was taken aback by the biblical claims offered by Jubilee supporters; the personal lobbying of several members of the Independent Presbyterian Church of Birmingham contributed toward changing his mind (Hoover 2001, 16). Bachus soon became a full-fledged supporter of debt relief, joining other conservative Republicans including John Kasich and Jesse Helms, both of whom were similarly persuaded by the movement's biblical appeals. During Banking Committee hearings Bachus announced that "I haven't read much by Catholics before, but I don't know how any Christian could read what the pope is saying here and not agree that we need to do something about the debt of these countries" (16). The zeal for debt relief among Bachus and other legislators was pivotal in encouraging the Clinton administration to push more actively for debt forgiveness, and it was indispensable for creating the critical mass needed in late 1999 to gain congressional approval for the necessary funding to help the U.S. fulfill its Cologne commitments (Grunwald 1999).

Although Jubilee 2000's ultimate goal—complete debt forgiveness for the forty-one most heavily indebted nations—remains on the distant horizon, it is not an overstatement to argue that the terms in which international debt relief is debated have changed dramatically in just a few years. The notion of a shared obligation to alleviate the plight of poorer nations through a renunciation of foreign debt draws on a vision of international justice substantially different from the heretofore reigning orthodoxy. As Will Hutton of the *Observer* puts it,

> Nobody argues that debt relief alone will solve world poverty. Economic development is a much more subtle process. But it is a beginning and it challenges one of the bedrocks of contemporary capitalism in a fundamental way. Private property and private finance are not independent of the world community—they are embedded in it. There cannot be a fatalistic view of the distribution of income internationally if it means unacceptable suffering. Creditors have social obligations apart from the insistence that they should eventually be repaid. (1999)

The biblical claims at the heart of Jubilee 2000 are not the only ones that can be offered on behalf of debt relief. Impoverished nations are more inclined to pursue environmentally destructive policies such as deforestation in order to raise needed money for debt repayment, and one can argue that industrialized nations have an interest in securing future markets for their exports (Edgar 2000). But these justifications, though they had been offered long before Jubilee 2000 was underway, had done very little toward making any meaningful progress in alleviating the foreign debt crisis. What Jubilee 2000 provided was a way to frame the dilemma in compelling *moral* terms, gesturing toward a generosity that could transcend national self-interest. And by relying on a biblical language to make its case, it was able to forge the kind of bipartisan legislative coalitions without which the movement's goals could never even have been seriously discussed. Jubilee 2000 thus provides an exemplary instance of how a particular religious vision can be used creatively and powerfully to challenge and reformulate political ideals.

Abortion: The Search for Alternative Approaches to a Vexing Debate

Determining public policy on abortion has proven to be one of the most elusive challenges facing American society. It has become the paradigmatic example of a moral conflict over the good, insofar as citizens' disagreements on abortion seem to be deeply rooted in their more fundamental differences over the purposes of life itself. It is not surprising therefore that many social theorists, political liberals among them, view religious and other comprehensive ideals as obstacles in the way of an acceptable resolution to the abortion debate. For if we inject these ideals into our collective deliberations, will we not be more likely to harden the lines of opposition, as we come to see our opponents not merely as disagreeing with us about a particular public policy issue, but as taking the wrong side in a struggle between good and evil?

Two recent arguments, Elizabeth Mensch and Alan Freeman's *The Politics of Virtue* (1995) and Kathy Rudy's *Beyond Pro-Life and Pro-Choice* (1996), seek in different ways to challenge the conventional wisdom on abortion and public discourse. Both books insist that an adequate response to abortion can *only* be obtained by engaging the substance of the moral traditions that inform Americans' views on the matter. The authors argue convincingly that it is only by taking these resources seriously that we can we arrive at a sound understanding of each other's perspectives and approach possible resolutions to the abortion debate that can avoid adversarial or coercive political strategies.

As Mensch and Freeman explain, the Supreme Court's *Roe v. Wade* decision in 1973 was widely perceived by its defenders as a way to circumvent political conflict over abortion. It was thought that by removing the debate from the legislative arena, it would thereby be drained of much of its divisiveness. But of course that did not happen. On Mensch and Freeman's reading, this is because the *Roe* decision preempted the vibrant moral debate that was taking place among theologians and ethicists during the 1960s and early 70s and that seemed to offer hope that a shared view on the ethics of abortion could perhaps become a reality. By rendering this dialogue "abruptly irrelevant for lawmaking purposes," *Roe* ended up polarizing and rigidifying the competing positions on abortion.

> People who were deeply troubled by the moral/religious implications of an absolute right to abortion—even throughout the second trimester of pregnancy—became hardened absolutists in their opposition to all abortion; any compromise became more, not less, unthinkable. Moreover, so long as *Roe* seemed securely in place, that absolutism too easily took on the character of moral highground at no political cost, with the fanciful Republican call, for example, for a "human life

> amendment" to the Constitution. . . . The pro-choice side, meanwhile, could too easily employ a close-out "rights" and "choice" rhetoric in an aggressive refusal to engage in moral discourse altogether. The result was an ever-deepening cultural divide. (1995, 4)

Mensch and Freeman argue that had the debate over abortion been allowed to continue to inform deliberations in the various state legislatures, it is conceivable that such a process "might have resolved the abortion issue through compromise more successfully than did the Court, even though many legislative compromises would not have been perfect from either the pro-life or pro-choice perspective" (128). Their speculation here is predicated on their contention that, by engaging the normative resources of Americans' religious traditions, a responsible discourse on abortion can illuminate the issues at stake in a much clearer fashion, by avoiding the opacity inherent in the "pro-choice" and "pro-life" markers. A good portion of their argument is dedicated to exploring the ideas of the Catholic natural law tradition and the Protestant theologians Karl Barth and Dietrich Bonhoeffer, in an effort to show that both of these theological strands are able to conceptualize abortion and its ethical ramifications in distinctive and valuable ways and are thus well-suited for informing public debate on the matter.

For Mensch and Freeman, the crucial factor that must be confronted in any discussion of abortion is that it is an issue of life and death—and thus to deny the perspective of religious traditions in grappling with it is to deny ourselves the ability to articulate fully what is involved in the act of abortion.

> To abort a fetus is to kill, to prevent the realization of a human life. But to say that much is not to answer the moral question involved. . . . That we choose to kill does not make it wrong on that score alone; but we surely need a vocabulary for talking about life-and-death issues in moral terms that underscore the seriousness of any choice for death. Our religious traditions have served for many hundreds of years to offer hope in the face of despair, to offer life in the face of inevitable suffering and death. We discard those traditions at our peril. (157)

Mensch and Freeman thus find Judith Thompson's famous thought-experiment on abortion, in which a woman has been involuntarily assigned to keeping an accomplished violinist alive by being plugged into a life support system for nine months, to be distortive and misleading. Thompson's hypothetical, which is intended to serve as a "close-out argument for choice," only shifts the balance in that direction by virtue of being "framed so starkly as a question of rights alone." Once other dynamics are taken into account, such as questions of virtue or duty, the scenario becomes significantly more complicated but also at the same time a closer approximation of the social reality in which the decision to abort or carry a pregnancy to term must be made (130–131).

Leaving religious traditions out of public debate on abortion becomes especially problematic when we consider that most Americans do in fact identify with a particular religious tradition and consider the issue of abortion with their religious convictions in view. A secular rationale of individual autonomous choice, while "undeniably empowering in its affirmation of the capacity of women to take control of their own lives," is nevertheless a vision that runs "counter to the religious traditions of most American women" (132). A discourse on abortion that wrestles with the contribution of theological traditions is thus able to "speak to" Americans in a way that secularized discussions cannot (109). If we are to hope for an approach to abortion that is both intelligible to and genuinely embraced by citizens, this is a crucial consideration to keep in view.

While Mensch and Freeman ultimately seek a compromise position on abortion, there is of course no guarantee that such a result would follow from a more expansive public debate.[28] Nor need we take the view that conscientious citizens must favor a compromise position in order to be welcomed participants in dialogue on this issue. Citizens who hold unswervingly to their stance on abortion reflect the seriousness of the issue, and the desire to pursue compromise at any price on such a weighty matter might itself signal a facile neglect of the significance of what is at stake. What taking our religious traditions seriously offers us, ultimately, is a much more substantive and genuine appraisal of the normative resources at our disposal, and a richer vocabulary with which to explore solutions to the dilemma of abortion. These are valuable goods in and of themselves, and to the extent they characterize our deliberations, we stand a better chance of negotiating the challenges of abortion both patiently and thoughtfully.

If what Mensch and Freeman demonstrate is the value of a sincere engagement over abortion, Kathy Rudy's contribution is her emphasis on the disciplined discourse that moral communities can offer to the debate. Rudy shares Mensch and Freeman's disapproval of adversarial pro-choice/pro-life abortion rhetoric, but she is much more wary of attempts to forge legislative compromises as a response to the dilemma. These, she finds, deny the way in which "the value of fetal life is constructed . . . community by community" (1996, 139). That is, what is at stake in the act of abortion is irreducibly conditioned by the normative understandings and interpretive frameworks that characterize the life of different moral communities: "Abortions only exist in the lives of concrete people in differing cultural locations. These locations, and the various political, religious, and ethical convictions which characterize and accompany them, construct different meanings and definitions for the term abortion. In these often competing locations, people do not at all see the same act when viewing an "abortion"; rather they see . . . different acts, dependent of course, on who they are and where they are located" (xiii). Approaches to abortion that privilege a legislative strategy are to some degree an attempt to circumvent this reality, by assuming that the boundaries separating moral communities are porous or nonexistent. What is needed, instead, is a process of engagement whereby we seek first and foremost to persuade others of the merits of our particular community's practices with regard to abortion. Only in this way can we be sure to avoid political strategies that will likely have the coercive effect of applying a singular approach to abortion that is insensitive to the different moral frameworks with which abortion is conceptualized and understood (142–149).

Rather than seeking first and foremost to legislate abortion policy, Rudy argues, each moral community should instead "spend more time and money . . . on making its world more plausible, internally coherent, and attractive" (143). She suggests that if "Christians see the world as a place where children ought to be welcomed, believers should work to make adoption services more humane and available; they should strive to make single mothers with unwanted pregnancies feel accepted and honored; they should live and act in ways that would allow pregnant women to feel positively about surrendering their babies to a Christian community." Similarly, those approaching abortion from a feminist perspective should focus their efforts on resisting "the things that make childrearing the exclusive burden of women and working toward ways in which raising children receives the support of the wider community," rather than pursuing a narrowly legal agenda that sees abortion solely as a rights-based issue (143). By enacting holistic visions of the good, moral communities have an opportunity to embody the values they espouse. And when they take this responsibility seriously, they can make their convictions publicly relevant without having to engage in coercive political tactics that will be more likely to polarize debate.

Although their approaches differ in important respects, both Mensch and Freeman and Rudy gesture beyond the current debate over abortion and envision ways in which particular moral communities can develop and offer their convictions on abortion with integrity and discipline. Neither approach views coercive political strategies favorably; even though Mensch and Freeman remain more hopeful than Rudy about the possibility (and desirability) of obtaining legislative compromises on abortion, they stress that

> when churches (and/or other "mediating structures") function with full vigor, providing the community with moral guidance, civil law will be required only as a last resort, to which, ideally, one need have recourse only rarely. In such a setting it would be a matter of relative indifference whether, for example, penal law addresses a question like abortion. Churches themselves, through their own freely chosen disciplines and in diverse ways, would uphold an underlying cultural respect for life, even while providing necessary contextual judgments in pastoral counseling, as well as providing a community of help and support for those who need it. That, of course, would be the model of churches as ideally functioning mediating structures, which not only lessens the need for a state-coerced morality, but also insures that the minimal morality embodied in the law will be widely shared and therefore relatively uncontroversial. (1995, 141)

To the extent that moral communities are engaging in the hard work of cultivating their distinctive practices and way of life, their energies can be channeled more productively and less divisively than if they see legislative politics as the principal venue for negotiating our moral differences.

With a sensitivity to the differences separating moral communities and a willingness to engage those differences patiently and diligently, we are best prepared for grappling collectively with those public policy challenges, such as abortion, that go to the heart of our deepest moral convictions. And as Mensch and Freeman note, the realm of public policy choices that touch on moral fundamentals is increasing: recent debates over animal rights and the environment similarly implicate our broader convictions about the purposes of life and our role as stewards of it (154). Arriving at compelling ways to conceptualize these debates and respond to their ethical challenges will require the imaginative solutions our diverse moral communities can provide. Remaining open to these visions and encouraging their presentation in public life thus becomes one of our paramount public responsibilities as citizens.

Preparing Ourselves for the Challenges of Moral Diversity

As American society becomes increasingly diverse and the cultural and religious differences separating us become more pronounced, finding ways to accommodate those differences while seeking shared political ideals must become one of our central political tasks. As I have argued, political liberalism's recognition of this need is one of its strongest features. Yet in the end, insofar as this approach to political life promises us a politics without significant moral disagreement or contestation, its conception of citizenship is inadequate for sustaining a vision of political life in which these dynamics are likely to be unavoidable. It is both unrealistic and undesirable to expect that the range of moral communities that cover the American landscape should withdraw their ideals of the good in the process of defining and instantiating public purposes. In fact, it is essential that these ideals be forwarded in public life, so that we might remain open to possibilities of political discovery, and seek ways to render our polity more hospitable to the variety of moral communities that inhabit it.

In another sense, too, it becomes crucial that we refrain from following political liberalism's approach of bracketing our fundamental convictions from the public sphere. For as the civil rights struggle demonstrates so vividly, our deepest convictions sustain our efforts to take part in the hard work and endurance required to attempt political change; this demands that our entire selves be a part of that process. Political liberals are willing to recognize the role our comprehensive convictions play in strengthening our adherence to political norms and in motivating our political activity. Yet the inordinate emphasis they place on quarantining the potentially harmful effects of these convictions in public life, when applied to the challenges of citizenship, can only work to sap the energy and imagination required for the most arduous political struggles. Citizens who must constantly scrutinize their political activity in order to satisfy the demands of the reasonable will be less inclined to draw from the well of particular moral resources that, as we have seen, give meaning to and the courage to persist in the difficult political challenges that we confront.

By shifting our approach to public life in the direction of sincerity and discipline, we make possible a politics that invites our entire selves and our traditions into public life, with the awareness that what matters most in this context is our desire to work with other citizens in a spirit of integrity and mutuality—rather than our ability to satisfy predetermined criteria of reasonable citizenship. And with the practices of creativity and forbearance, we are able to endure in the struggle to craft a mutually acceptable basis for public life in the midst of our divergent fundamental views. We thus retain the goals of achieving mutual respect and civic concord; indeed, these goals are reaffirmed all the more, because they are pursued honestly by taking our differences seriously and avoiding the false commonalities that cannot themselves successfully bring an end to moral conflict. What we must be committed to, in the end, is the hard work and courage needed for engaging our moral differences rather than avoiding them. We will not thereby arrive at a politics devoid of moral disagreements. But we will be better prepared for coming to terms with them when they arise.

Notes

Introduction

1. In addition to Rawls 1985, 1996, and 1997, recent arguments that have focused specifically on political liberalism's response to religious diversity include Charney 1998; Dombrowski 2001; Macedo 1995, 1996, 2000; Tomasi 2001; Weithman 1994; and Wenar 1995.

2. Gray draws especially from Isaiah Berlin's conception of value pluralism in articulating his version of modus vivendi liberalism. In addition to Gray 2000, see the essays in Gray 1993.

3. In this regard, see also the arguments by Mouffe 1993 and Honig 1993.

4. Tomasi argues that political liberalism should commit itself to addressing citizens' concerns about liberalism's spillover effects and should design institutional remedies to alleviate them, but must make sure that it does so while respecting "the architecture of public reason" (2001, 42). As I argue in chapters 2 and 3, however, the architecture of public reason in fact makes this kind of solicitude impossible.

5. For instance, Rawls 1996 discusses the religious dimensions of the political activity of the abolitionist and civil rights movements (li–lii, 247–252); Rawls 1997 focuses further on religion's relationship to public reason, including specific discussion of the Catholic Church's arguments against abortion and the contentious debate over religious liberty in eighteenth-century America (798–799, 794–795); Macedo 2000 addresses Christian fundamentalism and the evolution of American Catholicism in the context of public education.

6. Macedo 1995, 1996, 2000 most heavily reflects this impulse, although as I will argue in chapter 3, a reliance upon a narrative of religious conflict as a justification for political liberalism is also prominent in Rawls's thought.

7. Rawls expressly denies the idea that political liberalism relies upon "secular reason" as a way to regulate the public sphere; according to Rawls, this would involve "reasoning in terms of comprehensive nonreligious doctrines," which would be as inappropriate as reasoning on the basis of particular religious doctrines or worldviews (1997, 775).

8. For a nuanced discussion of the variegated dynamics of American liberalism and how multiple moral sources (including religion) influenced its development, see Kloppenberg 1998: "Viewed historically, the boundaries between religious, ethical, and political ideals, and those between liberal, republican, socialist, and social democratic ideas, have proved considerably more permeable in practice than some contemporary political theorists might suppose" (15).

9. Milbank offers an impressive account of the way in which philosophers from Hobbes to Derrida have depended crucially in their thinking on a narrative of conflict as being ontologically fundamental. Milbank argues that this narrative obscures other ways of narrating the social, and he articulates as an alternative an Augustinian rendering of the social in which peace is ontologically prior to conflict. This in turn opens up a different vision of the possibilities of politics, in which charity and forgiveness, and a reconciliation of virtue with difference, are considered the proper pursuits of a rightly ordered political community (1990, 423).

10. Particularly noteworthy examples are Hauerwas 1981 and Yoder 2001.

11. Again, as Kloppenberg argues: "Most of our predecessors drew on multiple traditions to balance competing values in a genuinely conflict-ridden polity marked by disagreements over policy rooted in genuine differences of conviction. Those differences persist in the compromises that have been worked out because of the shared commitment to democratic procedures. From the Constitution and the Bill of Rights onward, we Americans have committed ourselves to the provisionality of our principles as well as our policies" (1998, 18–19).

12. See also Neal, who holds that "the spirit of liberalism itself counsels a greater willingness to risk contact, contagion and common dialogue with nonliberal modes of life than is countenanced by the idea of the overlapping consensus" (1997, 11).

CHAPTER 1
Managing Moral Diversity in Rawls's *Political Liberalism*

1. In *Political Liberalism* Rawls denies that the evolution of his thought was prompted by "criticisms raised by communitarians and others" (1996, xix). It is certainly plausible, however, that these changes were influenced at least to some degree by Michael Sandel's forceful charge in *Liberalism and the Limits of Justice* that Rawls's project relied upon a metaphysical Kantianism to support its view of the autonomous self (1982). Rawls does refer directly to an article by William

Galston that argues that Rawls's account of moral agency in his earlier writings was essentially perfectionist (1982, 625). Rawls does not challenge Galston's assessment. See Rawls 1996, 191 and 198.

2. It is not coincidental that many analyses of the relationship between liberalism and religion center on communities such as the Amish or Christian fundamentalists. These are the "hard cases" for liberalism, much more so than mainstream religious denominations that have already made their peace with liberal modernity.

3. Rawls characterizes a moral doctrine as "general" if it "applies to a wide range of subjects, and in the limit to all subjects universally." A moral doctrine is "comprehensive" when it "includes conceptions of what is of value in human life, and ideals of personal character, as well as ideals of friendship and of familial and associational relationships, and much else that is to inform our conduct, and in the limit to our life as a whole. A conception is fully comprehensive if it covers all recognized values and virtues within one rather precisely articulated system; whereas a conception is only partially comprehensive when it comprises a number of, but by no means all, nonpolitical values and virtues and is rather loosely articulated." As Rawls goes on to explain, "many religious and philosophical doctrines aspire to be both general and comprehensive" (1996, 13).

4. In a similar vein, Charles Larmore argues that political liberalism requires a "minimal moral conception" that is "less comprehensive than the views of the good life about which reasonable people disagree" (1990, 341).

5. Evan Charney has explored some of these difficulties, noting that Rawls's characterization presupposes far too much agreement and consensus within religious (and for that matter, philosophical) traditions, and that the paradigm shifts that occur in all fields of knowledge would seem to challenge the notion that a "slow evolution" of development should be considered an indispensable feature of comprehensive doctrines (1998, 105–106).

6. This is a pivotal presupposition for Rawls, who, as noted earlier, is intent on refuting the notion that a metaphysical conception of the self undergirds his project.

7. John Tomasi refers to this process as the "ethic of individuation," as it concerns how citizens learn to negotiate the "interface" between the public and nonpublic aspects of their personal identity (2001, 79–85).

8. As Rawls puts it, "for the purposes of public life, Saul of Tarsus and St. Paul the Apostle are the same person. Conversion is irrelevant to our public, or institutional, identity" (1996, 32).

9. This narrative can be interpreted in different ways. Jeffrey Stout echoes the familiar view of Babel as a source of linguistic strangeness and confusion (1988). John Howard Yoder, on the other hand, sees Babel as God's beneficent proliferation of languages, representing opportunities for different communities speaking different languages to learn from one another (1996b).

10. This is not to say that Rawls's account of the intractability of moral diversity is untenable. Indeed, in my view it is a plausible empirical description of the kinds of disagreements citizens are likely to have over moral questions. What is at issue here is whether accepting a particular conceptualization of moral diversity should be viewed as a prerequisite for being considered a reasonable citizen. Because it does require this, Rawls's project will inevitably have an invidious impact on a number of currently widely accepted worldviews. To give one example, in Rawls 1985, 248, he notes that the assumption that "there are many conflicting and incommensurable conceptions of the good, each compatible with the full rationality of human persons," is at odds with the "Christian tradition as represented by Augustine and Aquinas."

11. What Rawls's account renders unreasonable, in other words, are views that would hold that "we cannot, as separate selves, say what our good is, because we have no sense of self in the absence of the good we share, that good being the intrinsic value of the relation between us" (1997, 39). If such a thick, community-constituted conception of the good is to be rendered consistent with Rawls's framework, it must be translated into liberal meta-theory: we as separate selves are said to *converge* in our allegiance to the same, independently held, comprehensive doctrine. But as Neal notes, this is precisely the view of moral personality that many moral traditions would resist; re-describing their self-understandings in this language could only result in distorting them (39–44).

CHAPTER 2
Religious Freedom within Political Liberalism?

1. Two especially helpful studies of the muddled state of religion clause scholarship and jurisprudence are Gedicks 1995 and Smith 1995.

2. Fish claims that despite the exploding volume of literature on the subject, "the discussion of this vexed issue has not advanced one millimeter" beyond Locke's framework in *A Letter Concerning Toleration* (1999, 163).

3. As Fish puts it:

> If it were truly possible to say "personal" and mean by it a realm whose boundaries were agreed on by everyone, the line between the personal and the public would draw itself, and merely personal confrontations would be avoided because they would instantly be distinguishable from principled, higher order confrontations. Settling the just bounds between church and state—between the private and the public (if you accept the distinction, and the hard question, remember, is what you do with those who don't)—would be a snap if the census of the two realms were already complete and authenticated; mutual respect would be a breeze (and cost-free) if everyone's "merely" personal moralities were safely quarantined in the private sector

> and you knew that what you were respecting wasn't going to inconvenience you in any serious way. (1999, 207)

4. For a vigorous challenge to Fish's antifoundationalist position, see Owen 2001. Owen argues that liberalism *must* be built upon a rationalism capable of articulating a convincing principle of religious freedom; if it is not, "the separation of church and state is in danger of becoming incoherent and disestablishment of becoming meaningless" (2).

5. Smith explains the theoretical "conundrum" we are confronting here: "The function of a theory of religious freedom is to mediate among a variety of competing religious and secular positions and interests, or to explain how government ought to deal with these competing positions and interests. To perform that function, however, the theory will tacitly but inevitably privilege, or prefer in advance, one of those positions while rejecting or discounting others" (1995, 63).

6. Paul Vitz, a New York University psychology professor who had extensively studied the treatment of religion in various textbook series, supported the plaintiffs' contentions about the neglect and disparagement of Christianity vis-à-vis the other religions presented in the readers. Vitz testified for the plaintiffs at trial. See in particular Bates 1993, 206–210.

7. Fish points out that this claim relies upon presuppositions that are crucial to a liberal psychology of education, which must explain how education can take place without raising the specter of coercive inculcation: "In that psychology, the mind remains unaffected by the ideas and doctrines that pass before it, and its job is to weigh and assess those doctrines from a position distanced from and independent of any one of them" (1999, 197). This is a contestable view, and not at all a self-evident one. For instance, Christian traditions that regard original sin as fundamental to human existence believe that the mind is susceptible to the competing influences (good or bad) that would contend for its allegiance, and thus would view with suspicion an approach to education that involves students sorting through conflicting positions with an eye toward "making up their own mind" about them (197–198).

8. As Fish explains, for the *Mozert* families the issue of indoctrination emerges "not at the level of urging this or that belief but at the more subliminal level at which what is urged is that encountering as many ideas as possible and giving each of them a run for its money is an absolutely good thing. What the children are being indoctrinated in is distrust of any belief that has not been arrived at by the exercise of their unaided reason as it surveys all the alternatives before choosing one freely with no guidance from any external authority" (1999, 198).

9. Taking note of this, Amy Gutmann argues that when we consider the implications of civic education from both the political liberal and the comprehensive liberal standpoints, we find them taking similar positions on issues of personal autonomy, tolerance, and critical thinking. However, she sees this not as a failure on political liberalism's part but rather as an unavoidable consequence of

a rigorous conception of citizenship: "It is probably impossible to teach children the skills and virtues of democratic citizenship in a diverse society without at the same time teaching them many of the virtues and skills of individuality or autonomy" (Gutmann 1995, 563).

10. Cf. Rawls 1997, 766–767, where Rawls makes it clear that political liberalism "does not engage" those whose comprehensive doctrines are at odds with political liberalism's view of justice. See also 805–806, where Rawls classifies "fundamentalist religious doctrines" as categorically incompatible with political liberalism.

11. The military exemptions given to Quakers and Mennonites would seem to constitute a paradigmatic case of public purposes narrowly understood (that is, preserving the liberal state) giving way to religious freedom. Macedo acknowledges the difficulty here, contending that while "as a public matter we believe the Quaker position on military service to be deeply mistaken," exemptions are granted to them because "the pacifism of the Quakers presents us with an intense version of some of our own values" (namely, "conscientious commitment to principle" and the reminder that "governments are apt to commit serious wrongs in our name") (2000, 209). As Macedo sees it, then, the Quakers' claim is not honored on its own merits; it is only because their appeal happens to resonate with other ostensibly more "political" values that it is given a solicitous hearing.

12. This is not to deny the fact that the honoring of these commitments will typically be conditioned by other considerations of a more pragmatic nature, for example, whether the group requesting an accommodation is an insular minority or a larger segment of the population. In *Wisconsin v. Yoder*, for instance, the case that exempted the Amish from a state requirement to educate their children beyond the eighth grade, the justices explicitly took into account the fact that the Amish were a small sub-community that had wished to remain largely separated from the rest of society. The possibility that the Amish exemption would disrupt or threaten the public educational process thus seemed minimal. These kinds of pragmatic considerations notwithstanding, the fact remains that for an exemption to be granted at all requires the acknowledgment of the importance of the free exercise of religion, a principle that must be, at the very least, considered a public good and thus balanced alongside other public purposes in order for it to be given its proper weight. My contention is that political liberalism cannot countenance such an approach, because it suggests the insufficiency of secular political values to resolve our most pressing moral conflicts.

13. On this point, see also the analysis of Philip Hamburger, who contends that the development of the American idea of separation of church and state cannot be accurately captured if it is "understood simply as the product of great men" or merely as an "institutional development." Rather, it must be viewed as in large part a product of "cultural and social contexts" that gave meaning to and helped propel the acceptance of that idea (2002, 17).

14. For my discussion of the early American struggles over religious liberty, I have relied extensively on both Miller 1986 and Curry 1986. Murphy 2001 offers a rich and detailed discussion of the evolution of religious toleration within seventeenth-century England as well as in the American colonies.

15. These "experiments" were not universally hailed as beneficial or as demonstrating the value of broad religious freedom, however. Rhode Island in particular was often referenced by those favoring establishment as having gone too far in its tolerance of dissenters. See Curry 1986, 91, and McConnell 1990, 1425–1427.

16. As William Miller explains, Madison's familiarity with the plight of persecuted Baptists, who were routinely horsewhipped and jailed until the time of the Revolution, was instrumental in the development of his convictions concerning religious freedom (1986, 3–7, 95–96).

17. While Jefferson's perspective was an important one in eighteenth- and nineteenth-century debates over religious liberty, the current popular estimation of Jefferson's genius in advocating church-state separation has probably exceeded its actual influence in shaping the debates in question. Philip Hamburger notes that Jefferson's now-famous letter to the Danbury Baptist Association in 1802, in which he first argued that the First Amendment constructed "a wall of separation between Church & State," had a relatively minimal impact on early nineteenth-century religious liberty debate (2002, 144–189). Jefferson's idea of a more radical separation conflicted with most Americans' assumptions that religion could exert a helpful influence on the political realm. Hamburger argues that the praise accorded to Jefferson's "wall" formulation is of relatively recent origin and that, measured culturally and politically, anti-Catholicism in fact played a much greater role in furthering Americans' embrace of the "separation of church and state" concept. Many nineteenth- and twentieth-century Americans found the idea of church-state separation a desirable strategy for limiting the political power of the "papists," who were seen as representing a unique threat to American democracy (191–251). Cf. the argument of Mark DeWolfe Howe, who faults an overreliance on Jefferson's metaphor among justices and academic elites for obscuring the crucial role faith communities played in infusing the First Amendment with religious significance (1965).

18. This is by no means to suggest that there was a consensus with respect to how these provisions were understood or implemented. On this point, see Smith 1995, 39–41.

19. As John Howard Yoder has observed, it is easy to overlook the many areas in which colonial legislative and administrative bodies extended free-exercise exemptions as a matter of course, since such policies were often implemented without fanfare or controversy (1989).

20. *Reynolds v. U.S.* (1879), the famous Mormon polygamy case. The 1940 case was *Cantwell v. Connecticut,* the first of many free-exercise cases involving Jehovah's Witnesses.

21. See Murphy 2001, 287: "Reifying 'toleration' into a discrete set of conditions that, once met, ends political debate fails to do justice to the ongoing quest for liberty of conscience in its many forms and risks ossifying an important political and philosophical principle."

22. The most notable example is *United States v. Seeger,* 380 U.S. 163 (1965).

23. It is also worth noting, of course, that many of the most pivotal cases have been initiated by members of religious communities *least* able to couch their claims in the "political values" of political liberalism.

24. Such an awareness would seem to offer better preparation for the kind of incremental, prudential approach Steven Smith gestures toward when he argues that "in a pluralistic community exhibiting a considerable degree of religious and secular diversity, civil peace and inclusiveness can be achieved only imperfectly and only through compromise, cultivated tolerance, mutual forbearances, and strategic silences" (1995, 117).

CHAPTER 3
The Secularity of Liberal Public Reason

1. Rawls 1997 contains an even stronger statement: In a well-ordered society "citizens realize that they cannot reach agreement *or even approach mutual understanding* on the basis of their irreconcilable comprehensive doctrines" (766, my emphasis).

2. See also Audi 1989; Audi and Wolterstorff 1997. Audi goes considerably further than most liberal theorists by insisting that citizens do not merely have a responsibility to use secular forms of argument in their public activity; even their motivations supporting particular positions should have a secular rationale (working alone or in harmony with other convictions, including religious ones). On Audi's conception of public reason, "one has a (prima facie) obligation to abstain from advocacy or support of a law or public policy that restricts human conduct, unless one is sufficiently *motivated* by (normatively) adequate secular reason, where sufficiency of motivation here implies that some set of secular reasons is motivationally sufficient, roughly in the sense that (a) this set of reasons explains one's action and (b) one would act on it even if, other things remaining equal, one's other reasons were eliminated" (Audi and Wolterstorff 1997, 28–29, emphasis in original).

3. For examples of this critique, see Perry 1991, 14–15; Audi and Wolterstorff 1997, 104–105. As will be discussed later in this book, political liberals find problematic not only religious arguments advanced in public debate but comprehensive secular ones as well (e.g., where a particular controversial norm, such as radical individualism, is set forth as grounds for a particular policy option). But

as Wolterstorff points out, this qualification doesn't entirely level the playing field. "Much if not most of the time we will be able to spot religious reasons from a mile away: references to God, to Jesus Christ, to the Torah, to the Christian Bible, to the Koran, are unmistakably religious. Typically, however, comprehensive secular perspectives will go undetected. How am I to tell whether the utilitarianism or the nationalism of the person who argues his case along utilitarian or nationalist lines is or is not part of his comprehensive perspective?" (Audi and Wolterstorff 1997, 105).

4. Rawls explains these transitions in his thinking in the expanded introduction to the paperback edition of *Political Liberalism* (1996). The fullest account of the "wide view" of public reason can be found in Rawls 1997.

5. Although Macedo is more than willing to take sides against unreasonable religious views, he seems determined to portray political liberalism as a modest, inclusive framework that makes few demands on reasonable religious citizens: "The political liberal offers a bargain to moderates in all comprehensive camps, whether fundamentalist Protestant or autonomy-pursuing liberal: let's put aside our wider convictions when designing commonly authoritative political institutions and focus on principles and aims that pass the tests of public reason. These concessions will not satisfy everyone, but they are significant" (1995, 482).

6. As examples of these institutions, which Hollenbach identifies as "the primary bearers of cultural meaning and value," he mentions "universities, religious communities, the world of the arts, and serious journalism." See Rawls 1997, 768 (citing Hollenbach 1994).

7. In "The Idea of Public Reason Revisited," Rawls adds another layer to this framework: the "nonpublic political culture," which includes "newspapers, reviews and magazines, TV and radio, and much else," and which "mediates" between the public political forum and the background culture. Rawls mentions the nonpublic political culture only in passing, so it is difficult to draw firm conclusions about its status in his larger framework, but he seems to view it as being closer in nature to the background culture than the political forum, since it is independent of the constraints of public reason (1997, 768 n13).

8. Thus voting becomes the paradigmatic activity in which all citizens have the opportunity to exercise public reason (Rawls 1996, 219–220). Citizens "are to think of themselves *as if* they were legislators and ask themselves what statutes, supported by what reasons satisfying the criterion of reciprocity, they would think it most reasonable to enact." They can then "repudiate government officials and candidates for public office who violate public reason" (Rawls 1997, 769, emphasis in original).

9. Rawls acknowledges the ambiguity of the "due course" requirement: "the details about how to satisfy this proviso must be worked out in practice and cannot feasibly be governed by a clear family of rules given in advance" (1997, 784).

10. Rawls is addressing in particular the explicitly religious arguments made by the abolitionists and civil rights activists during their respective struggles against slavery and segregation.

11. Similarly, Charles Larmore stresses that liberalism is fundamentally a "political doctrine," not a "philosophy of man" (1987, 25).

12. For another formulation, see Rawls 1997, in which political values include "those mentioned in the preamble to the United States Constitution: a more perfect union, justice, domestic tranquility, the common defense, the general welfare, and the blessings of liberty for ourselves and our posterity. These include under them other values: so, for example, under justice we also have equal basic liberties, equality of opportunity, ideals concerning the distribution of income and taxation, and much else" (776).

13. Insofar as the bishops are not public officials, they would not be formally included within Rawls's category of the public political forum (1997, 767).

14. In his analysis of the National Conference's *Economic Justice for All,* Jeremy Waldron observes the multifaceted nature of the bishops' address. "It might be thought that the Pastoral Letter is intended only to be used by Catholics in their conversations with other Catholics, but that is not the case. The bishops evidently expect the teaching and arguments of the document to be deployed by Catholics as they participate in the political life of the nation, alongside fellow citizens of other denominations. As we have seen, Catholics are called on to use the resources of their faith as they vote, deliberate, and interact with others in their capacity as legislators and officials if they happen to hold positions of special power, and certainly in their capacity as participants in the democratic political system" (1993, 819–820).

15. As Waldron points out, in *Economic Justice for All* the bishops note that they are writing "first of all, to provide guidance for members of our own Church as they seek to form their consciences about economic matters," but they go on to add that they "seek the cooperation and support of those who do not share our faith or tradition. The common bond of humanity that links all persons is the source of our belief that the country can attain a renewed public moral vision" (1993, 826 [citing National Conference of Catholic Bishops 1986, 13–14]).

16. As noted earlier, Rawls makes a brief reference to the "nonpublic political culture" that comprises various forms of media, but says nothing specific about the way in which that realm "mediates" between the public political forum and the background culture (1997, 768 n13). This seems a crucial omission. If in fact the nonpublic political culture is not simply an extension of the background culture, this would suggest that it bears at least some responsibility in shepherding public discourse—perhaps by orienting the discourse taking place in the background culture toward political values that could be rendered consistent with the overlapping consensus. Or conversely, the nonpublic political culture could serve as a

way of bringing to light new political concerns and questions that could alter the shape of the overlapping consensus in some significant way. Either of these possibilities would temper the rigidity of the separation between the two realms that otherwise characterizes Rawls's thought. But again, this is merely speculation, as Rawls does not discuss the issue at any greater length.

17. Or as he puts it elsewhere: "I propose that in public reason comprehensive doctrines of truth or right *be replaced by* an idea of the politically reasonable addressed to citizens as citizens" (1997, 766, my emphasis).

18. For a concise history of the various interventions of religious communities in American politics from the pre-Founding era to the early 1980s, see Reichley 1985.

19. I will be drawing primarily on Greenawalt 1988; Greenawalt 1995 is largely consistent with the arguments advanced in the earlier book.

20. Note that this differs markedly from the approach Rawls urges when public reason fails to provide a clear resolution to political disagreements: "if, when stand-offs occur, citizens simply invoke grounding reasons of their comprehensive views, the principle of reciprocity is violated. From the point of view of public reason, citizens must vote for the ordering of political values they sincerely think the most reasonable. Otherwise they fail to exercise political power in ways that satisfy the criterion of reciprocity" (1997, 797).

21. Greenawalt does allow certain exceptions to this general principle. He suggests, for example, that religious leaders may be justified in publicly advocating particular policy positions, and he notes that different forms of public argument may be appropriate depending upon the context in which they are offered (on the basis of a distinction similar to political liberalism's civil society/political domain paradigm). See Greenawalt 1988, 217–220.

22. Namely, that no religion can justifiably threaten civic peace on the basis of its own interpretation of social order. Even if such an assertion is made from the standpoint of "the political" without an explicit claim regarding the truth of any particular religious view, it seems hard to deny that to any believer convinced that his or her religious tradition cannot defend the good of civic peace as ultimate, this could only be construed as a denial of that religion's claim to truth.

23. In "The Idea of Public Reason Revisited," Rawls qualifies his position on abortion, by insisting that his claim in *Political Liberalism* regarding the unreasonableness of prohibiting first-trimester abortions was merely his "opinion" (1997, 798 n80). This does not affect the point I am making here, however: Rawls's stance on abortion is effectively determined by the relative weight he assigns to the political values he relies upon to decide the issue, and this weighing process would itself seem inevitably conditioned by Rawls's own comprehensive convictions.

24. In addition to Rawls, thinkers who see as paradigmatic liberalism's quest to secure the stability of the civil realm in the face of religious conflict include

Larmore 1987; Moon 1993; Macedo 2000. Rawls notes his own indebtedness in this regard to Judith Shklar's well-known "liberalism of fear" concept (Rawls 1996, xxvi, 374). For Shklar's account, see "The Liberalism of Fear" (1989).

25. See also Ashley Woodiwiss's helpful discussion on these points (2001, 76–80).

26. For a very different view see the work of Marcel Gauchet, who suggests that the secularization of the political is best understood as a product of changes that took place *within* the dynamics of transcendent religion, rather than an imposition forced upon religious communities. What led to the ultimate autonomy of the political, on Gauchet's reading, is the working out of the tension, "inherent to Christian being-in-the-world, between the principle of authority and that of freedom, between the obligation to submit to established powers and the intractable right to inner autonomy" (1997, 137). Thus the secular and the experience of political freedom that accompanies it do not represent a preexisting or "natural" phenomenon of human autonomy but rather are artifacts that emerge from the cultural core of Western religion (specifically, Protestantism). This is what allows Gauchet to suggest, rather provocatively, that all moderns are "Christians of a sort" (144).

27. As Greenawalt argues, if one's primary concern is political stability, the importance of social context in grappling with religious diversity is crucial. Each polity will have its own history, its own balance of religious forces, and its own set of social and political issues that occupy public debate in the political forum (1995, 128–132).

28. As Waldron observes, Rawls frequently writes "as if each comment that is made in public debate is nothing more than a proposal to use public power to forcibly impose something on everyone else so that what we have to evaluate, in each case, [is] an immediate coercive proposal" (1993, 841). For an illuminating example: "All the same, we can maintain that the political conception is a reasonable expression of the political values of public reason and justice between citizens seen as free and equal. As such the political conception makes a claim on comprehensive doctrines in the name of those fundamental values, so that those who reject it run the risk of being unjust, politically speaking. . . . In recognizing others' comprehensive views as reasonable, citizens also recognize that, in the absence of a public basis of establishing the truth of their beliefs, to insist on their comprehensive view *must be seen by others as their insisting on their own beliefs. If we do so insist, others in self-defense can oppose us as using upon them unreasonable force*" (Rawls 1996, 247, my emphasis).

29. For an excellent discussion of the Americanization movement, see Foner 1998, 163–193.

30. Rawls expresses uncertainty about whether the leaders of these movements thought of themselves as "fulfilling the purpose" of Rawls's proviso, which would require them to justify their political positions with political values. He

does say that they would have, "had they known and accepted the idea of public reason" (1997, 785–786 n54). This much seems tautological. The bigger question, perhaps, is whether they would have *needed* to fulfill the proviso in the first place. Could leading abolitionists or civil rights activists have been said to occupy the "public political forum" that Rawls formally limits to judges and politicians? Rawls is unclear on this point.

31. Or as Rawls states elsewhere: "the proviso was fulfilled in their cases, however much they emphasized the religious roots of their doctrines, because these doctrines supported basic constitutional values" (1997, 785–786).

32. Robert Audi's definition of a secular public argument, which draws on the understanding that a secular public sphere entails denying a lack of justificatory authority to religious claims, seems an accurate characterization of the kind of public argument political liberalism requires for approaching disputed matters via public reason: "A secular reason is roughly one whose normative force does not evidentially depend on the existence of God or on theological considerations, or on the pronouncements of a person or institution qua religious authority" (1993, 692). This rendering seems more appropriate than Rawls's more idiosyncratic definition of secular reason as "reasoning in terms of comprehensive nonreligious doctrines," since Rawls's formulation obscures the way in which his conception of public reason is designed to temper and constrain the force of public religious claims (1997, 775).

33. As John Gray argues, "Most late modern societies are far from exhibiting an overlapping consensus on liberal values. Rather, the liberal discourse of rights and personal autonomy is deployed in a continuing conflict to gain and hold power by communities and ways of life having highly diverse values. Where it exists, the hegemony of liberal discourse is often skin-deep" (2000, 13).

34. See for example West 1996.

CHAPTER 4
Approaching the Theological

1. See Habermas 1990.

2. Though Tracy is in agreement with much of Habermas's assessment of the challenges facing modernity, he departs from him in his embrace of theology's potential contributions to critical theory, and he criticizes him for his reluctance to take theology seriously as a possible resource for a renewed public sphere (1992, 35–42).

3. Thus far, Tracy has produced volumes addressing fundamental and systematic theology (Tracy 1975 and 1981a, respectively), but he has yet to produce a sustained work focusing on practical theology. For a noteworthy example of practical theology that is sympathetic to Tracy's concerns, see Coleman 1982.

4. Tracy makes clear that this division of labor is not intended to do away with each theologian's responsibility, at least on an implicit level, to address all three publics. See 1981b, 352; 1981a, 5–6.

5. See also Tracy 1994, where he argues that a publicly responsible Catholic social ethics is required to "correlate (as distinct from juxtapose) the arguments from inner-Christian resources and the distinct arguments from 'reason,' including some form of a general ethics and political theory" (196).

6. Or as Tracy states in another passage: "The questions which religion addresses are the fundamental existential questions of the meaning and truth of individual, communal and historical existence as related to, indeed as both participating in and distanced from, what is sensed as the whole of reality" (1981a, 157–158).

7. Tracy mentions as examples Christian fundamentalism and the theology of Karl Barth.

8. Tracy argues that we must recognize the ways in which "'religion' continues to operate in our common secular lives as an authentic disclosure which both bespeaks certain inevitable limits-to our lives and manifests some final reality which functions as a trustworthy limit-of life itself" (1975, 109).

9. Of course, Tracy's position here presupposes a *singular* "secular faith"—a notion that has been vigorously challenged by, among others, Ian Hunter in his *Rival Enlightenments* (2001).

10. This occasionally leads Tracy to make some unusual characterizations. The Puritans, for instance, come to be regarded not as a body of religious dissenters determined to establish a holy community, but instead as the progenitors of a distinctively American "covenantal" tradition "grounded in conversation with particular religious classics." Instead of instantiating a set of social practices designed to further God's purposes on earth, they are seen in a much more congenial light, as merely seeking to forge a "community of interpretation" (1994, 209–210).

11. As Tracy states, the "primary reference group of the systematic theologian will be the church as the primary mediator of the tradition" (1981a, 68).

12. Lindbeck observes that this understanding of religious engagement has an affinity with the approach favored by some nontheological disciplines, especially anthropology, which have begun to abandon the quest for universal categorizations and have instead sought to rely on the "description of religions from the inside" for their study of religious phenomena. "Scholarly nontheologians who want to understand religion are concerned with how religions work for their adherents, not with their credibility. Their interest, one might say, is in descriptive rather than apologetic intelligibility. The result, paradoxically, is that a postliberal approach, with its commitment to intratextual description, may well have interdisciplinary advantages, while liberal theology, with its apologetic focus on making religion more widely credible, seems increasingly to be a nineteenth-century enclave in a twentieth-century milieu" (1984, 129, 130).

13. The principal "ersatz" religion Neuhaus is referring to here is Soviet Communism, although he intends his point to be broadened to encompass authoritarian regimes generally. Neuhaus's contention, simply put, is that "democratic government is premised upon the acknowledgment of transcendent truth to which the political order is held accountable" (1984, 120).

14. This argument is presented most thoroughly in Neuhaus and Berger 1977.

15. Cf. the argument of Richard Wightman Fox, who questions whether the rhetoric of "defeat" is appropriate in this case: "Indeed, a key paradox of liberal Protestantism—one that must be a cornerstone of any history of liberal Protestantism—is that its goal has always been, in part, to sanctify the secular, to bring forth out of the natural and human worlds the divine potential contained within them. Secularization can be seen, in some of its forms, as a sign of success for liberal Protestantism, not a marker of defeat" (1997, 400).

16. In a telling passage, Neuhaus critiques Rawls's veil of ignorance because it imagines reasoning individuals who "have no history, no tradition, no vested interests, no self-knowledge, no loves, no hates, no fears, no dreams of transcendent purpose or duty. Living persons are distinguished by partiality, by passion, by particularity. Instead of re-linking life and law, Rawls subsumes life into a totally abstracted notion of justice that could not be further removed from the world in which the legitimacy of law must be renewed" (1984, 257–258).

17. Nor is this oppositional tension at all unfortunate from a Christian perspective. See for instance Jean Bethke Elshtain's commentary on Augustine, where she reminds us of Augustine's repudiation of the attempt to collapse the fundamental distinction between the *civitas dei* and the *civitas terrena,* and the different principles upon which they are ordered (1995, 98). On Augustine, see also John Milbank, who argues that Augustine's understanding of the *civitas dei* entails a counter-politics, with a basis for citizenship that is premised upon resistance to the exercise of *dominium* in all its forms (1990, 390).

18. Importantly, Yoder's lack of interest in harnessing the church to particular political agendas did not preclude him from noting certain points of convergence between the Christian ethos and liberal politics or from acknowledging the distinctive gains of liberal democracy. For instance, in responding to those who would rigidify the opposition between church and world, Yoder argued that "to take seriously the basic validity of the apocalyptic stance need not imply disrespect for the concrete values attained by democratic government in (e.g.) the defense of religious liberty, limited government, the franchise, etc. Such a systematic dualism as would refuse the vote or reject public social services need not follow" (1998, 8).

19. This idea is developed most comprehensively in Yoder 1972.

20. Niebuhr discusses the "Christ the Transformer of Culture" option, which of the five types he presents seems to be his preferred approach, in chapter 6 (1951, 190–229).

21. Yoder suggests that for Niebuhr, the state is assumed to be especially representative of what "culture" is (1996a, 55).

22. As Yoder explains further, "the tension will not be between a global reality called 'culture' on one side and an absolute spiritual distance called 'Christ' (or 'monotheism') on the other side, but rather between a group of people defined by a commitment to Christ seeking cultural expression of that commitment (on one hand) and (on the other) a group or groups of other people expressing culturally other values which are independent of or contradictory to such a confession. This latter group is what the New Testament calls 'the world'" (1996a, 74). See also Hauerwas 1981, 74.

23. See for instance Yoder 1996a, 75: "Suffering love can be seen as the way to which Christians are called, without our expecting the rest of society all to share in a radical obedience for which it is not prepared."

24. As Yoder explains, "Worship is the communal cultivation of an alternative construction of society and of history. That alternative construction of history is celebrated by telling the stories of Abraham (and Sarah and Isaac and Ishmael), of Mary and Joseph and Jesus and Mary, of Cross and Resurrection and Peter and Paul, of Peter of Cheltchitz and his Brothers, of George Fox and his Friends" (1984, 43). The role of narrative in sustaining the identity and practices of the church figures prominently in Hauerwas 1981 and Milbank 1990. For instance, Hauerwas argues that "as Christians, we claim that by conforming our lives in a faithful manner to the stories of God we acquire the moral and intellectual skills, as a community and as individuals, to face the world as it is, not as we wish it to be" (1981, 96).

25. See also 1996b, 132: "'Babel' is to be accepted as the human condition under God, as a good thing. . . . For every tribe to talk its own language, for all meaningful discourse to be community-dependent, is not a mistake. Neither is it the Fall nor the expulsion from Paradise. It is the way things ought to be."

26. As Yoder says elsewhere: "In their testimonies of their community identity, the Jewish and Christian communities confess having been called by grace to praise and serve a God who, although having 'chosen' them for a special role within history, is also the creator, sustainer, and ultimate savior of the other nations as well; such a community would be denying its own doxologies if it did not expect to find ways to reach beyond its own boundaries to communicate to those at home in other cultures the 'news' which they cannot receive otherwise than by being told it" (1996b, 136).

27. See also Yoder 1984, 55: the news proclaimed by the church is only properly "good" when it is "*received* as good," and therefore "it can never be communicated coercively; nor can the message-bearer ever positively be assured that it will be received" (emphasis in original).

28. On "middle axioms," see Yoder 1964, 33, 35–44. On "semantic frames," see Yoder 1984, 160–165.

29. See also Yoder 1984, 56: "What we need to find is the interworld transformational grammar to help us to discern what will need to happen if the collision of the message of Jesus with our pluralist/relativist world is to lead to a reconception of the shape of the world, instead of to rendering Jesus optional or innocuous."

30. On this point, see Lindbeck 1984, 128. On the church's role in presenting "imaginative alternatives for social policy," see Hauerwas 1981, 11.

31. In this respect, Yoder's thought offers an interesting parallel with Stanley Fish's claim about politics in the context of multiculturalism. Following Charles Taylor's call for "inspired adhoccery," Fish argues that "the solutions to particular problems will be found by regarding each situation-of-crisis as an opportunity for improvisation and not as an occasion for the application of rules and principles (although the invoking and the recharacterizing of rules and principles will often be components of the improvisation). Any solution devised in this manner is likely to be temporary—that is what ad hoc means—and when a new set of problems has outstripped its efficacy, it will be time to improvise again" (1999, 63–64).

32. See Weaver 1999 for a valuable overview of this and other political aspects of Yoder's vision.

CHAPTER 5
Envisioning a Politics of Moral Engagement

1. See Rawls 1996, 247–251, and Rawls 1997, 785–786.

2. My choice of the term "black church" is not intended to suggest that African American churches are homogeneous. I follow the approach of C. Eric Lincoln and Lawrence H. Mamiya, who view the commonalities among the historically African American religious denominations as much more significant than their differences; I use "black church" as a kind of shorthand for these general religious and sociological similarities. As the authors note, there are seven major historically black Christian denominations, which together include approximately 80 percent of African American Christians: the African Methodist Episcopal Church, the African Methodist Episcopal Zion Church, the Christian Methodist Episcopal Church, the National Baptist Convention, U.S.A., Incorporated, the National Baptist Convention of America, Unincorporated, the Progressive National Baptist Convention, and the Church of God in Christ. See Lincoln and Mamiya 1990, 1–19.

3. See also C. Eric Lincoln, foreword to Cone 1970, 8: "The black man's pilgrimage in America was made less onerous because of his religion. His religion was the organizing principle around which his life was structured. His church was his school, his forum, his political arena, his social club, his art gallery, his conservatory of music. It was lyceum and gymnasium as well as *sanctum sanctorum*."

4. W. E. B. DuBois's insightful comment on the multifaceted identity of the black preacher is relevant here: "The Preacher is the most unique personality developed by the Negro on American soil. A leader, a politician, and orator, a 'boss,' an intriguer, an idealist—all these he is, and ever, too, the centre of a group of men, now twenty, now a thousand in number. The combination of a certain adroitness with deep-seated earnestness, of tact with consummate ability, gave him his preeminence, and helps him maintain it." From DuBois, *The Souls of Black Folk,* quoted in Miller 1992, 27–28.

5. Taylor Branch provides an illuminating illustration involving Rev. Mike King (Martin's father), who preceded Martin in the pulpit at Ebenezer Baptist in Atlanta. King "advanced the notion that Ebenezer must help its people prosper financially as well as spiritually. They must pull together, help each other, and establish the church as a place not only of refuge in a hostile world but as a group of people who were going places. . . . If a barber joined Ebenezer, he would urge from the pulpit that the members patronize that barber. If the barber prospered, he would soon be reminded to make it known through his reciprocal contributions to the church" (1988, 41).

6. Branch mentions that King and his friends at Boston had wrestled with the question of whether it was advisable to consider race-related topics in their papers, and King concurred with the prevailing view that "to do so might cheapen their work in the eyes of influential Negroes as well as whites" (1988, 93).

7. Cornel West argues convincingly that the black church was "the most primordial and decisive source of [King's] thought. In his own writings and sermons, he simply presupposed this influence and always assumed that his being a black Baptist minister spoke for itself regarding this black church influence" (1990, 123).

8. See Branch 1988, 69–94, for an overview of King's graduate education. As Keith Miller notes, King also encountered the giants of the Western philosophical tradition, from Plato to Friedrich Nietzsche (1992, 7).

9. For good discussions of these influences, see Miller 1992 and Lischer 1997.

10. As Keith Miller notes, King was always rather vague when pointing to Gandhi's influence on his thinking (1992, 88–89, 94–99). Lischer observes that after 1960, King made no further reference to Gandhi in either his sermons or his speeches (1997, 214).

11. The full text of Johnson's stanza is as follows:

God of our weary years, God of our silent tears,
Thou who hast brought us thus far on the way;
Thou who hast by thy might led us into the light,
Keep us forever in the path, we pray.
Lest our feet stray from the places, our God, where we met thee.
Lest our hearts, drunk with the wine of the world, we forget thee.
Shadowed beneath thy hand, may we forever stand,
True to our God, true to our native land.

12. On "cosmic companionship," see King [1957a] 1986, 9; [1957b] 1986, 14. On the movement as "proving ground," see Branch 1998, 566–567; King [1958b] 1986, 438.

13. King was elected president of the Montgomery Improvement Association just hours before his first mass meeting speech at Holt Street Baptist. As King recounts, he had only twenty minutes to prepare "the most decisive speech of my life" ([1958b] 1986, 433).

14. Keith Miller estimates that King averaged between two and three hundred addresses per year (1992, 67).

15. The legal strategy was a crucial component of the civil rights struggle from the beginning, with a crucial early victory being the Supreme Court's 1954 decision in *Brown v. Board of Education* on the unconstitutionality of segregated public schools. The NAACP initiated the suit in *Brown* and aggressively pursued a wide range of civil rights litigation.

16. King would later claim during a 1965 interview that "nearly a million copies of the letter have been widely circulated in churches of most of the major denominations" ([1965] 1986, 351).

17. King's appropriation involved a slight rewording of Fosdick's original phrase ("We are intermeshed in an inescapable mutuality").

18. King goes on to cite Martin Buber and Paul Tillich for further support of this view.

19. For discussion of the "culture carrier" role, see Reagon 1990. Reagon emphasizes the way in which the work of "cultural transmission"—that is, "the work of passing on the stories of life in song, in ceremonies, in games, in the sounds around us"—has in African American churches largely been performed by women (207). This sociological observation would likely hold true in white churches as well, where women typically outnumber men by a considerable margin and are indispensable in the organizational life of their congregations, even when not exercising official leadership roles as pastors or priests.

20. Lischer notes the irony in the fact that much of the best evidence available of the mass meetings is due to FBI and local police surveillance; J. Edgar Hoover was not at all oblivious to the meetings' political significance. As "outsider" accounts, moreover, these records provide a particularly interesting glimpse into the peculiar power of the meetings. Lischer provides an amusing example from the notes of a detective who found himself trapped at a mass meeting when a visiting rabbi exhorted everyone in the audience to embrace those beside them: "Of course Officer Watkins and myself were sitting between two negroes and they really gave us the treatment" (Lischer 1997, 247; see in general 243–266).

21. King's understanding of *agape* reflects the term's traditional meaning of selfless giving and service to others, even to the point of returning good for evil: "*Agape* is understanding, creative, redemptive, good will to all men. It is an overflowing love which seeks nothing in return. . . . When one rises to love on this

level, he loves men not because he likes them, not because their ways appeal to him, but he loves every man because God loves him. And he rises to the point of loving the person who does an evil deed while hating the deed that the person does. I think this is what Jesus meant when he said 'love your enemies'" ([1961] 1986, 46–47).

22. Through these efforts the movement sought to draw national attention to the cause of the struggle. In a particularly insightful analysis, Mary Dudziak explains that this strategy had an international component as well. Civil rights leaders were well aware that foreign opinion could be used effectively to put international pressure on the United States to address racial inequality within its borders. In the context of the Cold War, demonstrations like those in Birmingham or Selma played a large role on the international stage in highlighting America's hypocrisy in proclaiming itself a champion of freedom and equality. These events embarrassed government officials and frustrated their attempts to present a favorable American narrative of racial progress that could be successfully exported abroad. While the United States Information Agency attempted to control this narrative, it could not compete with independent news sources around the world that provided their own coverage of the civil rights struggle. It eventually became clear that if the United States was to win its battle with the Soviet Union for global public opinion, it would have to engage in some kind of progress toward racial equality, in order "to make credible the government's argument about race and democracy" (2000, 14).

23. By asserting that the "doctrines" employed by the civil rights activists "supported basic constitutional values," Rawls is implicitly assuming that the constitutional values in question were already a reality (or at least conceptually embedded in the nation's founding documents); they needed only to be put into practice (1997, 786). If, on the other hand, the movement in fact had a hand in *shaping* the particular understandings of justice and equality that were eventually brought into being (as I am contending here), Rawls's formulation would clearly be inappropriate.

24. On a similar note, David Greenstone's *Lincoln Persuasion* contends that Abraham Lincoln's theological convictions allowed him to make a distinctive contribution to American liberalism during the slavery struggle, by taking seriously both the importance of preserving the union *and* elevating its moral condition. Amidst competing impulses in American liberal thought, Lincoln crafted a "covenantal synthesis" that bore a striking resemblance to the New England Puritan tradition, insofar as it refused to privilege political duties at the expense of moral duties or engage in instrumental rationality to the exclusion of a commitment to ethical perfectionism (1993, 276).

25. West adds as an aside, "I would find it difficult for King to be in any human society and not bring prophetic judgment to bear on it" (122).

26. King, quoted in King 1990, 139.

27. Cf. Jean Bethke Elshtain's discussion of "liberal monism," which, as she characterizes it, presupposes that "all institutions within a democratic society must conform to a single authority principle; a single standard of what counts as reason and deliberation; a single vocabulary of political discussion" (2003, 79).

28. In addition, by locating meaningful citizenship solely in the public political forum, political liberalism obscures the ways in which deeper comprehensive ideals work to inspire, shape, and motivate liberal citizenship as it is experienced by ordinary citizens on a regular basis. I am indebted to Tom Spragens for discussion on this point.

CHAPTER 6
The Promise of a Post-Secular Politics

1. For a fascinating discussion that explores the practice of *parrhēsia,* or "frank speaking," as it was embodied in ancient Athenian democratic culture, see Monoson 2000, chapters 2 and 6. Monoson explains that for the Athenians, *parrhēsia* was a deeply important practice characterized by truth-telling and a commitment to "speaking one's mind," especially in the context of delivering forceful criticism (52). It was, moreover, intrinsically associated with the character of the individual speaker. Only a speaker with demonstrated integrity and virtue, capable of "discrimination and moral seriousness," would be regarded by the assembly as a true *parrhēsiastēs* (160).

2. See also Andrew Murphy's analysis of the unequal burdens faced by "nonmainstream" religious citizens within Rawlsian liberalism and the incentives to dissemble that influence their political choices (2001, 250–258).

3. In this respect, Macedo's willingness to engage the perspectives of traditions such as Catholicism, as he does in his discussion of civic education and public school reform in *Diversity and Distrust* (2000), seems more appropriate than Rawls's pronounced reluctance to take up such a task. Rawls does state that "we may think of the reasonable comprehensive doctrines that support society's reasonable political conceptions as those conceptions' vital social basis, giving them enduring strength and vigor." At the same time, he insists that while political liberalism does "recognize the significance of these social roots of constitutional democracy," "*it need not itself undertake a study of these matters*" (1997, 785, my emphasis). Macedo's approach remains tendentious insofar as his engagement with other moral traditions is ultimately intended merely to determine whether or not they are consistent with his own conception of political liberalism. But in any event, these are the kinds of inquiries we must pursue if we desire an adequate understanding of the relationship between citizens' fundamental convictions and their political commitments.

4. I thank Elizabeth Kiss for this distinction.

5. For helpful historical discussions of the way in which core American "political values" have been used as cover for more destructive impulses, see Hamburger 2002 on the relationship between the idea of church/state separation and anti-Catholicism, and Smith 1997 on the ways in which understandings of American citizenship have been conditioned by racism, gender discrimination, and nativism.

6. As Neal notes, "if thirty years ago, there had been something resembling a Rawlsian 'pre-constitutional convention' in America, the matter of 'gay and lesbian rights' would not only not have been discussed, it would not have *existed* as a political matter" (1997, 124, emphasis in original).

7. The desire to divide citizens neatly into reasonable and unreasonable camps afflicts even versions of political liberalism that seek to be more attentive to its exclusionary impulses. For instance, Tomasi 2001 develops a four-category framework, ranging from comprehensive liberals on one extreme (A-people) to unreasonable groups and individuals (D-people) on the other. Among D-people Tomasi includes racists and "religious believers who express their piety by seeking to impose their views on other citizens" (17–18). Tomasi's central objective is not to condemn D-people but rather to render political liberalism more accommodating to citizens who fall within the two extremes of the continuum. Nevertheless, the irony of his categorization is evident, for once Tomasi advances his framework early in the book, D-people largely disappear from the remainder of his account. They are effectively rendered invisible, apparently unworthy of being seriously engaged. Tomasi thus aims for a more commodious political liberalism, but only within the boundaries he establishes in advance.

8. Or as Yoder puts it, "The hermeneutical problem of speaking across boundaries affects all forms of discourse. It matters little what I want to communicate to my neighbors in a different linguistic community—it could be the imperative of protecting the rain forests or the ozone layer, the affirmation of the superiority of IBM word processors to Macintosh, or the declaration of the valence rules of inorganic chemistry. The same concerns about intercommunity method would arise . . . Yet hermeneutical problems have seemed particularly disruptive and destructive of the peculiarly value-laden forms of discourse in which we express and enact our moral and religious commitments" (1996b, 136).

9. Cf. John Gray's argument regarding the limitations of rights-based approaches to politics, given the way they obscure the tragic outcomes that are endemic to politics in morally diverse societies (2000, 116).

10. I thank Tom Spragens for emphasizing the ramifications of these different purposes.

11. For helpful discussion on the Moral Majority's rise to prominence and its political activity in the 1980s, see Reichley 1985, 311–331. As Reichley notes, Falwell himself had once been convinced that Christians' political engagement (beyond paying taxes, voting, etc.) was unnecessary and unadvisable. The cultural and

political upheavals of the 1960s and 70s convinced him that this stance was no longer tenable and that a more assertive posture was required (315–316).

12. See Garrow 1986 for a helpful overview of the struggles King faced as he attempted to maintain the unity of the civil rights movement in the midst of political and ideological infighting, problems that plagued the movement especially after 1965.

13. See in particular the essays in Yoder 1998 and Yoder 1997.

14. Justice Boggs concurred with Justices Lively and Kennedy in the outcome of the case, although for different reasons. Boggs saw as dispositive "the present state of constitutional law," which as he interpreted it does not require a school board to demonstrate a compelling interest when free-exercise exemptions are requested. "Our holding requires plaintiffs to put up with what they perceive as an unbalanced public school curriculum so long as the curriculum does not violate the Establishment Clause" (*Mozert v. Hawkins*, 827 F.2d 1074, 1080–1081).

15. Vicki Frost, one of the *Mozert* plaintiffs, upon hearing that the Supreme Court refused to grant a writ of certiorari for their appeal, said "The state has exiled us. . . . They've put us outside and legally separated us from the public domain" (Bates 1993, 302). The plaintiffs' attorney, Michael Farris, exclaimed: "It's time for every born-again Christian in America to take their children out of public schools, and the quicker the better, to protest this decision" (301).

16. The group of parents that first organized to protest the readers understood their purpose in precisely these terms. As they explained in a newspaper advertisement, "The *Public* [*sic*] should actively participate in the operation and regulation of *public* schools, both economically and politically" (Bates 1993, 68, my emphasis).

17. Their perception that they were being treated contemptuously helped fuel the families' public agitation concerning the deficiencies of the readers. See Bates 1993, 33–37, 65–66. Bates suggests that the mutual animosity that developed between the board members and the parents was the principal reason for the board's decision to end the opt-out arrangement (77–89).

18. As one of the parents exclaimed, "The world thinks we lost, but we won. . . . Our children are out. They're getting a fine education, learning their heritage, how this great nation was built on Judeo-Christian principles. They're learning that there are penalties for misbehavior and rewards for right behavior. They're learning to be good citizens. They're learning to think, a lost art. . . . It was the best blessing that ever happened, having these children expelled from public school" (Bates 1993, 302).

19. One of the more striking aspects of current analyses of the *Mozert* case is the selectivity with which the facts of the case are described, depending upon the purposes for which the case is used. In his effort to demonstrate the compatibility between political liberalism and religious citizens, John Tomasi characterizes the *Mozert* families as entirely reasonable, "as exactly those kinds of citizens for the

accommodation of whom political liberalism was devised" (2001, 92–93). In a very different vein, Stanley Fish uses the case to reinforce the lines of battle between religion and liberalism, characterizing Vicki Frost and the other *Mozert* plaintiffs as religious militants whose goal is to oppose "the ground rules for modern political life" (1999, 220). Neither account does sufficient justice to the complexity of the families' appeals.

20. Recognizing the validity of these concerns, Shelley Burtt contends that "we should see parental requests for accommodation not as unacceptable threats to the transmission of needed civic virtues but as commendable efforts to assure that their families' legitimate (if not mainstream) moral and religious commitments are not directly undermined by children's classroom experience" (1994, 55). See also Burtt 1996.

21. For additional discussion of the families' early complaints against the readers see Bates 1993, 65–92.

22. The heavily contested debate over whether public schools teach secular humanism is an establishment-clause question (i.e., whether schools are in fact teaching a religion) rather than a free-exercise one. When the *Mozert* families made the decision to pursue a legal strategy, they focused their complaint on the free-exercise issue, which required them only to demonstrate that their faith had been burdened—not that the readers were teaching an ersatz religion. Although the parents did eventually renounce any desire to remove the readers from the schools, their earlier efforts to do so continued to haunt them. It helped turn the battle for public opinion against them, as they came to be portrayed as power-hungry extremists (Bates 1993, 120–152).

23. This discussion draws substantially from the argument presented in Coles and Dostert 2003.

24. It is worth noting that some of the individual teachers and school principals were more willing to pursue a flexible approach to the parents' complaints than the members of the school board, who were poorly informed about the specifics of the accommodations that had been negotiated and who persisted in viewing the parents in a caricatured light (Bates 1993, 88).

25. Administered by the World Bank and International Monetary Fund, the HIPC initiative does not entail complete debt forgiveness. It does, however, offer debt reduction to those countries willing to implement "structural-adjustment programs" that move their economies in a free-market direction. The merits of structural adjustment as a precondition for debt relief have been much debated; many argue that the heavy emphasis on eliminating trade barriers and privatizing public utilities and state-run businesses perpetuates these nations' inability to sustain economic development and compete fairly with wealthier nations. In addition to Rowden 2001, see Van Lier 1999.

26. Some scholars have cast doubt on whether the jubilee year provisions were ever actually put into practice on a widespread basis. But see Yoder 1972 for

evidence that the jubilee year was in fact regarded as normative and for discussion on the role it played in Jesus' teaching (64–77). Certainly the Old Testament prophets drew on the power of the jubilee vision as a "measuring stick" for determining the extent to which leaders were meeting the demands of social and economic justice. On this point see Myers 1998.

27. Also of some significance was celebrity involvement in the cause, particularly in Europe, where stadium rock concerts such as NetAid in 1999 and the Pope's own Great Jubilee Concert for a Debt-Free World in 2000 continued to enhance the visibility of the movement. See Hoover 2001 and Peterson 2001.

28. Mensch and Freeman express qualified approval of the *Planned Parenthood of Southeastern Pennsylvania v. Casey* (1992) decision, in which the Supreme Court upheld a number of constraints on abortion (e.g., informed consent and twenty-four-hour waiting periods) at the same time that it refused to overturn *Roe* (thus in effect making abortions more difficult to obtain, but preserving their legality) (1995, 148–150).

Bibliography

Alejandro, Roberto. 1998. *The Limits of Rawlsian Justice.* Baltimore: Johns Hopkins University Press.

Atkinson, Mark. 2000. "As the Jubilee 2000 Campaign Ends This Week, Guardian Writers Reflect on Its Achievements and the Battles Ahead." *Guardian* (London), 28 December [online database]. Available from LEXIS-NEXIS/Academic Universe. Accessed 5 June 2001.

Audi, Robert. 1989. "The Separation of Church and State and the Obligations of Citizenship." *Philosophy and Public Affairs* 18:259–296.

———. 1993. "The Place of Religious Argument in a Free and Democratic Society." *San Diego Law Review* 30:677–702.

Audi, Robert, and Nicholas Wolterstorff. 1997. *Religion in the Public Square: The Place of Religious Convictions in Political Debate.* Point/Counterpoint. Lanham, MD: Rowman & Littlefield.

Bates, Stephen. 1993. *Battleground: One Mother's Crusade, the Religious Right, and the Struggle for Our Schools.* New York: Henry Holt.

Branch, Taylor. 1988. *Parting the Waters: America in the King Years, 1954–63.* New York: Simon & Schuster.

———. 1998. *Pillar of Fire: America in the King Years, 1963–65.* New York: Simon & Schuster.

Burks, Mary Fair. 1990. "Trailblazers: Women in the Montgomery Bus Boycott." In *Women in the Civil Rights Movement: Trailblazers and Torchbearers, 1941–1965,* edited by Vicki L. Crawford, Jacqueline Anne Rouse, and Barbara Woods. Brooklyn, NY: Carlson.

Burtt, Shelley. 1994. "Religious Parents, Secular Schools: A Liberal Defense of an Illiberal Education." *Review of Politics* 56:51–70.

———. 1996. "In Defense of *Yoder*: Parental Authority and the Public Schools." In *Political Order: NOMOS XXXVIII,* edited by Ian Shapiro and Russell Hardin. New York: New York University Press.

Cavanaugh, William T. 1998. *Torture and Eucharist: Theology, Politics, and the Body of Christ.* Oxford: Blackwell.

Charney, Evan. 1998. "Political Liberalism, Deliberative Democracy, and the Public Sphere." *American Political Science Review* 92:97–110.

Coleman, John A. 1982. *An American Strategic Theology.* New York: Paulist.

Coles, Romand, and Troy Dostert. 2003. "Reconsidering the Politics of Education: Provinciality and Democratic Engagement." Unpublished article.

Cone, James H. 1970. *A Black Theology of Liberation.* Philadelphia: Lippincott.

———. 1991. *Martin & Malcolm & America: A Dream or a Nightmare.* Maryknoll, NY: Orbis Books.

Curry, Thomas J. 1986. *The First Freedoms: Church and State in America to the Passage of the First Amendment.* New York: Oxford University Press.

Dombrowski, Daniel A. 2001. *Rawls and Religion: The Case for Political Liberalism.* Albany: State University of New York Press.

Dudziak, Mary L. 2000. *Cold War Civil Rights: Race and the Image of American Democracy.* Princeton: Princeton University Press.

Dworkin, Ronald. 2000. *Sovereign Virtue: The Theory and Practice of Equality.* Cambridge, MA: Harvard University Press.

Dyson, Michael Eric. 1993. *Reflecting Black: African-American Cultural Criticism.* Minneapolis: University of Minnesota Press.

———. 2000. *I May Not Get There with You: The True Martin Luther King, Jr.* New York: Free Press.

Edgar, Bob. 2000. "Both Common Sense and Morality Dictate that We Help to End the Debt Crisis." *The Nation,* 24 April [online database]. Available from InfoTrac/Expanded Academic ASAP, A61410788.

Elliott, Larry. 2000. "Economics: Candle Lit for Debt Relief's Unfinished Business." *Guardian* (London), 27 November [online database]. Available from LEXIS-NEXIS/Academic Universe. Accessed 5 June 2001.

Elshtain, Jean Bethke. 1995. *Augustine and the Limits of Politics.* Notre Dame, IN: University of Notre Dame Press.

———. 2003. "Against Liberal Monism." *Daedalus,* summer, 78–79.

Falwell, Jerry. 1980. *Listen, America!* Garden City, NY: Doubleday.

Fish, Stanley. 1999. *The Trouble with Principle.* Cambridge, MA: Harvard University Press.

Foner, Eric. 1998. *The Story of American Freedom.* New York: W. W. Norton.

Fox, Richard Wightman. 1997. "Experience and Explanation in Twentieth-Century American Religious History." In *New Directions in American Religious History,* edited by Harry S. Stout and D. G. Hart. New York: Oxford University Press.

Galston, William. 1982. "Defending Liberalism." *American Political Science Review* 76: 621–629.

Garrow, David. 1986. *Bearing the Cross: Martin Luther King, Jr. and the Southern Christian Leadership Conference.* New York: William Morrow.

Gauchet, Marcel. 1997. *The Disenchantment of the World: A Political History of Religion.* Princeton: Princeton University Press.

Gedicks, Frederick Mark. 1995. *The Rhetoric of Church and State: A Critical Analysis of Religion Clause Jurisprudence.* Durham, NC: Duke University Press.

Gray, John. 1993. *Post-Liberalism: Studies in Political Thought.* New York: Routledge.

———. 2000. *Two Faces of Liberalism.* New York: New Press.

Greenawalt, Kent. 1988. *Religious Convictions and Political Choice.* New York: Oxford University Press.

———. 1995. *Private Consciences and Public Reasons.* New York: Oxford University Press.

Greenstone, J. David. 1993. *The Lincoln Persuasion: Remaking American Liberalism.* Princeton: Princeton University Press.

Grunwald, Michael. 1999. "GOP's Bachus Makes Debt Relief His Mission." *Washington Post,* 9 October [online database]. Available from LEXIS-NEXIS/Academic Universe. Accessed 5 June 2001.

Gutmann, Amy. 1995. "Civic Education and Social Diversity." *Ethics* 105:557–579.

Habermas, Jürgen. 1990. *The Philosophical Discourse of Modernity.* Cambridge, MA: MIT Press.

Hamburger, Philip. 2002. *Separation of Church and State.* Cambridge: Harvard University Press.

Hauerwas, Stanley. 1981. *A Community of Character: Toward a Constructive Christian Social Ethic.* Notre Dame, IN: University of Notre Dame Press.

Hollenbach, David. 1994. "Civil Society: Beyond the Public-Private Dichotomy." *The Responsive Community* 5:15–23.

Honig, Bonnie. 1993. *Political Theory and the Displacement of Politics.* Ithaca, NY: Cornell University Press.

Hoover, Dennis R. 2001. "What Would Moses Do? Debt Relief in the Jubilee Year." *Religion in the News* 4:15–17.

Howe, Mark DeWolfe. 1965. *The Garden and the Wilderness: Religion and Government in American Constitutional History.* Chicago: University of Chicago Press.

Hunter, Ian. 2001. *Rival Enlightenments: Civil and Metaphysical Philosophy in Early Modern Germany.* Cambridge: Cambridge University Press.

Hutton, Will. 1999. "The Jubilee Line that Works." *Observer* (London), 3 October [online database]. Available from LEXIS-NEXIS/Academic Universe. Accessed 5 June 2001.

John Paul II. 1994. *Tertio Mellenio Adveniente.* Apostolic letter dated 14 November. Available from http://listserv.american.edu/catholic/church/papal/jp.ii/jp2-3rd.html. Accessed 3 July 2001.

King, Martin Luther, Jr. [1956a] 1986. "Facing the Challenge of a New Age." In *A Testament of Hope: The Essential Writings of Martin Luther King, Jr.*, edited by James Melvin Washington. New York: Harper & Row.

———. [1956b] 1986. "Our Struggle." In *A Testament of Hope: The Essential Writings of Martin Luther King, Jr.*, edited by James Melvin Washington. New York: Harper & Row.

———. [1957a] 1986. "Nonviolence and Racial Justice." In *A Testament of Hope: The Essential Writings of Martin Luther King, Jr.*, edited by James Melvin Washington. New York: Harper & Row.

———. [1957b] 1986. "The Power of Nonviolence." In *A Testament of Hope: The Essential Writings of Martin Luther King, Jr.*, edited by James Melvin Washington. New York: Harper & Row.

———. [1958a] 1986. "The Current Crisis in Race Relations." In *A Testament of Hope: The Essential Writings of Martin Luther King, Jr.*, edited by James Melvin Washington. New York: Harper & Row.

———. [1958b] 1986. *Stride Toward Freedom.* In *A Testament of Hope: The Essential Writings of Martin Luther King, Jr.*, edited by James Melvin Washington. New York: Harper & Row.

———. [1960] 1986. "Pilgrimage to Nonviolence." In *A Testament of Hope: The Essential Writings of Martin Luther King, Jr.*, edited by James Melvin Washington. New York: Harper & Row.

———. [1961] 1986. "Love, Law, and Civil Disobedience." In *A Testament of Hope: The Essential Writings of Martin Luther King, Jr.*, edited by James Melvin Washington. New York: Harper & Row.

———. [1962] 1986. "The Ethical Demands for Integration." In *A Testament of Hope: The Essential Writings of Martin Luther King, Jr.*, edited by James Melvin Washington. New York: Harper & Row.

———. [1963a] 1986. "I Have a Dream." In *A Testament of Hope: The Essential Writings of Martin Luther King, Jr.*, edited by James Melvin Washington. New York: Harper & Row.

———. [1963b] 1986. "Letter from Birmingham City Jail." In *A Testament of Hope: The Essential Writings of Martin Luther King, Jr.*, edited by James Melvin Washington. New York: Harper & Row.

———. [1963c] 1986. *Why We Can't Wait.* In *A Testament of Hope: The Essential Writings of Martin Luther King, Jr.*, edited by James Melvin Washington. New York: Harper & Row.

———. [1965] 1986. "*Playboy* Interview: Martin Luther King, Jr." In *A Testament of Hope: The Essential Writings of Martin Luther King, Jr.*, edited by James Melvin Washington. New York: Harper & Row.

———. [1967a] 1986. "A Time to Break Silence." In *A Testament of Hope: The Essential Writings of Martin Luther King, Jr.*, edited by James Melvin Washington. New York: Harper & Row.

———. [1967b] 1986. *Where Do We Go from Here: Chaos or Community?* In *A Testament of Hope: The Essential Writings of Martin Luther King, Jr.*, edited by James Melvin Washington. New York: Harper & Row.

King, Richard H. 1990. "Martin Luther King, Jr., and the Meaning of Freedom: A Political Interpretation." In *We Shall Overcome: Martin Luther King, Jr., and the Black Freedom Struggle,* edited by Peter J. Albert and Ronald Hoffman. New York: Pantheon.

Kloppenberg, James T. 1998. *The Virtues of Liberalism.* New York: Oxford University Press.

Larmore, Charles. 1987. *Patterns of Moral Complexity.* New York: Cambridge University Press.

———. 1990. "Political Liberalism." *Political Theory* 18:339–360.

Lincoln, C. Eric, and Lawrence H. Mamiya. 1990. *The Black Church in the African-American Experience.* Durham, NC: Duke University Press.

Lindbeck, George. 1984. *The Nature of Doctrine.* Philadelphia: Westminster.

Lischer, Richard. 1997. *The Preacher King: Martin Luther King, Jr. and the Word That Moved America.* New York: Oxford University Press.

Locke, John. [1689] 1983. *A Letter Concerning Toleration.* Edited by James H. Tully. Indianapolis: Hackett.

Macedo, Stephen. 1992. *Liberal Virtues: Citizenship, Virtue, and Community in Liberal Constitutionalism.* New York: Oxford University Press.

———. 1995. "Liberal Civic Education and Religious Fundamentalism: The Case of God v. John Rawls?" *Ethics* 105: 468–496.

———. 1996. "Community, Diversity, and Civic Education: Toward a Liberal Political Science of Group Life." *Social Philosophy and Policy* 13:240–268.

———. 2000. *Diversity and Distrust: Civic Education in a Multicultural Democracy.* Cambridge, MA: Harvard University Press.

Madison, James. [1784] 1985. "A Memorial and Remonstrance." In *James Madison on Religious Liberty,* edited by Robert S. Alley. Buffalo, NY: Prometheus Books.

McConnell, Michael W. 1990. "The Origins and Historical Understanding of Free Exercise of Religion." *Harvard Law Review* 103:1409–1517.

Mensch, Elizabeth, and Alan Freeman. 1995. *The Politics of Virtue: Is Abortion Debatable?* Durham, NC: Duke University Press.

Milbank, John. 1990. *Theology and Social Theory.* Cambridge, MA: Blackwell.

Miller, Keith D. 1992. *Voice of Deliverance: The Language of Martin Luther King, Jr. and Its Sources.* New York: Free Press.

Miller, William Lee. 1986. *The First Liberty: Religion and the American Republic.* New York: Alfred A. Knopf.

Monoson, S. Sara. 2000. *Plato's Democratic Entanglements: Athenian Politics and the Practice of Philosophy.* Princeton, NJ: Princeton University Press.

Moon, J. Donald. 1993. *Constructing Community: Moral Pluralism and Tragic Conflicts.* Princeton, NJ: Princeton University Press.

Mouffe, Chantal. 1993. *The Return of the Political.* New York: Verso.

Mozert v. Hawkins County Board of Education. 1987. 827 F.2d 1058 (6th Cir.).

Murphy, Andrew R. 2001. *Conscience and Community: Revisiting Toleration and Religious Dissent in Early Modern England and America.* University Park: Pennsylvania State University Press.

Myers, Ched. 1998. "Jesus' New Economy of Grace." *Sojourners Magazine,* July–August. Available from http://www.sojourners.com/soj9807/980724.html. Accessed 3 July 2001.

Nagel, Thomas. 1987. "Moral Conflict and Political Legitimacy." *Philosophy and Public Affairs* 16:215–240.

National Conference of Catholic Bishops. 1986. *Economic Justice for All: Pastoral Letter on Catholic Social Teaching and the U.S. Economy.* Washington, DC: U.S. Catholic Conference.

Neal, Patrick. 1997. *Liberalism and Its Discontents.* New York: New York University Press.

Neuhaus, Richard John. 1984. *The Naked Public Square: Religion and Democracy in America.* Grand Rapids, MI: Eerdmans.

———. 1991. "To Serve the Lord of All: Law, Gospel, and Social Responsibility." *Dialog* 30:140–149.

Neuhaus, Richard John, and Peter L. Berger. 1977. *To Empower People: The Role of Mediating Structures in Public Policy.* Washington, DC: American Enterprise Institute.

Niebuhr, H. Richard. 1951. *Christ and Culture.* New York: Harper & Row.

Owen, J. Judd. 2001. *Religion and the Demise of Liberal Rationalism: The Foundational Crisis of the Separation of Church and State.* Chicago: University of Chicago Press.

Paris, Peter J. 1985. *The Social Teaching of the Black Churches.* Philadelphia: Fortress.

Perry, Michael J. 1991. *Love and Power: The Role of Religion and Morality in American Politics.* New York: Oxford University Press.

———. 1997. *Religion in Politics: Constitutional and Moral Perspectives.* New York: Oxford University Press.

Peterson, Jonathan. 2001. "The Rock Star, the Pope and the World's Poor." *Los Angeles Times,* 7 January [online database]. Available from LEXIS-NEXIS/Academic Universe. Accessed 5 June 2001.

Rawls, John. 1971. *A Theory of Justice.* Cambridge, MA: Harvard University Press.

———. 1985. "Justice as Fairness: Political Not Metaphysical." *Philosophy and Public Affairs* 14:223–251.

———. 1996 [1993]. *Political Liberalism.* John Dewey Essays in Philosophy 4. New York: Columbia University Press.

———. 1997. "The Idea of Public Reason Revisited." *University of Chicago Law Review* 64:765–807.

Raz, Joseph. 1986. *The Morality of Freedom.* Oxford: Clarendon.

Reagon, Bernice Johnson. 1990. "Women as Culture Carriers in the Civil Rights Movement: Fannie Lou Hamer." In *Women in the Civil Rights Movement: Trailblazers and Torchbearers, 1941–1965,* edited by Vicki L. Crawford, Jacqueline Anne Rouse, and Barbara Woods. Brooklyn, NY: Carlson.

Reichley, A. James. 1985. *Religion in American Public Life.* Washington, DC: Brookings Institution.

Rowden, Rick. 2001. "A World of Debt." *American Prospect,* 2–16 July. Available from http://www.prospect.org/print/V12/12/rowden-r.html. Accessed 2 July 2001.

Rudy, Kathy. 1996. *Beyond Pro-Life and Pro-Choice: Moral Diversity in the Abortion Debate.* Boston: Beacon.

Sandel, Michael. 1982. *Liberalism and the Limits of Justice.* New York: Cambridge University Press.

Shklar, Judith. 1989. "The Liberalism of Fear." In *Liberalism and the Moral Life,* edited by Nancy Rosenblum. Cambridge, MA: Harvard University Press.

Smith, Rogers M. 1997. *Civic Ideals: Conflicting Visions of Citizenship in U.S. History.* New Haven: Yale University Press.

Smith, Steven D. 1995. *Foreordained Failure: The Quest for a Constitutional Principle of Religious Freedom.* New York: Oxford University Press.

Stolzenberg, Nomi Maya. 1993. "'He Drew a Circle that Shut Me Out': Assimilation, Indoctrination, and the Paradox of a Liberal Education." *Harvard Law Review* 106:581–667.

Stout, Jeffrey. 1988. *Ethics After Babel: The Languages of Morals and Their Discontents.* Boston: Beacon.

Tomasi, John. 2001. *Liberalism Beyond Justice: Citizens, Society, and the Boundaries of Political Theory.* Princeton: Princeton University Press.

Tracy, David. 1975. *Blessed Rage for Order.* New York: Seabury.

———. 1981a. *The Analogical Imagination.* New York: Crossroad.

———. 1981b. "Defending the Public Character of Theology." *Christian Century,* 1 April, 350–356.

———. 1992. "Theology, Critical Social Theory, and the Public Realm." In *Habermas, Modernity, and Public Theology,* edited by Don S. Browning and Francis Schüssler Fiorenza. New York: Crossroad.

———. 1994. "Catholic Classics in American Liberal Culture." In *Catholicism and Liberalism: Contributions to American Public Policy,* edited by R. Bruce Douglass and David Hollenbach. Cambridge Studies in Religion and American Public Life. New York: Cambridge University Press.

Van Lier, Piet. 1999. "Crushed by Unpayable Debt, Cape Town Archbishop Asks Wealthy Nations to Forgive Poor." *Plain Dealer,* 12 December [online database]. Available from LEXIS-NEXIS/Academic Universe. Accessed 5 June 2001.

Waldron, Jeremy. 1993. "Religious Contributions in Public Deliberation." *San Diego Law Review* 30:817–848.

Weaver, Alain Epp. 1999. "After Politics: John Howard Yoder, Body Politics, and the Witnessing Church." *Review of Politics* 61:637–673.

Weithman, Paul J. 1994. "Rawlsian Liberalism and the Privatization of Religion: Three Theological Objections Considered." *Journal of Religious Ethics* 22:3–28.

Wenar, Leif. 1995. "*Political Liberalism*: An Internal Critique." *Ethics* 106:32–62.

West, Cornel. 1990. "The Religious Foundations of the Thought of Martin Luther King, Jr." In *We Shall Overcome: Martin Luther King, Jr., and the Black Freedom Struggle,* edited by Peter J. Albert and Ronald Hoffman. New York: Pantheon.

———. 1996. "The Prophetic Tradition in Afro-America." In *Let Justice Roll: Prophetic Challenges in Religion, Politics, and Society,* edited by Neal Riemer. Lanham, MD: Rowman & Littlefield.

Woodiwiss, Ashley. 2001. "Rawls, Religion, and Liberalism." In *The Re-Enchantment of Political Science: Christian Scholars Engage Their Discipline,* edited by Thomas W. Heilke and Ashley Woodiwiss. Lanham, MD: Lexington Books.

Yoder, John Howard. 1964. *The Christian Witness to the State.* Newton, KS: Faith and Life.

———. 1972. *The Politics of Jesus: Vicit Agnus Noster.* Grand Rapids, MI: Eerdmans.

———. 1984. *The Priestly Kingdom: Social Ethics as Gospel.* Notre Dame, IN: University of Notre Dame Press.

———. 1989. "Response of an Amateur Historian and a Religious Citizen." *Journal of Law and Religion* 7:415–432.

———. 1992. "On Not Being Ashamed of the Gospel: Particularity, Pluralism, and Validation." *Faith and Philosophy* 9:285–300.

———. 1996a. "How H. Richard Niebuhr Reasoned: A Critique of *Christ and Culture.*" In Glen H. Stassen, D. M. Yeager, and John Howard Yoder, *Authentic Transformation: A New Vision of Christ and Culture.* Nashville: Abingdon.

———. 1996b. "Meaning After Babble: With Jeffrey Stout Beyond Relativism." *Journal of Religious Ethics* 24:125–139.

———. 1997. *For the Nations: Essays Evangelical and Public.* Grand Rapids, MI: Eerdmans.

———. 1998. *The Royal Priesthood: Essays Ecclesiological and Ecumenical.* Edited by Michael G. Cartwright. Scottdale, PA: Herald.

———. 2001. *Body Politics: Five Practices of the Christian Community Before the Watching World.* Scottdale, PA: Herald.

Index

Troy Dostert

is an instructor of history at Cranbrook-Kingswood Upper School, Bloomfield Hills, Michigan.

CPSIA information can be obtained
at www.ICGtesting.com
Printed in the USA
LVHW082008091222
734913LV00002B/102